TO THE CHURCH IN ROME

TO THE CHURCH IN ROME

A COMMENTARY ON PAUL'S GREATEST EPISTLE

DOUGLAS WILSON

canonpress
Moscow, Idaho

Douglas Wilson, *To the Church in Rome: A Commentary on Paul's Greatest Epistle*
Copyright ©2020, 2022 by Douglas Wilson

Published by Canon Press
P. O. Box 8729, Moscow, Idaho 83843
800-488-2034 | www.canonpress.com

Cover design by James Engerbretson
Interior design by Valerie Anne Bost
Printed in the United States of America

Second edition: 2022. First edition published in 2020 by Blog & Mablog Press
as *A Gospel for All Nations: Sermon Notes on the Book of Romans.*

Unless otherwise indicated, all Scripture quotations are from the King James
Version. Bible quotations marked ESV are from the English Standard Version
copyright ©2001 by Crossway Bibles, a division of Good News Publishers.
Used by permission. Bible quotations marked NKJV are from the New King
James Version®. Copyright ©1982 by Thomas Nelson, Inc. Used by permis-
sion. All rights reserved.

Library of Congress Cataloging-in-Publication Data forthcoming

22 23 24 25 26 27 28 29   10 9 8 7 6 5 4 3 2 1

CONTENTS

This book is dedicated to Tertius (Rom. 16:22), who did a great job.

And it is also dedicated to Brian Marr, whose editorial suggestions and help were truly valuable.

INTRODUCTION

The book of Romans is a mountain range full of gold, and down through Church history it has been the location of more than one or two gold rushes. So many have been attracted to this mountain range over the centuries that entire denominational cities have been built there—with some of them even forgetting the gold beneath their feet, busy as they have been with importing modernist tinsel. Charles Hodge says somewhere that if it is true, it is not new, and that if it is new, it is not true.

> *As I went down in the river to pray*
> *Studying about that good ol' way...*

At the same time, I would like to supplement what Hodge observed by saying that if our teaching about the grace of

God in the gospel is both true and ancient, then it should also be *fresh*. The truth is certainly ancient, from before eternal times, but it is never stale.

Readers who follow recent theological currents will recognize that a "silent interlocutor" throughout the book is a movement that has come to be called the New Perspective on Paul (NPP). This is a movement that needs to be taken seriously in some of the questions it raises, but needs to be summarily dismissed with regard to others. Readers who are acquainted with the NPP will instantly recognize some of what is going on, but familiarity with that theological debate is not a prerequisite for grasping what I am seeking to set forward here.

This commentary initially began as a series of sermons for the saints at Christ Church in Moscow, Idaho. That series began in 2008, but since that time the outlines have been sandpapered a good bit until they showed up in this present form. But the fact that the genesis of this book was sermonic accounts for some of the tone and structure in what follows. As a consequence, this commentary may seem a bit more conversational than other commentaries, including even some of the other commentaries I have written.

It may be a help to the reader here if I give a broad structural outline of what is coming. This is more of a sketched-out roadmap than anything else, with details to follow. Think of the epistle to the Romans as divided into three broad sections. The first is where Paul sets out the gospel that he preaches, which would be chapters 1 through 5. The second section, 6 through 11, would be the Q & A session in the back of the synagogue. In this section, Paul is anticipating and answering objections to the gospel that he preaches. In chapters 12 through 15, he gives practical teaching on Christian living, and concludes with his greetings in chapter 16.

DOUGLAS WILSON

CHAPTER 1

The book of Romans is a first-century apostolic fund-raising letter, and the fact that it almost never strikes us this way simply demonstrates how divergent our practices are from the biblical practices. The Apostle Paul was seeking to minister in Spain, and he wanted the help of the Roman church. Modern fundraising tends toward a "blood on the envelope" approach. "Unless you send in twenty-five dollars now, our ministry will fail and our children will all starve." Paul's approach was much more responsible—so responsible, in fact, that many modern readers don't realize that it was a fundraising letter. Because he wanted help in bringing the gospel to Spain, he laid out the gospel as he understood it, in the spirit of full disclosure. This is why he determined to set before them a clear statement of the gospel as he preached it, so that they would know the nature of the ministry they were helping out, if in fact they decided to help out.

A GOSPEL FOR ALL NATIONS

> Whensoever I take my journey into Spain, I will come to you: for I trust to see you in my journey, and to be brought on my way thitherward by you, if first I be somewhat filled with your company. (Rom. 15:24)

THE BACKGROUND TO ROMANS

The letter to the Romans was likely written from Corinth. There are various reasons for thinking this, but the most they can do is establish a likelihood. Phoebe was a servant of the church at Cenchreae (right next to Corinth), and she is the one who delivered this letter to the Romans (Rom. 16:1). Paul identifies Gaius as his host (Rom. 16:23), and if this is the same Gaius of 1 Corinthians 1:14, then that would be suggestive. Erastus is mentioned in Romans 16:23, and a gent named Erastus remained in Corinth (2 Tim. 4:20). The KJV says that this Erastus was a "chamberlain," although we might render it as a steward or a treasurer. At any rate there was an important city official named Erastus in the first century, and an inscription that likely refers to him has been uncovered there.

Paul likely wrote this letter in the mid-fifties. Seneca was a Stoic philosopher who served as a tutor to the emperor Nero. Despite the awful name he garnered later, Nero was fairly decent for the first five years of his reign, which began in AD 54. Gallio was Seneca's brother, and he became proconsul of Achaia in AD 51 or 52. As you recall, Paul was hauled in front of Gallio in Acts 18:12–17, but Gallio refused to hear the case. In the next chapter, Paul establishes a very fruitful ministry in the Hall of Tyrannus at Ephesus, where he teaches for two years. Immediately after this is the first mention of wanting to visit Rome (Acts 19:21–22). This seems to be the most likely context for the letter.

Although Paul was a Roman citizen (Acts 22:28), there is no record of him ever visiting Rome before this. He wanted to minister in Spain, and Rome was on the way. This gave him the perfect opportunity to visit Rome and to make the acquaintance of the Christians there. At the same time, he had no desire to usurp the ministry of others, no desire to build on another man's foundation (Rom. 15:20).

The church in Rome was established in the capital city of the empire, and all the temptations you might expect came with that privilege. Paul was acutely aware of this, and he warns the Roman Christians of these temptations discreetly but very clearly. And he does so in a way that is woven together with his larger argument. There had been "visitors from Rome" present in Jerusalem at the first Pentecost, so a church had likely been established in Rome very early.

Priscilla and Aquila had been part of this early Roman church, and Paul befriended them when the Jews were expelled from Rome under Claudius (c. AD 49). Suetonius (seventy years later) said that this was because the Jews were constantly rioting at the instigation of a man named *Chrestus,* a variant Latin spelling of *Christus.* But if this referred to Christ, it would be odd for the Jews in Rome at the end of Acts not to know anything about this "sect" (Acts 28:22).

At any rate, after the death of Claudius in AD 54, there was a thriving Jewish Christian community in Rome, and when Paul wrote in 57, he could speak of the faith of the Roman church as a matter of universal knowledge (Rom. 1:8). In short, Rome was a happening place.

AN OVERVIEW OF ROMANS

Most of Paul's letters are pastoral responses to particular situations on the ground. Of necessity, this means that his teaching in the bulk of his letters is, generally speaking, *ad hoc*. But in this letter, he does not have particular pastoral responsibilities in Rome, and he is not responding to any particular crisis. Rather, he has the opportunity to go to Spain, and so he is setting forth his gospel as clearly as he can. The result is that the book of Romans is far more systematic than most of his other writings.

In taking an overview of the book here, we have to pass over a number of nooks and crannies, but we will address those as we proceed through the book. So take this as the *broad* overview, and remember that the original book did not have chapters and verses.

In the first chapter, Paul shows that the nations are trapped in sin. But lest the Jews vaunt themselves, in the second chapter, he shows that they are under the authority of sin as well. In the third chapter, he summarizes his point by showing that Jew and Gentile are both in bondage to sin. They both have the same dilemma. Thus far we have a statement of the problem—the problem of universal sin that the gospel was intended to address.

In chapter four, he gives us an exegetical basis for justification by faith alone, found in the example of Abraham as recorded in the book of Genesis. In chapter five, we have more of a theological statement of the same truth.

Given that we are justified by faith alone, apart from works of the law, Paul turns (in a sort of *refutatio*) to address a number of objections to his gospel. If we are justified by faith apart from the law, then doesn't that mean that we get to sin up a storm? In chapter six, Paul answers *no*. We are forgiven for our sins through the mechanism of dying to sin. If we are justified by faith apart from the law, then what was the law given for? Paul answers *that* question in chapter seven. The law was not given as a ladder to climb up to Heaven with. Rather, it was given to reveal to us how profoundly broken we all are (Rom. 3:20; 5:20; Rom. 7).

In chapter eight, Paul begins his glorious discussion of the relationship of God's sovereignty, on the one hand, to God's covenant promises and commitments on the other. Chapter eight gives us a discussion of God's commitment to the entire created order. Chapters nine through eleven describe God's saving work within the covenant that He had made with the Jews and how the Gentiles were eventually included in that.

So Paul laid out the basics of the gospel of free grace in chapters one through five. The human dilemma is sketched in the first three chapters, and then chapters four and five give us the way of salvation—justification by faith alone. That done, think of the next section as inspired by countless Q & A sessions in the back of synagogues. "One of you will say to me then." If we are saved by grace, won't that lead to moral disorder (Ch. 6)? If we are saved by grace, what was the law for then (Ch. 7)? If we are saved by grace, then how does sanctification work (Ch. 8)? If we are saved by grace, what was *Israel* for then (Chs. 10–11)?

And then, in accord with his custom, Paul gives the Romans a series of ethical exhortations, all of which line up with the gospel that has been articulated. Chapter twelve addresses body life within the congregation. Chapter thirteen has to do with our relationship to the unbelieving civil order. Chapter fourteen concerns debates about questionable matters that had arisen among Christians. Chapter fifteen addresses the subject of missions (remember the purpose of the letter). And chapter sixteen largely consists of greetings and a few remaining exhortations.

So here is a gospel for all nations. Evangelical Christians are accustomed to think of Romans as a tract outlining the way of individual salvation. This is certainly something that can (and *should*) be derived from this book, but it is important for us to note that Paul is proclaiming his gospel to the *church* at Rome, so that they would help him proclaim it to the *region* of Spain. The tribal nature of man is apparent throughout this entire book. It concerns individuals, of necessity, but we must begin where Paul begins: "By whom we have received grace and apostleship, for obedience to the faith among all *nations,* for his name" (Rom. 1:5, emphasis added).

You cannot talk about omelets without including eggs. But you can talk about eggs and never get to the omelet.

You cannot talk about nations without including men and women, boys and girls. But you can talk about men and women, boys and girls, and never get to the nations. This tendency to individualization among modern Christians is one of the devices that we use to keep the gospel from getting us into trouble.

As we study this book, we will discover that God's plan of salvation is far greater than a simple plan to save Smith, if only Smith believes. God loves the world, the Jews, the tribes, and the cosmos, and He fully intends to save all of it...and that includes Smith.

CALLED TO BE AN APOSTLE

In the first chapter, we considered the overall nature of the book of Romans and the fact that it was a fundraising letter. In this letter, Paul set out his gospel in a systematic fashion so that the Roman Christians would know the nature of the gospel that he desired to preach in his mission to Spain. If we want to understand the gospel in Paul's terms, as Paul sets it forth here, we have to take in the background of one other thing—the life of Saul or Paul himself.

> Paul, a servant of Jesus Christ, called to be an apostle, separated unto the gospel of God, (which he had promised afore by his prophets in the holy scriptures,) concerning his Son Jesus Christ our Lord, which was made of the seed of David according to the flesh; and declared to be the Son of God with power, according to the spirit of holiness, by the resurrection from the dead: by whom we have received grace and apostleship, for

obedience to the faith among all nations, for his name:
among whom are ye also the called of Jesus Christ: to
all that be in Rome, beloved of God, called to be saints:
grace to you and peace from God our Father, and the
Lord Jesus Christ. (Rom. 1:1–7)

THE BACKGROUND TO ROMANS

This letter is from Saul of Tarsus, commonly known as
Paul. He identifies himself in the first place as a servant
or slave of Jesus Christ (v. 1). He had been called to be an
apostle, which means "one commissioned and sent out,"
and the nature of the commission is made evident in that
Paul was consecrated or set apart for the gospel of God (v.
1). This gospel was not a new idea that had been cooked
up between the Testaments, but rather it was promised in
the Scripture by the prophets (v. 2). Specifically, the gospel
concerned God's Son, Jesus Christ our Lord—a Davidson
in his human line (v. 3). Jesus was the son of David, or Jesus ben David. The way we form our surnames, we would
say Jesus Davidson. But we must remember His lineage on
the other side too. He was declared to be the Son of God by
His resurrection (v. 4). It is important to add that this declaration was done with power and in accordance with the
spirit of holiness. This same God is the one through whom
the apostles had received grace and apostleship in order
to glorify His name by looking for obedience to the faith
among all nations (v. 5). This process was ongoing, and
the Roman Christians were included in that ingathering,
being called of Jesus Christ (v. 6). The letter is addressed
to all in Rome who were beloved of God and called to be

saints (v. 7). Paul blesses them with grace and peace from the Father and the Son in his initial benediction (v. 7).

In our overview of the entire book of Romans, we noted that the first chapter shows that the Gentiles were under sin, chapter two shows that the Jews were under sin, and chapter three shows them both up to their necks in the same kind of sin. This is important for us to note at the beginning of this book, because the gospel set forth here is a gospel that liberates the nations from wickedness, evil, sin, immorality, and so forth. This will be important for us to understand when we get to chapter seven and Paul's description of himself there as a representative Jew, but it is also important for us to see the nature of Saul's conversion to Christ rightly. Otherwise, we will get everything confused. For now, we need to see that the gospel directly addresses what preachers in another era used to call *sin*.

The pagan nations were wicked nations. In chapter one, Paul is grappling with all manner of sin among the Gentiles—all ungodliness and unrighteousness (1:18), vain imaginations (v. 21), vile affections (v. 26), a reprobate mind (v. 28), along with envy, murder, and deceit (vv. 29–31). There is much more than this. Among the Jews, Paul was concerned about hypocritical double standards (2:1), hard and impenitent hearts (2:5), thievery (2:21), adultery (2:22), and much more. Put them both together, and no one does good (3:12), they have throats that are open sepulchers (3:13), cursing and bitterness (3:14), and no fear of God at all (3:18). Nothing is plainer than that Paul sets his gospel over against all the doings of the carnal man, and *not* against the expectant but faithful Jew. The gospel is for the sinful and rebellious, whether Jew or Gentile. It is *not* a gospel that is set against the observant Jew who was looking forward to the coming of the Messiah in true faith.

We can learn a great deal about this by comparing the "blamelessness" of Saul of Tarsus before his conversion, and the blamelessness of Zacharias and Elizabeth, the parents of John the Baptist. One of the more serious errors found in what is called the New Perspective on Paul is that it tries to put these moral issues on the back burner and make the central thing a question about the boundary markers of Torah—circumcision, and other marks of Jewishness. In this view, when Luke tells us that Zacharias and Elizabeth were blameless according to the law (Luke 1:6), and when Paul says something that sounds similar (Phil. 3:6), New Perspective advocates claim that they must be referring to the same thing. But this is plainly false. Zacharias and Elizabeth were righteous, and Saul was self-righteous. Zacharias and Elizabeth were conscientious and faithful Old Covenant members, looking forward to the Messiah as did all the prophets, Simeon, Anna, and our Lord's mother. Luke is *praising* Zacharias and Elizabeth.

So Paul is referring to his previous "blamelessness" as so much dung (Phil. 3:8), and wants us to know that those who were *still* holding to what he *used to* hold to are dogs, *evil* workers, and flesh mutilators (Phil. 3:2). Paul held himself to have been an awful man before his conversion. He describes himself as a chief among sinners (1 Tim. 1:15), as a blasphemer (v. 13), and insolent (v. 13, NKJV). When Christ appeared to him on the Damascus road, He was showing great kindness to a vile man. Christ delivered him from much more than an overly sentimental attachment to the boundary markers of the Old Covenant.

Unless this is understood, the book of Romans will never be.

We do not want to examine these things on the surface. The prophet Jeremiah describes those who would say peace when there is no such thing. He talks about those who heal the wound of the people lightly (Jer. 6:14; 8:11). We naturally flinch from any treatments of the wound that really get down to business. A great deal of contemporary scholarship on Paul is dabbing around the edges of humanity's gangrenous wound with a damp washcloth, not really wanting to admit the obvious. To change the metaphor, the solution will be to take the book of Romans as if it were an extraordinary whiskey—straight. Let the gospel make you cough and catch your breath.

This is true gospel. Christ Jesus was declared with power to be the Son of God by His resurrection from the dead. The fact of death reveals that we are dealing with no minor problem. The measures that God took to save us indicate the greatness of our dilemma. God Himself took flesh and dwelt among us, born into the line of David. This was not merely to help us figure out how to dispose of our phylacteries.

We have already considered how the gospel is for the nations, and not *just* for individuals as individuals. But let us never try to hide from the holiness and graciousness of God by taking refuge in some corporate shelter.

THE HEART OF ROMANS

The gospel is not faith, but the gospel cannot be understood or appropriated apart from a living and evangelical faith. As the Westminster Confession puts it, the faith that justifies is "no dead faith" (WCF 11.2). Another name for "not dead" is alive or *living*. The gospel is objective and outside us. But the beating heart of Romans is the centrality of a living faith, the only kind of faith that ever believed God for anything.

> First, I thank my God through Jesus Christ for you all, that your faith is spoken of throughout the whole world. For God is my witness, whom I serve with my spirit in the gospel of his Son, that without ceasing I make mention of you always in my prayers; making request, if by any means now at length I might have a prosperous journey by the will of God to come unto you. For I long to see you, that I may impart unto you some spiritual gift, to the end ye may be established; that is, that I may be comforted together with you by the mutual faith both of you and me. Now I would not have you ignorant, brethren, that oftentimes I purposed to come unto you, (but was let hitherto,) that I might have some fruit among you also, even as among other Gentiles. I am debtor both to the Greeks, and to the Barbarians; both to the wise, and to the unwise. So, as much as in me is, I am ready to preach the gospel to you that are at Rome also. For I am not ashamed of the gospel of Christ: for it is the power of God unto salvation to every one that believeth; to the Jew first,

> and also to the Greek. For therein is the righteousness
> of God revealed from faith to faith: as it is written, The
> just shall live by faith. (Rom. 1:8–17)

The church at Rome was not an insignificant body. Their faith was spoken of throughout the entire world (v. 8). Although Paul was not connected to that church formally, he nevertheless lifted them up to God unceasingly (v. 9). This point was apparently important enough for Paul to swear to (v. 9). He served God in his spirit in the gospel of the Son (v. 9). In his prayers, one of his requests was that he would be able in the will of God to make it to Rome in order to visit with them there (v. 10). He had a deep desire to be a blessing to the Romans (v. 11). But, he hastens to add, this edification would by no means be a one-way street (v. 12). He wanted them to know that he had attempted to come many times, wanting some fruit there in Rome just as he had been fruitful among other Gentiles elsewhere (v. 13). Paul saw himself under obligation both to the Greeks (among whom he had already done much work) and to the barbarians (in Spain perhaps). His obligations were to the wise and unwise, to those in the seats of power and those in the hinterlands (v. 14). So as far as Paul's strength is concerned, he is prepared to spend it in Rome (v. 15). Why? Because he is not ashamed of the gospel (v. 16), the gospel he serves faithfully (v. 9). This gospel is not shameful, and it is the power of God to salvation to everyone who believes—to the Jew first, then the Greeks, and then the barbarians (v. 16). For in the gospel, the righteousness of God is revealed from faith to faith (v.

17). Scripture teaches us this—the just shall live by faith (v. 17; Hab. 2:1–5).

Remember the point of the book of Romans—Paul is looking to the Romans to help him in his mission to Spain. But he does not simply use them in a callused or pragmatic way. If they are going to be his partners in this work, he wants to meet them first, wanting a relationship of mutual support. He does not want to minister in Spain with their support unless he has first ministered to them. And neither does he want to minister in Spain with their support unless they have been a blessing to him. In short, he is not just after their money. All biblical giving occurs in the context of communion and fellowship. It is not to be an impersonal or bureaucratic affair.

And so we come to what might be considered the thesis statement of Romans. The phrase that Paul introduces here—the just shall live by faith—is taken from the minor prophet Habakkuk (2:4). This is the first quotation from the Old Testament in an epistle saturated with such quotations. And it is not just a phrase taken at random. The entire book of Habakkuk is a chiasm, and this verse that Paul cites is found at the center of the chiasm. It is the central point of that book—not to mention being the central point in this one.

Here's a diagram of the chiasm:

A Habakkuk complains about how long he must wait for justice. (1:2–4)

> **B** Yahweh answers him by describing the arrival of the incredibly powerful Babylonians. (1:5–11)

>> **C** Habakkuk complains a second time—why do You allow the wicked to destroy nations more righteous than they are? (1:12–17)

>>> **D** Wait patiently. The wicked will die, and *the righteous will live by faith.* (2:1–4)

>> **C'** Yahweh answers the second complaint: everything will be put right. (2:5–20)

> **B'** Yahweh gives a final answer: His army is far more powerful than the Babylonians. (3:1–15)

A' Habakkuk resolves his first complaint. He will wait for God's salvation. (3:16–19)

So the point of Habakkuk is to urge believers to a patient and tenacious faith in the face of incredible adversity. The context makes it clear that this faith is not raw propositional assent. Connected to this, the word rendered *faith* here (*emunah*) includes "faithfulness" or "fidelity." This is not "justification by works," but rather "justification by faith that lives." The fidelity is not fidelity in works, but rather fidelity to itself, to the true nature of faith. There is a lot of scholarly discussion about whether to render this as *faith* or *faithfulness*, but in this context I don't really want to choose. The faith that lives by faith is faithful, and faithfulness without true faith is actually faithless. The just shall live by faith that is *alive*.

Now Paul says here that in the gospel "the righteousness of God" is revealed. What does that mean? I have already mentioned the New Perspective on Paul, and one of the things emphasized in that theology is that the righteousness of God refers to His covenant faithfulness in keeping His promises, and not to an imputed righteousness—the righteousness of Christ credited to the one who believes.

To take it in this latter sense, *as we must*, does not mean that we are denying that God is righteous Himself and is a faithful, covenant keeping God. That is also true. But notice what Paul is claiming here. The just shall live by faith, meaning that the just shall live *from* faith *to* faith. This faith is what reveals or manifests the righteousness of God. If we come at it from the other direction and say that God has kept His promises righteously, we have to ask what those promises are. The answer to that is that Jesus is Immanuel, God with us. He is the one who became the last Adam so that many might be made righteous (Rom. 5:19).

This gospel is potent indeed. When we are ashamed of the gospel, it is either because we have not reflected on how powerful it is, or it is because we have tinkered with it, thinking to improve things, and have only succeeded in creating something to be ashamed of.

THE GLORY OF THE OBVIOUS

God the Father is prominent in the first three chapters of Romans. God the Son figures largely from the middle of chapter three to the end of chapter five. And then the Holy Spirit is central from chapters five through eight. We have, in turns, the wrath of the Father, the propitiation of the Son, and the liberating deliverance of the Spirit. Remember that all three persons of the Trinity are working in harmony together and that they are not trying to balance one another by leaning in opposite directions. It is *not* that the Father exhibits a wrath that the Son does not share. The Father's wrath speaks for the whole triune God, the sacrifice of Christ reveals the whole triune God, and the liberation of the Spirit does the same.

So as we work through the first part of the book of Romans, let us remember that God reveals Himself in His Word, and not just in His creation.

> For the wrath of God is revealed from heaven against all ungodliness and unrighteousness of men, who hold the truth in unrighteousness; because that which may be known of God is manifest in them; for God hath shewed it unto them. For the invisible things of him from the creation of the world are clearly seen, being understood by the things that are made, even his eternal power and Godhead; so that they are without excuse: because that, when they knew God, they

glorified him not as God, neither were thankful; but became vain in their imaginations, and their foolish heart was darkened. Professing themselves to be wise, they became fools, and changed the glory of the uncorruptible God into an image made like to corruptible man, and to birds, and fourfooted beasts, and creeping things. Wherefore God also gave them up to uncleanness through the lusts of their own hearts, to dishonour their own bodies between themselves: who changed the truth of God into a lie, and worshipped and served the creature more than the Creator, who is blessed for ever. Amen. (Rom. 1:18–25)

In this passage, Paul outlines what the wrath of God is directed against, which is all ungodliness and unrighteousness (v. 18). He also reveals to us the way in which God's wrath functions (v. 24). Men in rebellion suppress the truth in unrighteousness, holding it under (v. 18). Paul is explicit that men sin against *light*. God has shown to man what is manifestly true about Him. He has shown it to them and *in* them (v. 19). How did God do this? God's invisible characteristics are understood by inference from the things that are made (v. 20). Specifically, Paul means God's eternal power and Godhead, and this means that men are without excuse in their rejection of Him (v. 20). This is because they started from a position of knowing God (v. 21), but then refused to do two things.

They refused to acknowledge the Godness of God, refusing to glorify Him as God (v. 21), and they refused to be thankful (v. 21). As a result, their imagination veered into vanity, and their foolish hearts were darkened (v. 21). Of course, this was not *their* perspective on what was happening (v. 22). As they became increasingly foolish, they puffed themselves up as wise. The glory of the incorruptible God that they refused to glorify was changed (in their imagination only) into images of corruptible creatures, like man, birds, quadrupeds, and creeping things (v. 23). Therefore, God let them go, giving them over to uncleanness in the lusts of their hearts and the dishonoring of their bodies (v. 24). This is what happens to those who swap out the truth of God for a lie (v. 25) and who worship and serve the creature more than the Creator—the one who is forever blessed (v. 25). *Amen.*

We are accustomed to think that the wrath of God comes on men for their sins. We understand the concept, or so we think. We sin in history, and the wrath of God comes at the end of history. This is certainly true enough (see v. 32), but it is not the *entire* truth.

The Bible teaches not only that sin brings the wrath of God, but also that, in an important sense, sin *is* the wrath of God. In this passage, the wrath of God is revealed against sin (v. 18). But how is it revealed (v. 24)? When God "lets go," that is a form of His wrath. When He takes away His restraining hand, the pit of evil that we fall into is a consequence of His anger and not just an occasion for additional anger later.

We can see the same principle elsewhere in Scripture. "The mouth of strange women is a deep pit: he that is abhorred of the Lord shall fall therein" (Prov. 22:14). This adultery is not just something that God will judge later on; it is a judgment in its own right. Sodom was judged, therefore, *before* the fire fell, and America is under judgment as we speak. As Lewis points out in *The Great Divorce*, the mercy of God is when we say to God, "Thy will be done." The wrath of God is when He says to us, "No, no, *thy* will be done."[1]

We see that the human dilemma is summed up by the three words suppression, substitution, and subversion. The sin starts with rebellion and ingratitude. That is the first step. God takes our head in both His hands and points it toward the greatness of His glory. We refuse to look at it because to do so would obligate us. We take the greatness of His glory and thrust it away from us, holding it under, *suppressing* our knowledge of it. The second stage is to *substitute* something else in place of God—images of men, or birds, or beasts, or crawling things. The final stage of judgment (and remember, all of this is the wrath of God) is *subversion*. The glory of God in the image of God (man) is still too clear, and so that image must also be dishonored. In its extremity, that dishonor takes the form of homosexual practices. This is not something where we can agree to differ. It is not that we believe such practices are dishonoring while they believe it is honoring. They also know it is dishonoring and degrading—that is the whole *point*. Self-loathing is not an unfortunate consequence of homosexuality. It the *point* of homosexuality.

You cannot dishonor the glory of God in the Godhead and then sustain an appropriate honor for the image of God in

1. C.S. Lewis, *The Great Divorce* (New York: MacMillan, 1946), 72.

man. Incidentally, the word *Godhead* here is not related to the word *head*, but rather from the Middle English *hed* to our word *hood*. So this word refers to the Godness of God, the *Godhood* of God, meaning the divine nature of God.

This means that, among other things, apart from Christ, human rights are an incoherent concept. If you hate the person, you won't honor their picture. If your whole orientation is a rejection of the goodness of God, then what are you going to do with the reflection of that goodness that is found in the human body? You are going to figure out ways to degrade it, and unnatural sex acts are one of the most obvious ways to accomplish that kind of degradation.

Never undertake to prove what everybody knows already. When you are in discussions with the office atheist or with the radical secularist in your family at the Christmas reunion, do not accept their invitation to step into a neutral place from which you can prove to them that God exists. To do this grants legitimacy to the heart of their rebellion—you have acquiesced to his claim that he really does not know and that he would really like to know. He is holding an overinflated beach ball underwater and has been doing it so long that his arms are quivering, and he invites you to accept the challenge of proving to *his* satisfaction that beach balls in fact do exist. He is *terribly* interested and wants nothing more than to know the truth. He wants you to prove the existence of beach balls. What you ought to do instead is poke his arms a little bit.

Remember that he professes that what he is doing is wise (v. 22). But God's evaluation is different (v. 22). They say they want nothing other than respect, mutual affirmation, an elimination of hate crimes, and all the rest of it. God calls it the dishonoring *of one another*.

VILE AFFECTIONS

Recall that we have learned that the wrath of God *is* revealed in the world, and it is revealed as God "lets go" of a culture, allowing that culture to run headlong into various suicidal and fruitless practices. In this passage, we find a deepening expansion of this point Paul has already made.

> For this cause God gave them up unto vile affections: for even their women did change the natural use into that which is against nature: and likewise also the men, leaving the natural use of the woman, burned in their lust one toward another; men with men working that which is unseemly, and receiving in themselves that recompence of their error which was meet. And even as they did not like to retain God in their knowledge, God gave them over to a reprobate mind, to do those things which are not convenient; being filled with all unrighteousness, fornication, wickedness, covetousness, maliciousness; full of envy, murder, debate, deceit, malignity; whisperers, backbiters, haters of God, despiteful, proud, boasters, inventors of evil things, disobedient to parents, Without understanding, covenantbreakers, without natural affection, implacable, unmerciful: who knowing the judgment of God, that they which commit such things are worthy of death, not only do the same, but have pleasure in them that do them. (Rom. 1:26–32)

The wrath of God, considered in this light, is clearly not limited to homosexual practices. But Paul certainly places that particular perversion at the very center of his argument. Notice that men do not embrace vile affections despite everything that God could do. No, it says that God "gave them up unto" these vile affections (v. 26). The reason we have gay pride parades is that *God* is doing something to us. As a result, Paul argues, even the *women* gave up the natural use of men (v. 26). And the men did the same, turning in an unseemly desire toward one another (v. 27). Just as they did not *want* to retain God in their knowledge, so God *let* them not retain Him in their knowledge (v. 28). As a result, they then filled up with all kinds of spiritual sludge (vv. 29–31). Sins are like grapes; they come in bunches. This happened despite the fact that *they* knew it to be the judgment of God (v. 32). This means their suppression of the knowledge of God did not really work. They did not want to retain the knowledge of God, but they still *knew* the judgment of God (v. 32). That judgment is that sin warrants death, as they well know, but they insist on becoming cheerleaders for that way of death anyway (v. 32).

God created mankind, male and female, in His image (Gen. 1:27). This means that attempts to rearrange how everything goes are foundational attempts at trying to make a heretical theology stick in some way to the world. By defacing the image of God, we assault God Himself. By rearranging the components, rebellious mankind is trying to recreate God, trying to make Him into something other than what He eternally is. Homosexual actions are therefore a high-profile revolt against the Trinity. All sins do the same thing, but this shows up the problem in stark relief.

Remember that God does not just reveal Himself in Scripture. He reveals Himself in nature, and the natural use of the female by the male, and the natural use of the male by the female, are important parts of that revelation. Homosexual practice is contrary to the design of God, not just because God says so in Scripture (Lev. 20:13), which He of course does, but also because we discover in the natural world that *the parts don't fit*. This is not just physiological, although it is that also. If you keep all the nuts in one bag and all the bolts in another, you won't ever build anything. But the parts don't fit anywhere else, either. They don't fit spiritually, mentally, emotionally, or culturally. Homosexual advocates like to represent this point as a cheap laugh line from traditionalists, but Paul shows it to be a cogent point, an unanswerable argument.

This is true at every level, but consider just one aspect of it. A man who turns to another man for sexual gratification is not just rejecting marriage to one woman—he is rejecting half of the human race. A woman who turns to another woman is doing the same thing. And this is a way of striking at God. Just as rebellious peasants who cannot kill their king frequently settle for hanging him in effigy, so it is here. God has painted His own portrait, His own image, and the predominant colors He used were the colors *male* and *female* (Gen. 1:27). The choice to turn away from this to embrace someone of the same sex is art vandalism. It rejects the other half of the painting and, still worse, it displays hatred for the painter.

So when Paul says that God gave them up to "vile affections," he does not just mean that they are vile "from our perspective, though others might differ." Remember that this is at the very center of God's judgment. When men desired to think as though God were not there, God granted their wish *in judgment*, and gave them over to a reprobate mind (v. 28). This is how we know that wrath is occurring—God gives them up, God gives them over (vv. 26, 28). Remember that Paul is echoing the judgment themes found in Psalm 106, and here is another one. God granted their request, but He sent leanness to their souls (Ps. 106:15). God judges in wrath by saying *yes* to them.

The sins that follow, a grim list indeed, are not just sins that the culture in question dabbles in. They don't just happen from time to time. When God's wrath is being poured out, what happens? The *pouring* corresponds to a *filling*. "Being filled with all unrighteousness" (v. 29). This particular cultural jug is filled with all unrighteousness, sexual uncleanness, wickedness of various kinds, covetousness and *wanting*, malice and spite, green envy, murder, disputes and tangles, lies and more lies, a surly malignity, whispering campaigns, backstabbing, God-hating, contempt for others, overweening arrogance, boasting and bragging, evil inventions, disobedience to parents, stupidity and stupor, oath-breaking, lack of natural affection, hard-heartedness, and unmercifulness (vv. 29–31).

And please note the ironic twist: in the modern parlance, to oppose the root that produces all this kind of corrupt fruit is called *hate*. Yeah, right, whatever.

Those who know God suppress the knowledge of God in unrighteousness, but nevertheless retain their awareness of the judgment of God (in which they live). Nevertheless, they persist in their rebellion. They know that sin is worthy of death, but they nevertheless do these things and *take pleasure* when others follow the way of death along with them. This makes these people cheerleaders of death. Truly the words that Wisdom speaks in Proverbs are manifest in this instance: All who hate wisdom *love death* (Prov. 8:36).

And this is how we know that America is currently under judgment. Note again, we do not know in the abstract that America, like all nations, will be headed for judgment *if*...We are dealing with a very concrete situation, not an abstract one.

Suppose there was a nation awash in consumer goods, a nation that gained the world, but which lost its own soul (Matt. 16:26). Suppose that nation cut off its future by slaughtering over sixty million of her own citizens. Suppose further that this was urged as a noble and constitutional thing to do. Suppose that this nation began to sanctify sodomite marriages and laughed at every form of righteousness. Suppose that there were millions of Christians in this country who longed for America to deliver herself by returning to her noble, true self, instead of longing for Christ to save her from her corrupted, wicked self.

Such a nation would be suffering under a true spiritual delusion, and would be in desperate need of the message found throughout this book of Romans.

CHAPTER 2

THE SPIRIT OF ACCUSATION

God's wrath is taught very clearly in Scripture. Our great problem with it is that we confound it with a spirit of accusation that belongs to the devil, and we show that we do not understand how righteousness—the *real* thing—interacts with sin. We think we know, but we tend to know only how *self*-righteousness would deal with unrighteousness.

> Therefore thou art inexcusable, O man, whosoever thou art that judgest: for wherein thou judgest another, thou condemnest thyself; for thou that judgest doest the same things. But we are sure that the judgment of God is according to truth against them which

commit such things. And thinkest thou this, O man, that judgest them which do such things, and doest the same, that thou shalt escape the judgment of God? Or despisest thou the riches of his goodness and forbearance and longsuffering; not knowing that the goodness of God leadeth thee to repentance? But after thy hardness and impenitent heart treasurest up unto thyself wrath against the day of wrath and revelation of the righteous judgment of God; (Rom. 2:1–5)

Having indicted the entire Gentile world, the Apostle Paul turns to the Jews. This is seen in the judgments he describes as delivered against pagan practices in the first part of this chapter, but then it is made explicit in v. 17. "Behold, thou art called a Jew..."

But it is interesting that as he does so, addressing those who would *approve* of his treatment of the Gentiles in chapter one, he speaks to them as "O *man*" (vv. 1, 3). His point in the second chapter is that you Jews have the same problem with sin, "you are *men* after all," and you have compounded all of it with the hypocrisy of a double standard. The Gentile pagan looking at the stars was "without excuse" (1:20). In the same way, this one who would judge the Gentiles is also inexcusable (2:1). Why? Because he does the same sorts of things himself. But the judgment of God rests on those who *do* such things (v. 2), and it is not possible to avert that judgment simply because you disapprove of them on paper or because your sacred Torah condemns them. Do you really think, O man, that it is okay with God that you judge those who do such things while doing the same deeds? Do you think that God will let it go? That He will somehow *not* judge (v. 3)? The absence of judgment thus far is not meant to communicate that all is well. It is meant to lead to repentance (v. 4). To think otherwise is to despise the riches of His goodness, forbearance and longsuffering (v. 4). To resist the plain intentions of God in all this is to treasure up wrath for yourself against the day of wrath and revelation of God's righteous judgments (v. 5).

Paul knew that the despicable behavior of the Gentiles really was atrocious in the sight of God, and he said so. He also knew that their behavior was atrocious in the sight of the Jews, but for completely different reasons. God disapproved of them the way *God* would. The Jews disapproved of their immoralities the way the *devil* would, in a spirit of diabolical accusation. Chapter one followed by this in chapter two was a Pauline setup, and it is evidence of our blindness that we still walk into it. Is the Gentile world, gay pride parades and all, without excuse? Absolutely. They are without excuse in the same way that their evangelical disapprovers are—those who live in the same kind of moral squalor, but with the furniture rearranged.

Do unto others as you would have them do unto you, right (Matt. 7:12)? But this is not just a positive statement that can be applied to every aspect of life (Eph. 5:28). We have the most trouble with the flip side of this expression of God's character. Just a few verses before the Golden Rule, Jesus unloaded this on us: "Judge not, that ye be not judged. For with what judgment ye judge, ye shall be judged: and with what measure ye mete, it shall be measured to you again" (Matt. 7:1–2). Clearly, Jesus is not prohibiting any form of moral discernment. Consider what He requires a few verses later concerning the false prophets—beware of ravening wolves (Matt. 7:15). Rather, He is prohibiting a double standard, which keeps others away from addressing *my* sin by bringing up *their* sin first. The best defense is a good offense, right? *Wrong.*

God really is righteous, and when true righteousness comes into contact with unrighteousness, there must be either wrath or mercy. But wrath is not fussy indignation, self-importance, and self-righteousness—or any other thing the devil does. The righteousness of God is not the devil's bony finger, pointing in accusation (Rev. 12:10). God *is* righteous. The devil *thinks* he is righteous.

The whole point of the diabolical is *not* the Miltonic "evil be thou my good." What is Satanic and diabolical is to believe that you understand righteousness better than God does. Religious people do this all the time, believing that their standards are better, righter, tighter, and more holy than God's. But this was refuted and destroyed by the cross, when the "righteous accuser" let his hatred get away from him and perpetrated a gross injustice by executing the world's only sinless victim. Why would anyone believe the accuser now? Why would we even *trust* the spirit of accusation? The cross has conquered the spirit of accusation.

We become like what we worship. This principle is clearly taught by Paul in the first chapter, and he is resting on a long prophetic tradition. This is a fundamental spiritual law. "And he gave them their request; but *sent leanness into their soul*" (Ps. 106:15, emphasis added). "Their idols are silver and gold, the work of men's hands....They that make them *are like unto them*; so is every one that trusteth in them" (Ps. 115:4, 8, emphasis added). "Thus saith the LORD, What iniquity have your fathers found in me, that they are gone far from me, and *have walked after vanity, and are become vain*?" (Jer. 2:5, emphasis added). "And they rejected his statutes, and his covenant that he made with their fathers, and his testimonies which he testified against them; and *they followed vanity, and became vain,* and went after the heathen that were round about them, concerning whom the LORD had charged them, that they should not do like them" (2 Kings 17:15, emphasis added). "I found Israel like grapes in the wilderness; I saw your fathers as the firstripe in the fig tree at her first time: but they went to Baalpeor, and separated themselves unto that shame; and *their abominations were according as they loved*" (Hos. 9:10, emphasis added).

This great principle is not altered if the idol is hidden away where no one knows about it or *pretends* to not know about it. We think our picture of Dorian Gray is hidden away in the attic, but we can only keep up the pretense for a time. The *idol* may be hidden in the attic (Deut. 13:6), but our reflection of that idol's characteristics is out there for all the world to see. You become what you worship, *and what you are actually becoming is a public revelation of your true worship*. What many call a midlife crisis is simply idolatry catching up with a person. If you are falling apart, don't waste your time trying to catch and gather the pieces. *Destroy the idol.*

Now bring all this back to Romans 2. The Jews had a double standard that cheered when Paul lit into the Gentiles. They liked hearing about how sinful the Gentiles were. But this meant what? It meant that while the Gentiles were becoming like Baal, Zeus, and Moloch, the Jews were becoming like the devil. They said they worshiped the God of Abraham, but then turned His holy law into an instrument of accusation. And there is a warning here for us. Any believer who understands that the law of God really is holy, and this would include evangelical Christians, will be tempted to use that holy law as a club reserved for use on others. The definition that Ambrose Bierce gave to the word *Christian* comes to mind: "One who believes that the New Testament is a divinely inspired book admirably suited to the spiritual needs of his neighbor."

GLORY, HONOR, IMMORTALITY

Paul has already stated his great theme for us—that *the just shall live by faith*. This is the great epistle of justification by faith, apart from works of the law. At the same time, it is quite striking that there is no more of a contradiction between Paul and James than there is between Paul later on in Romans and Paul here in Romans 2. James says that as the body without the spirit is dead, so also faith without works is dead (Jas. 2:20,26). In this chapter of Romans, Paul says that God will render to every man according to his deeds (Rom. 2:6), and eternal life is the destiny of those who by patient continuance in doing good seek for glory, honor, and immortality (Rom. 2:7).

Who will render to every man according to his deeds:
to them who by patient continuance in well doing seek
for glory and honour and immortality, eternal life:
but unto them that are contentious, and do not obey
the truth, but obey unrighteousness, indignation and
wrath, tribulation and anguish, upon every soul of man
that doeth evil, of the Jew first, and also of the Gentile;
but glory, honour, and peace, to every man that worketh good, to the Jew first, and also to the Gentile: for
there is no respect of persons with God. For as many
as have sinned without law shall also perish without
law: and as many as have sinned in the law shall be
judged by the law; (for not the hearers of the law are
just before God, but the doers of the law shall be justified. For when the Gentiles, which have not the law,
do by nature the things contained in the law, these,
having not the law, are a law unto themselves: which
shew the work of the law written in their hearts, their
conscience also bearing witness, and their thoughts the
mean while accusing or else excusing one another;) in
the day when God shall judge the secrets of men by
Jesus Christ according to my gospel. (Rom. 2:6–16)

In the judgment that is sure to come, God will render to
each man according to his deeds (v. 6). Those who seek glory, honor, and immortality through good deeds, God will
grant eternal life (v. 7). But for those who are stiff-necked,
and who do not obey truth, God will pour out on them
indignation, wrath, tribulation, and anguish (vv. 8–9), to
the Jew first and then to the Gentile. But glory, honor,

and peace to those who do good, to the Jew first and then to the Gentile (v. 10). This is because God does not play favorites (v. 11). Those like the Gentiles who have sinned apart from the Torah shall perish outside the Torah. Those like the Jews who sinned under the Torah will be judged by it (v. 12). God doesn't care what you listen to, He cares what you *do* with it (v. 13). And when Gentiles, who do not have Torah, do by nature the precepts contained there, they demonstrate that they have access to a natural law, a general law (v. 14). This natural law is within them and is read by their consciences, enabling them to accuse or excuse one another (v. 15). When will this happen (v. 12)? It will happen on the day that God judges the secrets of men by Jesus Christ, and all this in accordance with the gospel that Paul calls "my gospel" (v. 16).

We should begin by looking at the relationship between the Torah and natural law. One of the great problems we have with interpreters of Paul is that they rarely have minds as supple as his. They want to define a term, and then they want it to stay put. A great example of this would be Paul's use of the word *law*. Interpreters want it to mean the Mosaic Torah, or they want it to mean a timeless code of moral truths, and they don't like it when Paul jumps back and forth between meanings, frequently within the space of one verse (v. 14). The Gentiles don't have the Torah, but they do have nature, and this nature teaches them a number of the tenets found in the Torah. So they don't have the Torah, but they do have natural law, and these two are consistent with one another. The idea of natural law is thoroughly Pauline. And by natural law, I simply mean that men, apart from the Bible, can look at the created order and see that God is majestic and holy.

It is a commonplace for Christians to see a tension between Paul and James. Paul says that by the deeds of the law no flesh shall be justified (Rom. 3:20). And James famously says that we are not justified by faith alone (Jas. 2:17). What are we to do about that?

But let's solve a different problem first. Paul says that by deeds of the law no flesh shall be justified (Rom. 3:20). But here he talks about those who in "patient continuance in well doing seek for glory, honour and immortality," and he promises "glory, honour, and peace" to every man "that worketh good." Listening to the law won't justify you, Paul says, but the *doers* of the law shall be justified (v. 13).

Any attempt to make Paul the master of raw faith, with a few necessary good works sprinkled in there by James, is a futile and silly task. Paul and James extended to one another the right hand of fellowship (Gal. 2:9), which means that James was good with what Paul taught about faith alone, and Paul was good with what James said about the necessity of good works. The necessary connection between living faith and living works is *organic*, and this is as clearly stated in Romans 2 as it is in James 2. The solution? Obey the truth (v. 8), and this includes the truth that good works that a man does in his own name, on his own authority, will only send him deeper into Hell. Christ alone, grace alone, by faith alone. *Obey* that, and God will raise you to life, and life is not possible unless the body and spirit are *together* (Jas. 2:26).

So what kind of Gentiles are we talking about in vv. 14–15? Some have suggested that the Gentiles of verses 14–15 are believing Gentiles, Christians. This gets us away from the possibility that some pagans might actually be justified if their conscience excuses them on the day of judgment (v. 15). But this is unlikely for two reasons. First, if these were Gentile *Christians*, then why would nature have to teach them these things? Christian Gentiles have the Old Testament, and by this point, they also have a bunch of the New Testament. Paul is talking about natural law here, not a fuller form of special revelation which the Gentile Christians had.

Secondly, we are solving a problem we don't really need to solve. The Gentiles as a group prior to this moment in history were mostly unsaved unbelievers. But a number of them, not Jewish at all, were saved. So there is no need to have the same ratio of now accusing/now excusing for the whole lot. The Gentiles prior to Christ did *not* occupy a place that is today occupied by non-Christians. Now that Israel has become international in scope, it *is* necessary for everyone to become an Israelite, to come into the Christian Church, which is the new Israel, as we will see in the rest of this letter. But the old Israel was to be a priestly nation on behalf of all the nations (Ex.19:6). While a Gentile could become an Israelite if he *wanted* to, there was no obligation to do so. In the Old Testament, a Gentile *while remaining a Gentile* could be saved, and many tens of thousands of them were. Some of these Gentiles had some of their information from special revelation (through contact with the Jews), but there is no reason for thinking, for example, that Melchizedek got his information from the Jews. There weren't any Jews until Abraham.

Melchizedek was no Jew, and was a priest (Gen. 14:18), and yet Abraham, the father of all the faithful, paid tithes to him (Heb. 7:6). Jethro was a priest in Midian, not in Israel, and yet was a godly man (Ex. 3:1). Naaman the Syrian became a worshiper of the true God (2 Kings 5:17). The Lord referred to the fact that God had mercy on a Sidonian woman (Luke 4:26). Many thousands were saved in Nineveh, under the preaching of Jonah (Jonah 3:6–10), much to that prophet's dismay. When Solomon dedicated the Temple, he did so with the prayer that God would heed the prayers of Gentiles directed there (1 Kings 8:41–43). The Temple had a dedicated court for the Gentiles, because it was to be a house of prayer for all *nations* (Mark 11:17). The truth of God—from any and every quarter—is for the entire world, and always has been.

THE GENESIS OF HYPOCRISY

We have already seen in the first chapter of Romans that the unbelieving Gentile world is without excuse in its rebellion against God. We have also seen (in this second chapter of Romans) that believing Gentiles are not in the same position. And here in this passage, we come to the point of emphasis, which is that the Jews are also under sin and in need of a Savior.

> Behold, thou art called a Jew, and restest in the law, and makest thy boast of God, and knowest his will, and approvest the things that are more excellent, being

instructed out of the law; and art confident that thou thyself art a guide of the blind, a light of them which are in darkness, an instructor of the foolish, a teacher of babes, which hast the form of knowledge and of the truth in the law. Thou therefore which teachest another, teachest thou not thyself? Thou that preachest a man should not steal, dost thou steal? Thou that sayest a man should not commit adultery, dost thou commit adultery? Thou that abhorrest idols, dost thou commit sacrilege? Thou that makest thy boast of the law, through breaking the law dishonourest thou God? For the name of God is blasphemed among the Gentiles through you, as it is written. (Rom. 2:17–24)

Paul begins by naming the Jews explicitly—you who are called a Jew (v. 17). Not only does he call himself a Jew, but he also rests in the law (v. 17) and makes his boast in God (v. 17). What is this but the great Reformation principle of *soli Deo gloria*? The Pharisee who insulted the publican in his Temple prayer did the same—"I thank thee, *God*..." Not only so, but this Jew knows the will of God, and knows it because he is instructed by God from the law. As a result, this Jew approves *excellent* things (v. 18). He is also confident that he has the ability to teach—he is a guide to the blind (v. 19), a light for those in the dark (v. 19), an instructor of the foolish (v. 20), a teacher of little babies (v. 20), as someone who has the right form of knowledge and truth in the law (v. 20). Very good, Paul says, but let's start somewhere else.

Those who teach must first teach themselves, and more-over, those who expect others to learn the lessons must learn the lessons themselves *first* (v. 21). It doesn't count if you teach yourself first, but the pupil is stupid. If you preach against stealing, do you steal (v. 21)? If you say not to commit adultery, how's it going in *your* life (v. 22)? If you abhor idols, and good for you, do you commit sacrilege yourself (v. 22)? The word literally here is *temple-robber*, and Paul is exonerated of a similar charge at Ephesus (Acts 19:37). There had apparently been some shenanigans on the part of someone that the Roman Christians would have known about. You boast in the law, but you in fact dishonor God through your breaking of the law (v. 23). Because of you Jews, Paul says, the Gentiles blaspheme the name of God (v. 24). Not only so, but you have been doing this for a long time—long enough for both Isaiah and Ezekiel to have noticed it centuries earlier (Isa. 52:5; Ezek. 36:22).

Orthodoxy is heavy on teaching, knowing, and approving. But notice how Paul then uses the verbs—*teach*, *preach*, *say*, *abhor*, and *boast*. You teach the right, you preach the right, you say the right, you abhor God's rivals, and you boast in Him alone. Yes, but what do you *do*? Don't hide behind the creeds and confessions.

Paul objects to the fact that the hypocrisy of the Jews has provided unbelieving Gentiles with some cheap entertainment. But there is a common mistake here that we make, and Paul shows us how to avoid it. The hypocrisy of God's people does *not* create a valid excuse or defense for the unbeliever. Take the most obnoxious televangelist you can construct in your imagination, the randiest pope ever in

Church history, and the smarmiest Scripture-twister ever, and everything they ever said or did is shouted down by one sunrise, one midnight at sea, or five minutes of contemplating the complexities of a single cell. The unbeliever is *always* without excuse (Rom. 1:20).

The plain fact is that God *hates* hypocrisy, and He will judge it at the last day (Isa. 9:17; Matt. 6:2; 22:18). What sense does it make to oppose the living God, who alone will judge the hypocrites, and to do so because *you* disapprove of hypocrites? If you hate the behavior of certain people on a particular team, then why do you engage in the same behavior? Blasphemers "because of hypocrisy" and the hypocrites themselves will both be thrown into the lake of fire, and if God goes in alphabetical order, those who *pretended* to hate hypocrisy in their blasphemies will have to go first.

When we get to the point of denunciation, it is not hard to condemn hypocrisy as Paul does here, and to use a canoe paddle on it. But why and how is hypocrisy a snare that works so easily? It is among the most contemptible of sins—we all hate it—so why do so many fall into it? What contributes to the setup? Remember that Paul expects the Gentile Christians to learn the lessons that the unbelieving Jews failed to learn (Rom. 11:20).

Rain doesn't fall from a clear, blue sky, and hypocrisy doesn't come from nowhere either. When glaring hypocrisy is evident, this means that it is glaringly obvious to *others*. In the experience of the hypocrite himself, things can be pretty tangled and obscured. There can be many motivations for our inconsistencies. For example:

- We are pious and unwilling to mock holy things...the way God does (Jer. 7:4). We absolutize the things of God instead of recognizing that God is the absolute.

- We bask in the reflected glory of things that God actually praises (Rom. 2:18). As Thomas Watson once put it, not everyone who hangs about the court speaks with the king.

- We are afraid of blowback (John 7:13; 9:22). This happens when our hypocrisy is the result of fear.

- We are careless of the fact that big hypocrisies grow from little hypocrisies (Ps. 19:12–13). What began as secret sins moved on to presumptuous sins, and then on to great transgression.

- We refuse to make our own deep motivations an object of serious contemplation (2 Cor. 13:5). While there is a kind of self-examination that is morbid, there is another kind that is essential.

- We don't understand the mimetic nature of human motivation and behavioral contagion (Jas. 4:5–6). Human beings are born imitators, and we frequently do not recognize when we are doing it.

- We judge others by their actions, but we want to be judged by our intentions (Prov. 20:10). But when we compare ourselves to others, it really should be apples to apples.

- We say that mere possession of the truth works as a talisman (Jas. 2:14). But James says that head knowledge without doing it is simply self-deception.
- We rest in external privileges, instead of improving them (Rom. 11:22). If we are blessed in our situation, we need to remember that much is expected from those who have been given much.
- We stare at Scripture as though it were a mural, instead of through Scripture as a window (John 5:39). The Scriptures are not simply words *about* God. They are His vehicle for communicating Himself to us.
- We don't understand what God is *actually* like (Ps. 16:11). God is the fountainhead of all happiness and joy, and hypocrisy is never anything like that.

THE ABSOLUTE NECESSITY OF THE NEW BIRTH

We left off with Paul's observation that the Gentiles blasphemed God's name because of the behavior of God's people, the Jews. In this passage, he goes on to show the root cause of the discrepancy between the holy name by which God's people were called, on the one hand, and the unholy lives which disgraced that calling, on the other. The root cause was the lack of personal regeneration. As Jesus told Nicodemus, a man *must* be born again. To take the larger argument of Romans, not all Israel are Israel. We may (and we must) extend this to say that not all Christians are Christians.

> For circumcision verily profiteth, if thou keep the law: but if thou be a breaker of the law, thy circumcision is made uncircumcision. Therefore if the uncircumcision keep the righteousness of the law, shall not his uncircumcision be counted for circumcision? And shall not uncircumcision which is by nature, if it fulfil the law, judge thee, who by the letter and circumcision dost transgress the law? For he is not a Jew, which is one outwardly; neither is that circumcision, which is outward in the flesh: but he is a Jew, which is one inwardly; and circumcision is that of the heart, in the spirit, and not in the letter; whose praise is not of men, but of God. (Rom. 2:25–29)

What good is circumcision? Who needs it? Paul says that circumcision does profit a Jew if he keeps the rest of the law (v. 25). Circumcision is obedience to the Torah at the doorway (Deut. 11:20), but if disobedience is pervasive through the rest of the house, then God treats the sign of allegiance at the doorway as though it were the opposite (Rom. 2:25). And what happens when you flip this around? If an uncircumcised person keeps the righteousness of the *moral* law (remember, he is not keeping Torah, because he is uncircumcised), then won't God place him in the ranks of the honorary circumcised (v. 26)? Not only so, but the uncircumcised in this position will be in a position to judge the person who "by letter" and "by circumcision" transgresses the law (v. 27). This person could be either a pagan Gentile of verse 14, or a baptized Gentile in the church at Rome— Paul's argument works either way. *Why* does it work this way? Paul then says that a man is not a true Jew who is simply one outwardly, and that true circumcision is not a matter of what is done to the flesh (v. 28). A true Jew is a Jew on the inside, and true circumcision is a matter of the heart and spirit, not the letter (v. 29) The praise for such a man is not from men, but from God (v. 29).

We now come to the place where we will discuss the Torah and the righteousness of the law. The distinction between the Torah and what might be called the essence of the law is a very important one if we are to understand the letter to the Romans. We have noted it before, and we have to make a note of it again here. Paul clearly distinguishes between formal law-keeping and essential law-keeping— but this is not possible if we say that his only interest has to do with the relationship of the old Torah and the new gospel. Paul insists here that an uncircumcised person by nature can nevertheless keep the essential law, what he identifies as the "*righteousness* of the law."

A similar thing must be said about a very crucial word here, one that is also essential to a right understanding of Romans. It occurs in our passage here, and that word is *logizomai* (λογιζομαι). It is the kind of word that is remarkably flexible—it was rendered as "thinkest" in 2:3, but it occurs here as "counted" (2:26). Elsewhere in Romans it is translated as "reckon" (4:4), "account" (8:36), or, most famously, "impute" (4:6). We will muddy everything if we understand this word as any kind of *infusion*. We will not do a great deal with this now, but it will be very important later—so mark this spot. For the moment, let us just say that we are justified on the basis of a forensic declaration of righteousness concerning us (an imputation, or a reckoning), and not on the basis of an infusion of righteousness into us.

Sin creates rebellious dualisms. God created us so that our spirit, soul, and body would all live in harmonious union. But rebellion against Him fractured this harmony and made it possible for an individual to be one man on the outside and a completely different man on the inside. This was not what we were created for, but our sin made such hypocrisy possible. But that is not our concern in this message now— the basic problem of hypocrisy was addressed earlier.

Here is a different problem. Some Christians, discovering that there ought not to be this inside/outside divide, have falsely concluded that there is no such thing as a fundamental inside/outside divide. But this is saying, ultimately, that hypocrisy is impossible. However, Paul is blunt here. He knew men who were Jews on the outside, but he did not consider them to be Jews on the inside. What needed to occur in order for them to be Jews on the inside? Paul says that it amounted to heart circumcision, in the spirit and not in the letter (v. 29). As it was, their outside testified against their inside (v. 27). By the letter and by their circumcision they transgressed.

This is the great contribution of historic evangelicalism—teaching the absolute necessity of the new birth. This should not be confused with the accretions of pop evangelicalism or certain traditions within evangelicalism which seek to put that new birth in a can, prepackaging it for the upcoming revival meetings, prescribing just what it looks like in every instance—going forward, signing the card, that kind of thing. But the Spirit moves as *He* pleases. Reformation and revival are not a commodity.

So what is at issue? How does it all translate? Does this warning at the end of Romans 2 translate over to Christians? Can we say that "he is not a *Christian* who is one outwardly, neither is baptism that which is outward in the flesh"? Can we say he is a Christian who is "one inwardly," and baptism is "of the heart, in the spirit, and not in the letter." Of course we can, and we *must*.

Paul here is spelling out the root causes of the great Jewish failure. The Jews had not kept the law in truth even though they were circumcised—precisely because they had not obeyed the *law* by receiving the circumcision of the heart (Deut. 10:16; 30:6; Jer. 4:4). This doctrine of the new birth is no innovation of Paul's—God required it in the Old Testament times as well. And Paul elsewhere tells the covenanted Christians that they were capable of failing in just the same way that the Jews had (Rom. 11:20–21; 1 Cor. 10:6), *and for the same reasons* (2 Cor. 13:5). A brief glance at Church history shows us the wisdom of this warning, as does a moment's reflection on our own circumstances. A man, if he wants to see the kingdom of God, must be born again. Is this your desire? Then look to Christ—Christ on the cross, Christ in Heaven, Christ in the Word, Christ in the water, Christ in the bread and wine. But always this is looking *through* to Christ, not staring *at* whatever the vehicle or messenger was.

CHAPTER 3

BEGIN WITH THE CONCLUSION

We learned from the end of chapter two that not all Jews are Jews along with the corollary that not all Christians are Christians. But keeping up with the apostle can be a strenuous effort sometimes, and we now learn in the first part of chapter three that the Jews who are not really Jews are, nevertheless...Jews. And the same goes double for Christians.

> What advantage then hath the Jew? Or what profit is there of circumcision? Much every way: chiefly, because that unto them were committed the oracles of God. For what if some did not believe? Shall their unbelief make

the faith of God without effect? God forbid: yea, let God
be true, but every man a liar; as it is written, That thou
mightest be justified in thy sayings, and mightest overcome when thou art judged. (Rom. 3:1–4)

Chapter two concludes with Paul offering the definition
of the true Jew, the inward Jew. But now, without missing a beat, he returns to the conventional use of the word
Jew. It is as though he is asking that if a bunch of Jews ar-
en't really Jewish, then what good does it do them being
Jewish? We would say, having thought we got his point,
"Well, no good at all." But what does he say? "Much every
way" (v. 2). The chief reason there is profit in external
circumcision (the kind of Jewishness he is talking about
now) is that the externally circumcised were entrusted
with the oracles of God, the Scriptures (v. 2). Some did
not believe, and Paul responds to that with a *So what?*
Can the unbelief of covenant members undo the covenant? No way (v. 3). Their unbelief cannot make "the
faith of God" without effect. One important question here
is whether this is subjective (God's faith, or perhaps His
faithfulness) or objective (the faith that God established,
i.e., the Christian faith). But no matter which we take it,
can a Europe filled with baptized infidels undo the glorious truth proclaimed in baptism? Not a bit of it, and God
forbid. Every last covenant member could be a skunk, and
God remains true (v. 4). Our task is not to conform the
sacrament to the behavior of people, but rather to conform the people to the nature of the sacrament. And then
Paul quotes Psalm 51:4, to powerful effect (v. 4).

So we may begin with Paul's conclusion. The first thing to note is that Psalm 51 was composed after David had received the rebuke of Nathan for his sin with Bathsheba. That was the occasion. So what is the psalm about? It is about true confession, internal cleansing, and the comparative value of the externals in God's sight. David pleads for cleansing and forgiveness (vv. 1–2). He confesses his sin honestly and in the right direction, so that God would be justified when He speaks, clear when He judges, and might conquer when He is judged (vv. 3–4). David, a covenant member, was conceived in iniquity (v. 5). God wanted David to possess truth in the inward parts (v. 6). For that to happen, God must do the cleansing and restoring (vv. 7–12). After this, and only because of this, teaching the transgressors and sinners can occur (v. 13). God is rightly praised when men are truly forgiven (vv. 14–15). God wants sacrifices in the heart, not on the altar (vv. 16–17). God is invited to build His city (v. 18), and *after that* He will be pleased with the external sacrifices (v. 19). The distinction between an outward Jew and an inward one was, again, gleaned from the *Old* Testament. Heart circumcision was required in the Old Testament, as we saw earlier, and here we see God's rejection of mere external conformity to His sacrificial law.

As an aside, Paul says here that the chief value of institutional Judaism was the fact that the Jews possessed (and transmitted to us) the oracles of God, the Scriptures (v. 2). He echoes this same thing again later in an expanded list—they had the adoption, the glory, the covenants, the law, the worship of God, the promises, the fathers, and the privilege of being the people of the Christ (9:4–5). But here in chapter three, he places possession of the Scriptures in the chief place—and we can see a number of the blessings that will be named in chapter nine as subsumed under that. This being the case, then why has the Church today relinquished control of the Scriptures, the *full* corpus of the oracles of God, turning them over to an alliance of big business and textual critics in the academy? Whose idea was that? And why do we persist in acting like it was a good one?

Returning to our theme, we can see that Paul sets up a parallel between verses 3 and 4. In verse 3, the two elements are "unbelief" and "the faith of God." In verse 4 they are "every man a liar" and "God be true." We should therefore understand unbelief being equivalent to man lying, and the faith of God as the equivalent to God being true. And when Paul caps it off with his citation of Psalm 51, the whole thing should come into focus. God being true despite the sinfulness and lies of covenant members does not primarily mean that God wins the argument (although He *does* always win the argument); it means that despite our sinfulness and uncanny ability to get everything wrong, He will still win the world. Remember how Psalm 51 ends— with pure worship in the world, pure internally and externally both. The result of God remaining true to David despite David being untrue to God is that transgressors are taught, and *sinners are converted*. Thus we ultimately do not have to choose between the faithfulness of God and our faith in God. The latter is only possible because of the former, and the former necessitates the latter.

Honest confession of sin does not get in God's way. God does not need our bright and shiny righteousness in order to advance His kingdom. What He wants is for us to acknowledge what we are by nature, which is iniquitous from conception (Ps. 51:5). He wants us to acknowledge what we are by choice and action—which is transgressors in need of forgiveness (Ps. 51:1–2). Remember that Paul is quoting this psalm after Romans 1 placed all the unbelieving Gentiles under the condemnation of sin and Romans 2 placed all the unbelieving Jews under the condemnation of sin. He is writing this on the threshold of his point in Romans 3, which is that Gentiles and Jews are *together* in the same terrible fix. David, one of the greatest covenant kings in the history of God's covenant people, confessed that he was conceived in sin and that the amniotic fluid in which he was formed was the fluid of iniquity. So stop trying to protect *God's* reputation by hiding *your* sin. He doesn't care. Christ died for sinners, and God is reconciled. We should therefore stop trying to win the I-didn't-have-to-be-forgiven-for-as-much-as-you-did contest.

True confession means acknowledging what your sin actually was and doing so with complete honesty before God (1 John 1:9), and it also means acknowledging the true identity of the one insulted by the sin. David says, "Against thee, thee *only*, have I sinned" (Ps. 51:4, emphasis added). Mark that. David was guilty of adultery, disloyalty to a faithful subordinate, then murder, and then a political cover-up and scandal. Lots of other people were involved, but against "thee only have I sinned." But take heart—all sin is aimed at God, seeking to topple Him from His throne. But

He is true, even if you are full of lies. You might as well come quietly...cleansing awaits.

RIGHTEOUS VENGEANCE

Paul is walking the world through the meaning of honest confession before God. The unbelieving Gentiles don't want to honor God as God or give Him thanks, so Paul sets the grandeur of God right in front of them as displayed in every created thing. The Jews don't want God, so Paul condemns them according to the standards of Torah, the same Torah that they thought they were so pleased with. He is driving to the conclusion of the first part of his letter, which is the sinfulness of every man. But human pride doesn't want to talk about human sin and would much rather talk about divine sins. So Paul takes a moment to swat at the gnat that some call the greatest philosophical problem *ever*—the problem of evil.

> But if our unrighteousness commend the righteousness of God, what shall we say? Is God unrighteous who taketh vengeance? (I speak as a man) God forbid: for then how shall God judge the world? For if the truth of God hath more abounded through my lie unto his glory; why yet am I also judged as a sinner? And not rather, (as we be slanderously reported, and as some affirm that we say,) let us do evil, that good may come? Whose damnation is just. (Rom. 3:5–8)

Some men can be counted on to get huffy with this kind of Pauline talk—"every man a liar," and so forth. And they determine that the best defense against the ultimately holy

God is a good offense, and they come up with stumpers for the Q&A after an evangelistic presentation. First, they say, if our unrighteousness sets off God's righteousness, putting it in a good light so to speak, then what must we say? Speaking carnally, is God unrighteous when He takes vengeance (v. 5)? Of course not, Paul says. First, he is speaking "as a man," that is, carnally and as one of his questioners. That would mean that God couldn't judge the world (v. 6). And since it is a nonnegotiable reality that God *will* in fact judge the world, the question must be bogus. Philosophy doesn't judge God's day of vengeance. God's day of vengeance judges philosophy and, while He is at it, philosophers also. Paul then repeats the same argument in different words—if my lie glorifies God by setting up a glorious contrast with His truth, then why does He then get to judge me as a sinner (v. 7)? *Hmmmm?* And some of them have taken their incoherence to the next level, which was probably the whole point, slanderously representing *Paul* as arguing that we should do evil so that God will be glorified (v. 8). Given the way Paul phrases this, this utterly unserious argument is being attributed to him. Those who do this are under a just condemnation (v. 8).

The Apostle Paul had to deal with this issue, so there is no real reason why we who have learned from him should not have to deal with it also. What do we do when men attack the Calvinistic straw man? The teaching that God is exhaustively sovereign (a teaching that is pervasive in this book of Romans) is *easy* to twist, caricature, misrepresent, and slander. The move is a simple one. You take the teaching, cash out what you believe its logical implications to be, turn white in the face, and then attribute those appalling conclusions to those who hold to the premises that you have just mangled. This is a mistake in argumentation that Paul links to damnation (v. 8). At the same time, Calvinists need to remember the Golden Rule. If you don't like it on the receiving end, then you shouldn't like it on the giving end.

Is God unrighteous when He takes vengeance (v. 5)? Absolutely not, Paul says. His judgments are necessarily righteous. Is it up for discussion whether or not God will judge the world (v. 6)? No—Paul does not reason to the *conclusion* that God will judge all creatures. He does that elsewhere, reasoning from the fact of the resurrection to the conclusion that Jesus will judge (Acts 17:31). Rather, the fact that God in Heaven is the judge of all nations is his *premise* here (v. 6).

God is the only lawful possessor of wrath, and no man may step in as His deputy without God's express teaching in Scripture. In the book of Romans alone, God's wrath is clearly displayed (1:18; 2:5; 2:8; 4:15; 5:9; 9:22; 12:19; 13:4–5); His judgments are just and sure (1:32; 2:2–3; 2:5; 5:16–18; 14:10); and His vengeance is honored (3:5; 12:19). But here is the problem. Man is in the dock, and man therefore wants (*desperately* wants) God to be in the dock instead.

But think about this for a moment. If man is to be judged by God, where does the standard for judgment come from? From God's holy, infinite, and entirely righteous character. If God is to be judged by man, where does the standard for judgment come from? And how incoherent is that? "Who art thou that repliest against God?

Shall the thing formed say to him that formed it, Why has thou made me thus? Hath not the potter power over the clay...?" (Rom. 9:20–21). Our problem with all of this— Hell, damnation, wrath, judgment, or vengeance is *not* that it is all too unjust. Don't we know our hearts any better than that? Our problem with God's judgment is not the potential for grave injustice, to be guarded against by *us* and policed by *us* (!), but rather the much more frightening prospect of real justice.

Knowing this about God's righteous character is not a setup for theological paranoia. Those who understand it that way do not understand it. High views of the *triune* God's righteousness will lead directly to higher views of His grace and mercy. We now have "peace with God" (5:1). There is now *no condemnation* for those of us who are in Christ Jesus (8:1).

In the book of Romans, Paul's questioners are worldly men, and they do theology like a cheeky sophomore. And one of the most natural worldly tendencies out there is the attempt to magnify God's grace by minimizing His holiness and consequent wrath. But doing that will not give you the faith once delivered; rather it will give you a pile of mush. It is that impulse that drives every form of theological liberalism, including the forms of it that are rampant in the evangelical world today.

Lowering the bar to shouts of "Grace!" will only have the effect of trying to make God's kindness to us something that He owes us rather than something that overflows from the good counsel of His will and the very nature of His being. He doesn't *owe* us a blessed thing. He doesn't owe us forgiveness, or cleansing, or salvation, or a place in Heaven. He doesn't even owe us a participant ribbon. He gives us all these things, but not because we are entitled to them. There is no entitlement here, only free grace.

I emphasized the word *triune* a short while ago. If there is no God, or if there are many gods, there is no such thing as justice. If God is a solitary being, a unitarian god, then we are all crushed under the weight of something *called* justice. If God is the ultimate hermit, alone and utterly solitary, then He cannot be love. Prior to the creation, there would be no one or nothing to love, and in the uncreated realm there would only be the Monad. But Scripture teaches us that God is love (1 John 4:8). Because God is triune, the Father loves the Son everlastingly, and the Son returns the love. Apart from anything created, God is love. Men who beat their wives worship the solitary kind of god. But our triune God, the living God, is the only one who can rule a universe in which mercy and truth may kiss each other (Ps. 85:10).

THAT EVERY MOUTH MAY BE STOPPED

One difficulty that presents itself while working through a book like Romans in small segments is that it is very hard to find a place to stop...and this is because Paul frequently doesn't stop. Consequently, in this section we need to run a little ahead and stop in mid-thought, and in the following section we will back up in order to be able to finish the thought. And that thought revolves around the connection to being shut up under sin without one thing to say, on the one hand, and God's intent to justify us fully and freely, on the other hand.

> What then? Are we better than they? No, in no wise: for we have before proved both Jews and Gentiles, that they are all under sin; as it is written, There is none righteous, no, not one: there is none that under-standeth, there is none that seeketh after God. They are all gone out of the way, they are together become unprofitable; there is none that doeth good, no, not one. Their throat is an open sepulchre; with their tongues they have used deceit; the poison of asps is under their lips: whose mouth is full of cursing and bit-terness: their feet are swift to shed blood: destruction and misery are in their ways: and the way of peace have they not known: there is no fear of God before their eyes. Now we know that what things soever the law saith, it saith to them who are under the law: that every mouth may be stopped, and all the world may become guilty before God. Therefore by the deeds of the law there shall no flesh be justified in his sight: for by the law is the knowledge of sin. But now the righteousness of God without the law is manifested, being witnessed by the law and the prophets; even the righteousness of God which is by faith of Jesus Christ unto all and upon all them that believe: for there is no difference: for all have sinned, and come short of the glory of God. (Rom. 3:9–23)

Paul has been comparing Gentiles with Jews, and he now asks if the Jews are better than the Gentiles (v. 9). The astonishing answer is that they are not—he has already proved that Jews and Gentiles are "all under sin" (v. 9). He then launches into a string of quotations from the Old Testament Scriptures that make the point bluntly enough. Verses 10b-11 are from Psalms 14:1–3 and 53:1–3 (cf. Eccles. 7:20). The first part of verse 13 is from Psalm 5:9. The second half of that verse is from Psalm 140:3. Verse 14 is Psalm 10:7. The next three verses are from Isaiah 59:7–8. The last component in this string of quotations (v. 18) is Psalm 36:1. The resultant picture is quite grim.

These citations are all from the law, so Paul quite rightly points that they are directed to those who are in fact under the law (v. 19). The point of doing this is to shut every mouth, Jewish and Gentile mouths alike, and establish the whole world as guilty before God (v. 19). This is why law is excluded as a way of justification for all men (not just for Jews). No *flesh* will be justified by law (v. 20)—law simply brings us a knowledge of the problem. The speed limit sign has no control over your gas pedal. But now there is a righteousness of God that the law and prophets testified to, but which is manifested "without the law" (v. 21). This righteousness of God is embodied in the faithful obedience of Jesus Christ (v. 22), and this righteousness of God is "unto all and upon all" that believe (v. 22). There is no difference in their gospels (v. 22) because there is no difference in their plight (v. 23).

We should note first that for Paul "the law" which shut the Jews up under sin was not limited to the Torah—it included the entire Old Testament. His citations here do not include anything from the Mosaic books, which would be the Torah proper. He quotes from Psalms and Isaiah, and he says that the result is moral instruction from "the law" addressed to Jews "under the law."

Psalm 14 makes a distinction between the "workers of iniquity" and "my people." The same thing is true of Psalm 53, although the initial judgment is made against all the "children of men." The hat tip to Ecclesiastes 7:20 says that there is no such thing as a just man on the earth. Psalm 5 makes a distinction between those who do evil and those who put their trust in God. Psalm 140 makes a distinction between the wicked and the afflicted, poor, and righteous. Psalm 10 makes a distinction between the wicked on the one hand and the poor and humble on the other. The passage from Isaiah assumes an apostate and unfaithful Israel. Psalm 36 makes a distinction between the wicked and the "upright in heart."

So put all this together. The string of citations is directly aimed by Paul at those "under the law," and he says quite clearly that he is talking about them. This means that the primary application of these citations from the Old Testament are directed against Jews, against members of God's covenant family. But what are we to do with all the references to the righteous and upright within Israel, standing in contrast to these wicked ones? Does this condemnation not apply to them? Not at all—they are righteous because they *accept* what Paul says here as being applicable to them. The wicked reject it—that's how we can tell who they are. Paul makes a clear distinction within Israel between the sons of Sarah and the sons of Hagar. The sons of Sarah are those who admit that they are by nature sons of Hagar. We are (*all* of us) by nature objects of wrath (Eph. 2:3).

Paul expects us to reason from the Jews to the whole world by extension. We are all in the same boat. If the Jews cannot be justified in this way, then nobody can be. God says these things to the Jews *so that* every mouth will be stopped, and the whole world will be found guilty.

The law, whether found in the Torah, or cited elsewhere in the Old Testament, or seen in the stars, or found in the conscience of a Gentile, is incapable of bringing a declaration of righteousness. What it does is bring the news about sin. The law, in whatever permutation, is simply a messenger of trouble. It is not a savior. It is not a ladder to Heaven. It is not a way of making you better than others. God gave it as a surefire instrument of making you *worse* (Rom. 3:20; 5:20). All good little Christian kids growing up in a conservative church with strong family values should take note.

The righteousness of God is mentioned twice here (vv. 21–22). N.T. Wright, a theologian in the school of thought called the New Perspective on Paul, says that this cannot refer to the imputed righteousness of Christ, but rather must refer to the covenant faithfulness of God the Father keeping His promise to Abraham. But this is a false dichotomy. *It must be both.* If it were just the latter, then why would Paul have added "without the law" (v. 21). Why would God have to fulfill His promise to Abraham without relying on the law? This is talking about His righteousness becoming ours without *us* having to keep the law. And then his comment in verse 22 cinches the point. What is the *destination* of the righteousness of God? It is "unto all and upon all" that believe. What is the mediating mechanism of this righteousness of God's? It is the faithful obedience (*righteousness*) of Jesus Christ.

In his magisterial *Institutes,* John Calvin makes a wonderful point about the nature of self-knowledge. He says that we do not know ourselves rightly unless we have grasped two things. The first is the primal greatness of man—what we were created to be, and what we were before the Fall. The second is a knowledge of how great our fall has been. When we learn this, we have learned the first lesson of the gospel—all have sinned. All have fallen short of the *glory* of God. This truly humbles us and prepares the way for us to be lifted up in the resurrection of Jesus Christ.

THE JUST GOD WHO JUSTIFIES

If God failed to fulfill His promise to Abraham, then He would be unjust. If God fulfilled His promise by simply *declaring* that everyone was now justified, then He would be unjust under that circumstance as well. If He doesn't save the nations, then He is unjust. If He saves the nations, then He is unjust. But He has declared His intention to Abraham to do this anyway—He will be true, even though *every* man fails. How will He be able to do that? This passage answers that question.

> But now the righteousness of God without the law is manifested, being witnessed by the law and the prophets; even the righteousness of God which is by faith of Jesus Christ unto all and upon all them that believe:

for there is no difference: for all have sinned, and
come short of the glory of God; being justified freely
by his grace through the redemption that is in Christ
Jesus: whom God hath set forth to be a propitiation
through faith in his blood, to declare his righteousness
for the remission of sins that are past, through the forbearance of God; to declare, I say, at this time his righteousness: that he might be just, and the justifier of
him which believeth in Jesus. Where is boasting then?
It is excluded. By what law? Of works? Nay: but by
the law of faith. Therefore we conclude that a man is
justified by faith without the deeds of the law. Is he the
God of the Jews only? Is he not also of the Gentiles?
Yes, of the Gentiles also: seeing it is one God, which
shall justify the circumcision by faith, and uncircumcision through faith. Do we then make void the law
through faith? God forbid: yea, we establish the law.
(Rom. 3:21–31)

The righteousness of God, His faithfulness to Abraham, is
now manifested. The law and the prophets testify to this,
and His righteousness is now manifested "apart from law"
(v. 21). What do those who believe receive? Unto all and
upon all that believe, this righteousness of God comes *in
the form of Jesus Christ's faithful obedience* (v. 22). There
is no difference between Jew and Gentile (as we have already learned), so we see that all have sinned and come
short of the glory of God (v. 23). But as they share in the
dilemma, they also share in the gospel that delivers them
from the dilemma—justified freely by His grace through

the redemption that is in Christ Jesus (v. 24). This Jesus was "set forth" to be a propitiation for those who have faith in His blood (v. 25). This propitiation (defined as an averting of wrath) was necessary to vindicate God's righteousness—His forbearance of sins in the past could have led to false conclusions (v. 25). This propitiation in the present time declares His righteousness—for the one who believes in Jesus, He may be both just *and* the one who justifies (v. 26). This kind of salvation excludes boasting because it excludes works, that is, any works of *ours* (v. 27). This is why a man (Jew or Gentile) is justified by faith apart from the deeds of the law (v. 28). The Jew is justified apart from Torah, and the Gentile is justified apart from natural law. This glorious provision of justification *apart from law* is given to both Jew and Gentile (v. 29). One God, one new mankind, one faith (v. 30). Does this mean the Torah was worthless? No, not at all. This fulfills the whole *point* of the Torah (v. 31), which was to prepare for the Messiah.

The righteousness of God is not mediated to us directly. God promises to bring a Messiah, and His righteous Word is fulfilled when He does so. And what does that Messiah do? He reveals or manifests the righteousness of God in two ways. First, God shows His righteousness by fulfilling His promise (v. 21). Second, God shows His righteousness by having His Son live a perfect, sinless life—God sent an Israelite who would finally live as Israel was required to live by the Torah (v. 22). He would be perfect. God shows His faithfulness by sending a Messiah who would be faithful on our behalf. Since all have been shut up into the same prison house of sin (v. 23), it only makes sense that the key that will unlock that common prison house will be the same key—the key of faith. Faith in what? Faith in whom? Faith in the righteous God who sent Jesus Christ to be faithful on our behalf (v. 22).

It is important for us to note that Paul is talking about the salvation of the *world*. He does not have a truncated focus, that of trying to get a handful of individual souls into Heaven when they die. Now it is just *fine* to go to Heaven when you die, and you have the Church's blessing for those of you who want to do so. But the salvation plan that Paul is outlining here is nothing less than a restoration of Eden and a great deal more than that (Rom. 5:20). Eye has not seen, ear has not heard, and it has not yet penetrated the heart of man what God has in store for us. But all of it is connected in some way to that word *glory*.

Too often we just lump all the biblical words together that describe some aspect of our salvation and treat them as though they were synonyms. But they are not. So here is a brief glossary. The words *justify* and *righteousness* are, in the Greek, part of the same *dikai-* (δικαι-) word group. When someone is *justified,* he has been *declared righteous*— in the courtroom sense of that word. *Redemption* refers to a purchase (v. 24), the purchase price being the blood of Jesus Christ (v. 25). *Propitiation* is the means to deflect or avert wrath. So Christ in His death was a propitiation, a substitutionary sacrifice, and His blood was the redemption payment. Because He died, the holy wrath that was due to sin was fully satisfied, and it became possible for a holy God to declare "not guilty" over those who were...guilty.

So we have two declarations of righteousness going on here. One is the declaration of *our* righteousness, our vindication in the courtroom of God's justice. This is what is meant by justification, a verdict which we appropriate by faith alone. But there is *another* declaration, mentioned in both verse 25 and verse 26. God is declaring His righteousness, not simply because the Messiah showed up as promised, but because the Messiah died as a propitiation. Why was this necessary? Well, it was needed because God in His forbearance had left previous sins unpunished (v. 25). The cross is the declaration of God's righteousness in that all our sin is now dealt with. When sin in the past is remitted, and when our sin in the present is remitted, the question naturally arises: how can a holy God *do* that?

What we need is a just God who justifies. Unbelievers like to pretend that the great moral dilemma is "how a loving God could send anyone to Hell." But that is not a real problem. It doesn't even approximate a problem. He could do that by just issuing everyone their paycheck. The *wages* of sin is death. The real problem, the one requiring the death of Jesus as a solution, is how a holy God can let anyone into Heaven. And this is the place where Paul describes just how it all works. God wants to declare His righteousness two ways. He wants to declare that He is just *and* the one who justifies. He could be just and damn us all. He could forgive us in a boys-will-be-boys kind of way, but that would make Him unjust along with us. The gospel is found in that glorious word *and*.

If we are saved in this fashion, what is therefore excluded (v. 27)? Faith in the death of Jesus excludes boasting.

We are justified by faith alone, and not by any form of moralistic scurrying around (v. 28). To go any other way would exclude the Gentiles, who did not have the Torah, and it would also, incidentally, exclude the Jews, who did not keep the Torah (v. 29). God is the God of both groups. We worship and serve one God, who has made one justified people, and there is one way to become a member of that people. That one way is faith (v. 30).

CHAPTER 4

BLESSED IS THE MAN

The word *imputation* may seem like one of those technical theological words, the kind that make your head hurt, but it is really quite straightforward—and *full* of blessing.

> What shall we say then that Abraham our father, as pertaining to the flesh, hath found? For if Abraham were justified by works, he hath whereof to glory; but not before God. For what saith the scripture? Abraham believed God, and it was counted unto him for righteousness. Now to him that worketh is the reward not reckoned of grace, but of debt. But to him that worketh not, but believeth on him that justifieth the

ungodly, his faith is counted for righteousness. Even as David also describeth the blessedness of the man, unto whom God imputeth righteousness without works, saying, Blessed are they whose iniquities are forgiven, and whose sins are covered. Blessed is the man to whom the Lord will not impute sin. (Rom. 4:1–8)

What did Abraham, our father, discover (v. 1)? He would have had something to boast about if he had been justified by works (v. 2). The problem is that this is not possible for any flesh, so Abraham wouldn't have been able to boast before God (v. 2). So what does the Bible say about his justification? It says that Abraham believed God, and that this was *reckoned* to him, *counted* to him, *imputed* to him, as righteousness (v. 3). The basic division between works and grace is then outlined—work gets a paycheck, and this is the antithesis of grace (v. 4). But for the one who does not work, but instead believes in the one who justifies the ungodly, his faith is reckoned, counted, imputed to him for righteousness (v. 5). David describes the blessed condition of a man who has received this grace, and it is a twofold grace. First, God imputes righteousness apart from works (v. 6). Paul then quotes the place where David says this (Ps. 32:1–2), and he does so to double effect. Blessed is the man whose sins are forgiven (v. 7) and whose sins are covered (v. 7). He continues—blessed is the man to whom the Lord does not impute sin (v. 8). We have two kinds of imputation here. The positive imputation of righteousness, and the nonimputation of sin.

Remember that in chapter three, the apostle has already established the basis for how God does this without ceasing to be holy. He is the God who wants to be just *and* the one who justifies. Reckoning, counting, and imputing righteousness (apart from a propitiatory sacrifice offered by a genuine and lawful substitute) is acquitting the guilty without a foundation, a thing that a holy God cannot and will not do. This is why Jesus died and rose again—He did so as our representative. Fix it in your hearts and minds— Jesus did not die so that we might live. He died so that we might die, and He lives so that we might live.

Paul is here setting Abraham before us as the paradigm of faith, but in the Bible, faith is always preceded by repentance. Abraham is our father in repentance, not just in faith. He did all that we need to do (4:23), and we certainly need to repent. Here in verse 5, we see that Abraham (like us) was trusting in the God who justifies the *ungodly*. And last, the Bible is plain that Abraham himself was called out of idolatry and sin (Josh. 24:2). Abraham began as an ungodly man. Abraham, the father of pilgrims, was himself a pilgrim.

We also have to take a moment to decipher some Pauline shorthand. He says here that Abraham's belief of God was counted unto him for righteousness (v. 3). This is also a general truth—anyone who believes God has his faith counted for righteousness (v. 5). But does this mean that God is taking my faith (as imperfect as anything else I do) and treating that faith *as* my righteousness? No, not at all. The *ground* of our righteousness is the life and death of the Lord Jesus—our representative. That righteousness of another is apprehended by us using the *instrument* of faith.

When Jesus tells someone "your faith has saved you," this is a comparable form of shorthand (Luke 7:50; 18:42). Of course, *Jesus* saved these people, not their naked faith. We see the same thing here. The person who is justified here "believeth on him that justifieth the ungodly." So *faith counted as righteousness* is short for *faith in the representative substitute who is counted as that righteousness.* Don't fall into the trap of trying to have faith in your faith. Your isolated faith can't justify anyone or anything.

We must shake loose of our individualism. The problem is in the *ism,* not in the individual as such. True individuality does exist, but autonomous individuality, individuality that seeks to be independent of God, does not. We are not individuals in the sense that marbles in a box are—we are like individual leaves on a tree. One differs from another, *but they are all still connected.*

The connection is a covenantal one. There are two human races, and each one has a covenantal head, a federal head. A covenant head represents a particular group or body, and when he acts, the group acts through him. Adam is the head of the first human race, and Jesus is the head of the new human race, and there is a covenantal or imputational bridge between the two races—thus making it possible for us to be transferred from the old humanity to the new.

Here are the three great imputations: First, Adam sinned as your representative, and so his rebellion against God was imputed to you. In Adam, you rebelled against God.

Second, God in His mercy caused that original sin (in which you participated through your representative) and all your individual sins, to be imputed to Jesus Christ on the cross (2 Cor. 5:21). This is the imputational bridge, and it is referred to here in our text (v. 8). And finally, God imputes the righteousness of the new Adam to every member of His race.

So Adam's sin was yours. All your sins are Christ's. And all Christ's righteousness is now yours in the resurrection. Lift up your *heads*.

Grace and works do not mix, and this is good news. Works are connected to things that men would love to have, but which they cannot have. Men outside Christ would love to boast, but they cannot boast before God (v. 2). They would love to receive a reward in the judgment, a reward through which God pays them what He owes them—as a matter of debt (v. 4). Men love the idea of being a standard of righteousness unto themselves, and this is why they loathe and despise every form of free and sovereign *grace*. And free and sovereign grace repulses every form of works, striving, earning, moralistic tip-toeing, meriting, goody-two-shoe-ing, shucking, or jiving.

But there is an upside. The reason you are saved at *all* is because you are saved by *grace*.

FATHER ABRAHAM

We rightly refer to *Father* Abraham. He is the central model for us from the pages of the Old Testament, living out the implications of radical faith, the implications of faith at the root. As we walk in imitation of him, we are his children indeed. As we walk in imitation of him, we have the family resemblance that Jesus once looked for in the Pharisees and did not find (John 8:39).

> Cometh this blessedness then upon the circumcision only, or upon the uncircumcision also? For we say that faith was reckoned to Abraham for righteousness. How was it then reckoned? When he was in circumcision, or in uncircumcision? Not in circumcision, but in uncircumcision. And he received the sign of circumcision, a seal of the righteousness of the faith which he had yet being uncircumcised: that he might be the father of all them that believe, though they be not circumcised; that righteousness might be imputed unto them also: and the father of circumcision to them who are not of the circumcision only, but who also walk in the steps of that faith of our father Abraham, which he had being yet uncircumcised. For the promise, that he should be the heir of the world, was not to Abraham, or to his seed, through the law, but through the righteousness of faith. For if they which are of the law be heirs, faith is made void, and the promise made of none effect: because the law worketh wrath: for where no law is, there is no transgression. Therefore it is of faith, that it might be by grace; to the end the promise might be sure to all the seed; not to that only which is of the law, but to that also which is of the faith of Abraham; who is the father of us all. (Rom. 4:9–16)

Remember where we are in Paul's argument. The universal enemy of our souls is sin, and it afflicts Gentiles and Jews alike. The entire human race is shut up under sin, but God is not intervening at the last moment in a panic, trying to troubleshoot a problem that is beyond Him. He has been declaring His universal plan of salvation for the entire world through Abraham, and He has been doing so from the very first book of the Bible. God's plan through Abraham is for all kinds of men and women, and always has been.

Is this Abrahamic blessing for Jews only (v. 9)? We can answer the question by remembering that faith was reckoned to Abraham for righteousness, and remembering when this happened (v. 10). Abraham was right with God through faith *before* he was circumcised (v. 10). He received circumcision after he received righteousness in order that uncircumcised Gentiles might consider him their father as well (v. 11). His circumcision was a seal *after* the fact. At the same time, he did get circumcised, so that he might be the father of a certain group of Jews—those who walk in the kind of faith that Abraham had while still uncircumcised (v. 12). For the promise that Abraham would inherit the world was a promise to be received through the righteousness of *faith* (v. 13) and was *not* to be received through the Torah. For if the Torah could do it for us, then both faith and promise are made void (v. 14). So the Torah can't do it—but it *can* bring wrath. For if there is no law, there is no transgression of the law (v. 15). And this is why the salvation of the world is by faith, so that it might be gracious (v. 16). This ensures that the promise extends to all Abraham's seed—both those circumcised in infancy and those who share his faith only, without ever being circumcised. This is what makes him the father of us all (v. 16).

We come now to the importance of the Abrahamic timeline. The Apostle Paul bases his argument here on the chronology of events, and we need to be careful as we reconstruct that chronology ourselves. We have already noted that Abraham came out of the idolatrous city of Ur (Josh. 24:2) and that he had trusted in the one who justifies the *ungodly*, Abraham himself included (Rom. 4:5). This means that Abraham began his pilgrimage as an idolatrous sinner. The first biblical mention of Abraham's personal faith is when he left Ur of the Chaldees (Heb. 11:8). When he left his country, the Bible says that he obeyed God, and God told him to go in conjunction with the promise (Gen. 12:1–3). So Abraham went, believing in that promise (Heb. 11:8–10). He was seventy-five when this happened. Then, three chapters later, when God promised Abraham descendants like the stars of the sky, Abraham believed God, and it was credited to him as righteousness (Gen. 15:5–6). He was around eighty-six at this time. *Twenty-four years after* his departure from Ur, God established the covenant of circumcision with Abraham (Gen. 17:1–14). This means that Isaac was begotten after Abraham was circumcised, and Ishmael was not. Abraham spent seventy-five years as a sinner, twenty-four years as an uncircumcised believer in God, and seventy-six years as a circumcised believer (Gen. 25:7). This helps to put Paul's timeline argument into good perspective.

Put another way, before he became the first Jew, for many years Abraham was a believing "Gentile." Paul is arguing that Abraham was a believer in the true God, and he was a true believer in the true God, for twenty-four years. He was righteous, *and he was not a Jew*. He was simultaneously not a Jew and declared righteous for a long time. Gentiles (who had been promised to Abraham back in Gen. 12) are therefore invited to look to him as their father in the faith. He had faith, and that's all, and they had faith, and that's all. Believing Gentiles can look back at the uncircumcised Abraham, and believing Jews can look back at the circumcised Abraham.

Is circumcision nothing, then? As Paul might say, "May it never be!" Circumcision has value in many ways. But the central value is only for those who share the *faith* of Abraham. Note carefully how Paul limits this. The uncircumcised Abraham is father of the Gentiles, but only those Gentiles who believe. In the same way, he is the father of the Jews, but only those Jews who believe. He is very clear on this. He is the "father of circumcision *to them* who are not of the circumcision *only,* but who *also* walk in the steps of that faith of our father Abraham, which he had being yet uncircumcised" (v. 12, emphasis mine). In other words, a circumcised Jew who has faith may rise to the level of that famous Gentile Abraham. But if not, he does not.

Perhaps this might help us smooth relations between Presbyterians and Baptists. Circumcision and baptism are not precise counterparts, but they come pretty close (Col. 2:11). There is a great deal of overlap in what they signify. This being the case, let us reason by analogy. The thing that matters is true faith, faith that lives, walks, breathes, and loves. Did you take the sign of baptism after you believed? Then you are a credobaptist the same way that

Abraham was a credo-circumcisionist. Were you baptized in infancy? Then you are a paedobaptist the way that Isaac was a paedo-circumcisionist—provided you *believe*. If that faith is there, if faith is present, be fully convinced in your own mind, and don't sweat it.

All the promises given to Abraham were pointing toward the same thing—*a saved world*. Scripture expresses this in many different ways, but all these expressions are directed at God's love for *all* the nations of men. Abraham was looking for a city with foundations built by God (Heb. 11:10). Abraham looked forward to Christ's day; he saw it and was glad (John 8:56). All the families of the earth would be blessed through him (Gen. 12:3). His descendants in the faith would be like the stars for number (Gen. 15:5). God would multiply Abraham exceedingly (Gen. 17:2), and many nations would come from him (Gen. 17:6). Paul interprets all this definitively when he says that the promise (expressed in these places) that he would *inherit the world* was set before him (and before us) as something to be obtained through the righteousness of faith. Abraham was heir of the world. But it was not for him, or for us, to be obtained through Torah. What is it that overcomes the world (1 John 5:4)? Is it not our *faith*?

So let us close this section with an observation on one other curiosity. In all the debates and wrangles over justification by faith, it is curious that too many in our day are obsessed with believing in the *way* that Abraham believed, but they want to dispense (almost entirely) with *what* he believed. But we are told what to believe—that Jesus rose from the dead (Rom. 4:24)—and the entire context of this shows that in His resurrection we are to see the resurrection and salvation of the entire world.

FATHER OF NATIONS

We are continuing to follow the apostle's discussion of Abraham's faith. We finished our treatment of Romans 4:16 by acknowledging that Abraham was the father of believing Jew and believing Gentile alike.

But what do we mean by that word *believing*? Abraham sets the pattern, and in this passage, we learn what his faith was actually like. It is not enough for Abraham to have real faith and for us to have something merely *called* faith.

> (As it is written, I have made thee a father of many nations,) before him whom he believed, even God, who quickeneth the dead, and calleth those things which be not as though they were. Who against hope believed in hope, that he might become the father of many nations; according to that which was spoken, So shall thy seed be. And being not weak in faith, he considered not his own body now dead, when he was about an hundred years old, neither yet the deadness of Sara's womb: he staggered not at the promise of God through unbelief; but was strong in faith, giving glory to God; and being fully persuaded that, what he had promised, he was able also to perform. And therefore it was imputed to him for righteousness. Now it was not written for his sake alone, that it was imputed to him; but for us also, to whom it shall be imputed, if we believe on him that raised up Jesus our Lord from the dead; who

was delivered for our offences, and was raised again
for our justification. (Rom. 4:17–25)

We have noted *that* Abraham believed, but we have also
taken special note of *what* he believed. In this place, Paul
notes that he believed the promise of Genesis 17:5, which
is that he would be the father of many nations (v. 17). Now
Abraham is the father of all (v. 16) before Him whom he
believed (v. 17). The one he believed was God, and is He
a worthy object of our faith? He is the one who raises the
dead, and who speaks to nothing as though it were something—and then it is something (v. 17). The promise cited
in the next verse that Abraham believed was the promise
from Genesis 15: "so shall your seed be." Against hope he
believed this particular word in hope (v. 18). He was not
weak in faith (v. 19), so he looked to the promise and not
to the circumstance. The circumstance was his own body,
virtually dead, and Sarah's aged and barren womb (v. 19).
Not a lot to go on. He did not stagger at the promise in
unbelief (v. 20) but was strong in faith. What did that look
like? He gave glory to God (v. 20). Abraham was *fully persuaded* that God was able to do what He had said He would
do (v. 21). And this is why it was imputed to him as righteousness (v. 22). Abraham was a man of faith, and he was
an all-in man of faith. But this word is not recorded as a
historical curiosity—as in "Look what happened to Abraham!"—it was not written for *his* sake alone (v. 23). It was
also written for us, who will have this righteousness imputed to us if we believe *in Him* who raised Jesus from the

dead (v. 24). This Jesus was delivered over for our sins (v. 25), and He was raised to life for our justification (v. 25).

Notice the parallel between what Abraham did and what we are to do. Abraham gave glory to God (v. 20). He believed in God (v. 17), not in certain random occurrences. Abraham did not just believe the dead were quickened, and that certain inexplicable things happen. He believed in God, the One who brought these things about. He believed what was *spoken* (v. 18) precisely because he believed the *Speaker*.

In the same way, in an identical way, we must do more than believe *that* Jesus came back from the dead. We must believe in Him who raised Jesus from the dead. We believe in a *Person* who says and does things; we do not proceed straight to an abstracted proposition *about* what was said and done. But we may not detach them from the other side either. Just as we cannot be justified by the predicate apart from the subject, neither can we be saved by the subject apart from the predicate

We must learn to see that, at bottom, Abraham believed the same promise that we do. Abraham believed in the God who quickens the dead (v. 17), and we believe in the God who quickens the dead (v. 24). Abraham believed in the God who gave him the nations of men (4:13, 17, 18), and we believe in the God who raised Jesus for *our* justification (v. 25). Who does that pronoun refer to? Remember that we have learned that Abraham is the father of believing Jews and Gentiles both, and that he understood this as meaning that God was giving the *world* to him (4:13). *Our* justification is, therefore, over time, the *world's* justification. Our justification is part of the fulfillment of the promise that the nations would be blessed through Abraham.

The world *will* be Christian. The nations *will* come to Christ. The swords *will* be beaten into plowshares. The earth *will* be as full of the knowledge of the Lord as the waters cover the sea. From the rising of the sun to the going down of the same, the name of the Lord *will* be praised (Ps. 113:3). The ensign *will* be raised, and the ends of the earth *will* stream to the Lord Jesus (Is. 2:2). Is this too big to swallow?

Doesn't this just take the breath away? Is this too glad to be true? After all, scores of wars are continuing around the planet as I write these words. Millions live in grinding and unbelievable poverty. Our secular establishment has nothing but contempt for the right of the unborn to live. Sexual immorality continues to spiral out of control. We insist that our public square be kept stripped of all reference to the true and living God and blithely still expect Him to bless us with anything. A glance at the newspapers would not lead you to the conclusions outlined in the previous paragraph.

"I see your point, certainly," Abraham said. "I *am* an old man. How could I possibly beget a son? And look at Sarah...she was barren when she was young, and she is old now." Is that what you want to be remembered for—pointing at our newspapers and persuading Abraham that he ought not believe the promises of God?

Abraham wouldn't have listened to this kind of unbelieving chatter. He was fully persuaded. God had promised him the world, remember, and he believed God, giving glory to Him (v. 20). What did Abraham do with all the information that was contrary to that promise? *He ignored it.* He had nothing whatever to do with it. He looked instead to the promise made by the God who does...what? The God who is not hog-tied by *our* circumstances. We believe in the God who quickens the dead, proving that He does this through His raising of Jesus from the grave. We believe in the God who calls *those things which are not as though they were.* And what are Abraham's children to do? They do the same, calling nonexistent realities into reality. We are to do this by faith, never by sight. We know this world will come about because we are the instruments God is using to build it.

If Abraham was promised the world, then that would include all the nations within it. And that means it would also include the Roman Empire, which also contains a lesson for Americans. According to Virgil, Aeneas was the legendary Trojan who laid the foundations of the great Rome. "And Peter said unto him, Aeneas, Jesus Christ maketh thee whole: arise, and make thy bed. And he arose immediately" (Acts 9:34). This would be as if Peter walked up to a lame man named Uncle Sam and told him that Jesus Christ made him whole. Note that Peter doesn't flatter him; he *heals* him. America is not a picture of health; we are laid up with the palsy. Arise, then, and *walk.* America is not vibrant with life. We are like Israel in the valley of dry bones. Rise, then, and *live.* So you believe that America can be restored this way, by mere words from a pulpit of wood?

Well, yes, I do.

CHAPTER 5

RIGHTEOUSED

Recall that the first three chapters of Romans address the universal problem, the problem of sin. Sin afflicts the Gentiles, as we saw in the first chapter. It afflicts the Jews, as Paul shows in the second chapter. Sin has both Jew and Gentile in its grip, and in the same way—that is the argument of the third chapter. In the fourth chapter, Paul begins his discussion of the glorious solution—a solution promised repeatedly in the first book of the Bible. That solution was the establishment of a new humanity through Abraham. And now Paul comes to the paradoxical truth—the seed of Abraham, the one through whom this new way of being human will be brought about, is a new Adam. This means that this second Adam has a *father*, Abraham.

Paul begins his articulation of God's solution for man's sin and rebellion by giving us an exegetical case—pointing to Abraham's example of faith in Genesis. That is the theme of chapter four. Now, coming to chapter five, we have his theological and typological case for the same thing. Adam was a type of the one to come, and Christ, the second Adam, is the antitype.

> Therefore being justified by faith, we have peace with God through our Lord Jesus Christ: by whom also we have access by faith into this grace wherein we stand, and rejoice in hope of the glory of God. And not only so, but we glory in tribulations also: knowing that tribulation worketh patience; and patience, experience; and experience, hope: and hope maketh not ashamed; because the love of God is shed abroad in our hearts by the Holy Ghost which is given unto us. For when we were yet without strength, in due time Christ died for the ungodly. For scarcely for a righteous man will one die: yet peradventure for a good man some would even dare to die. But God commendeth his love toward us, in that, while we were yet sinners, Christ died for us. (Rom. 5:1–8)

We have believed in the God who quickens the dead, who raised Jesus from the dead. On this basis, we have been justified (that is, "righteoused") by faith (v. 1). As a result, we have (as our present possession) peace with God through our Lord Jesus Christ (v. 1). In addition to this, we also have access by faith into the status of grace (v. 2). Consequently, we rejoice in hope—hope that looks forward to the glory of God (v. 2). On top of that, we glory in our tribulations now because we know that tribulations are part of this process (v. 3). Tribulation works its way out to patience (v. 3). Patience, the next link in the chain, leads to experience, and this experience leads to hope (v. 4). This hope does not let us down, and why? Because the love of God is poured out in our hearts by the Holy Spirit who has been given to us (v. 5). In our experience, when did this grace start? We had no strength to do anything, and while we were in that condition, Christ died for the ungodly (v. 6). For us it is a big thing to die for a righteous man, and sometimes some of us attain to that level (v. 7). But God's love is quite different—Christ died for us while we were still all messed up (v. 8).

This passage focuses on the present and on the future both. Because we have believed (the same way that Abraham did), what do we have *now*? In the first place, Paul says, we have justification (v. 1). As a result of that, we have peace with God (v. 1). We have the privilege of standing in grace (v. 2). We also have the joy that hope brings (v. 2). We also have tribulation coupled with a right perspective on those tribulations (v. 3), which is to say, we glory in them. When we look at Paul's life, it should be obvious that the persecutions he endured were in the forefront of these tribulations. But if we look at the way he lumps everything together elsewhere (2 Cor. 12:10), we should not strictly limit it to that.

Now the joyful hope that we currently have looks forward to the coming glory of God (v. 2). Remember from a chapter or so ago what sin causes us to fall short of? Right, the *glory* of God (Rom. 3:23). And Abraham, justified by faith, did what? He gave *glory* to God (Rom. 4:20). What was at the center of the Gentiles' idolatry? It was that they exchanged the glory of God for the image of mere creatures (Rom. 1:23).

In between now and the glory to come, what can we look forward to? The answer is threefold—patience, experience, and more mature hope (v. 4).

The word *glory* is fascinating and helps us to understand its relationship to tribulation. Though they are different words in the Greek, notice that we glory in tribulation now as we look forward to the coming glory. What do tribulation and glory have in common? Well, they are both heavy, and Paul is very clearly using the image of training for something. This is not just training—it is *weight* training.

A Christian approach to tribulation therefore strains toward a goal. It is not the response of one who just hunkers down to take it. Our trials are teleological—which means they all have a *point*. And this means we must interact with our tribulations with both faith and intelligence. Faith is first, and intelligence follows the argument through patience, experience, and hope.

But if tribulation is a set of training weights, who is the trainer? Well, of course, the answer in our text is the Holy Spirit. But as many who have had this experience can tell you, there will often come a temptation to think that your personal trainer is a maniac and a sadist. That's what training *does*. That is what weight training makes you *think* about your trainer. Why is He doing this to me?

And that is why Paul turns immediately to a *discussion* of the nature of the Holy Spirit's work in our hearts. There is no real point in submitting to this process without personal trust. What has He shed abroad in our hearts? The answer is *love*, not aimless, mindless torture. Notice that God has not sent a sense of love from a distance. He has not *sent* love to us, He has *brought* it. The Holy Spirit is given to us, and the love He sheds abroad in our hearts came with Him.

God gives us things because He gives Himself and brings the stuff with Him. He does not give as a substitute for giving Himself, but rather as part and parcel of giving Himself. The Holy Spirit is given unto us (v. 5). Christ was given to die for the ungodly (v. 6), that is, for *us* (v. 8).

When we are tempted to falter in the course of tribulations, what should we tell ourselves? We should tell ourselves the very same thing that the Spirit in this text tells us, and which the Spirit in our hearts tells us. Here is the argument, and it is very simple.

What were you like when God undertook you as His project? What condition were you in? And while you were in that condition, what did God do for you? The answer is that we were "without strength" (v. 6), and "ungodly" (v. 6). We were sinners (v. 8). Now, while we were in *that* condition, Christ died for us, and this was intended as a commendation of God's love for us (v. 8). The argument looks ahead a few verses (vv. 9–10). If God did all this for His enemies, what will He do for those of us who are now His friends? Remember, we have peace with God (v. 1).

We are justified (v. 1). After what God did for His enemies, what do you think He might do for His friends?

THE RECONCILIATION

We have a tendency to describe our conversions as single-faceted events. But in the Scripture, conversion to Christ is multifaceted, and the different words we use for it are not precise synonyms. We will be considering some of those terms in the context of this passage, and it is important to note that they describe different spiritual realities. For example, to be *converted* means to be turned. To be *saved* means to be delivered. To be *reconciled* means the establishment of peace where there was hostility before. These realities all fit together, but they are not all identical.

> Much more then, being now justified by his blood, we shall be saved from wrath through him. For if, when we were enemies, we were reconciled to God by the death of his Son, much more, being reconciled, we shall be saved by his life. And not only so, but we also joy in God through our Lord Jesus Christ, by whom we have now received the atonement. (Rom. 5:9–11)

Recall the argument from the previous section, which was the argument that extended into this passage. If God did so much for us while we were His enemies (v. 8), why would He start to stint now that we are His friends? The point of Paul's emphasis in verse 9 is "how much more." Given that we are now justified by His blood (v. 9), how much more shall we be saved from wrath through Him (v. 9)? And if we were reconciled while we were enemies (by the death of His Son), how much more now, being reconciled, shall we be saved (v. 10)? And on top of all that, we also have joy in God, through Jesus, through whom we have received "the atonement" (v. 11). Literally this is "the reconciliation," the same word that is used in verse 10.

At the end of chapter four, we saw that we are justified in the resurrection of Jesus (v. 25). But here we see that we are described as having been "justified by his blood" (v. 9), that is, by His death. The death and resurrection of Jesus are a salvific and justifying unity. And even though we have been saved, notice that the salvation spoken of in verses 9–10 is a *future* salvation. We have been saved, we are being saved, and we shall be saved. Distinguishing these things is important, but it is not like separating the red buttons from the blue buttons. It is more like distinguishing height from depth.

Remember that in this section, Paul is balancing what has been done with what shall be done. He is arguing from the former to the latter. Because of what God did for us while we were enemies, we may be confident that He will do a great deal more for us now that we are His friends. In this context, he says that we "shall" be saved from wrath, and the reason given is that we have already been saved from wrath. We were enemies of God, and what (in Romans) is characteristic of enemies?

The wrath of God is found at both ends, which means that deliverance from wrath is found at both ends. For example, the wrath of God is revealed from Heaven against His enemies *already* (1:18). And what was waiting for His enemies in the future? Hypocrites were storing up wrath for themselves (2:5). Those who pursued the law were pursuing wrath (4:15). This means that those who used to be enemies have already been delivered from the 1:18 kind of wrath, and this is grounds for believing that they will be delivered from the 2:5 kind of wrath as well.

But the argument works both ways—those professing Christians who have not been delivered from the current manifestations of wrath have no reason for believing that they will be delivered from future wrath. What treasures up wrath (2:5)? It is a hard and impenitent heart, and it doesn't matter if the flesh has been circumcised (2:28) if the heart has not been (2:29). In the same way, it doesn't matter if the body has been baptized if the heart has not been. And, of course, when I say it doesn't matter, this simply means that it doesn't matter as far as averting wrath goes. It matters very much in other ways. It matters, for example, as a method of bringing down additional wrath.

Not only are we saved from wrath, we are saved "by his life." By this we should understand the equation of wrath with death. The way of wrath is the way of death. Christ has been raised to *life* for our justification (4:25), and it is in this life that we have received reconciliation. God is the God of life, and there is a necessary animosity between Him and death. We cannot live in death and *not* be at odds with His life. To anticipate, how can we who are dead to sin still live in it (Rom. 6:2)? And if we are raised in His life, then we are necessarily raised in His newness of life (6:4). The logic is simple. Those who used to be dead can be saved "by His life," but it is impossible for those who continue in death to be saved by His life. God does remarkable things in salvation, but He doesn't square the circle.

When this is rightly understood, when the argument is followed, what results? What is the crowning glory? Not only is all the foregoing so, but we have joy. This is not a glib *happy happy joy joy,* but is rather an impressive edifice of towering joy, possible only because of the bedrock it is built on. That bedrock is the bedrock of sovereign grace, nothing but grace, and grace all the way down. So we joy in God, and we joy in Him through our Lord Jesus, through whom we have been reconciled. The fruit of that reconciliation is joy, and the Person through whom we rejoice is the same Person through whom we were reconciled.

And saved means *saved.* You cannot be saved from drowning and remain on the bottom of the pool. You cannot be saved from wrath and remain underneath an ocean of it. One of the advantages of wrath in the present is that it enables us to see the disposition of wrath in the future. We are not to associate with those who call themselves brothers, but who are living under wrath (1 Cor. 5:9–13). After listing the manifest works of the flesh, Paul says that "they which do such things shall not inherit the kingdom of God" (Gal. 5:21). The rule of thumb is straightforward—*wrath now means wrath later*—unless full repentance divides the two. Hard and impenitent hearts now mean hard and impenitent hearts later. No one in Hell is repentant—they may be sorry enough, but they are not repentant. Repentance is a gift of God, remember.

Those who minimize the importance or significance of manifestations of wrath now are therefore minimizing the importance of the wrath to come. Preaching on sin now—for example, saying that sodomy is a deep corruption despite recent hate crimes legislation—is not a contemptuous way of telling the world to go to Hell. It is standing in the way of them going to Hell.

HUMANITY 2.0

In Adam, with what we might call Humanity 1.0, the system crashed. God could have written it off as a wasted project, but in His grace He did not. In Christ, the prototype for the next version was revealed, and all subsequent human history has been the period of beta testing for Humanity 2.0. The last day will be the final rollout, with every bug finally and completely removed. No more will a man say to his neighbor, *"That's* the blue screen of death."

> Wherefore, as by one man sin entered into the world, and death by sin; and so death passed upon all men, for that all have sinned: (for until the law sin was in the world: but sin is not imputed when there is no law. Nevertheless death reigned from Adam to Moses, even over them that had not sinned after the similitude of Adam's transgression, who is the figure of him that was to come. But not as the offence, so also is the free gift. For if through the offence of one many be dead, much more the grace of God, and the gift by grace, which is by one man, Jesus Christ, hath abounded unto many. And not as it was by one that sinned, so is the gift: for the judgment was by one to condemnation, but the free gift is of many offences unto justification. For if by

one man's offence death reigned by one; much more they which receive abundance of grace and of the gift of righteousness shall reign in life by one, Jesus Christ.) Therefore as by the offence of one judgment came upon all men to condemnation; even so by the righteousness of one the free gift came upon all men unto justification of life. For as by one man's disobedience many were made sinners, so by the obedience of one shall many be made righteous. Moreover the law entered, that the offence might abound. But where sin abounded, grace did much more abound: that as sin hath reigned unto death, even so might grace reign through righteousness unto eternal life by Jesus Christ our Lord. (Rom. 5:12–21)

This is a tightly reasoned portion of Romans, and we need to take special care as we repeat and summarize the teaching of each verse. One man, Adam, brought sin into the world, and death followed. Death came to all men because sin came to all men (v. 12). Before the Torah, sin existed, but sin against the Torah is not imputed when the Torah had not yet come to be (v. 13). (We will explain what this means in just a moment.) Nevertheless, sin against *some* standard had to exist, otherwise there would not have been any death between Adam and the giving of the Torah by Moses (v. 14). Those who sinned and died between Adam and Moses did not sin against an explicit command as Adam did (v. 14). Adam, of course, was a type of the last Adam, Christ (v. 14). But Adam is a contrasting type, not a parallel type. The offence of Adam *is not like* the free gift of the last Adam (v. 15). Both of them bequeathed something to "many," but the work of the last Adam is qualitatively different (v. 15)—life instead of death, and grace instead of penalty. The one who sinned is not like the gift—one brought condemnation, but the free gift brought justification (v. 16). For if the one man's offense caused death to reign (v. 17), shouldn't we use *that* as a measuring rod to show how much more we are going to reign in life through Jesus Christ (v. 17)? How screwed up the world is should be taken as a standing testimony for how good it is going to be when God is done. Before Paul has said that the parallel is that both deal with "many." He now says "all" (v. 18). Condemnation came to all Adam's descendants, and justification of life will come upon all the last Adam's descendants. In both cases, those descendants were reckoned, in their respective times, as the true humanity. One act of disobedience was imputed to many. One act of obedience was imputed to many (v. 19). The reason God brought the Torah into history was to stir up trouble (v. 20). He wanted to make the offence abound, which it did, especially in Israel. But where sin abounded (Israel), grace abounded much more (v. 20). This is where Christ came. God poked the hornet's nest of Israel with the stick of Torah, and then sent Christ into it. All this was done so that we might know that just as sin reigned to the point of death, so also, and by so much more, we might know that grace is reigning through righteousness to eternal life (v. 21). And how? All through the Lord Jesus, the last Adam, the new human race. He is the perfect man, and He is the one into whom we must mature and grow.

We already saw that the typology here has both a parallel and a contrasting function. The parallel is that Adam and Christ are both founders of races. They are both the fathers of their respective descendants. They are each fathers of "many," and when it comes to their own children, théy are the respective fathers of "all." This is the parallel. But the contrast is qualitative. Adam brought disaster; Christ brought salvation. Adam brought sin, condemnation, and the reign of death; Christ, the last Adam, brought the free gift of obedience, justification, abundance of grace, and the reign of life.

Because of the revelation of God's character that we saw in the first chapter of Romans, it was certainly possible for sin to exist and function in the time between Adam and Moses. Adam sinned against an explicit commandment, and he fell from innocence into the offence. When the Torah came through Moses, sinners found themselves stirred up and their lusts exacerbated by the explicit teaching found in Torah. Christ obeyed an explicit command. But even when there was no explicit command (as there was not between Adam and Moses), there was still an implicit and clear moral order, which men knew and understood. This is why sin and death existed before the Torah. God is just, and He judges us against what we know. But, to our dismay, this simply makes the judgment more certain, inevitable, and holy.

Adam sinned against God by disobeying His *explicit* command. When the Israelites wandered away from Him, they were doing the same thing, sinning against the explicit commands of the Torah. The biblical principle is "to whom much is given, much is required." That means that sinning against explicit requirements of God brings in greater judgment. To sin against greater light is a greater sin. So what about those who were not given such explicit requirements? Were they not sinners also? Were they not under God's judgments also? Yes, they were, but God does calibrate His judgments in accordance with the available light. He never calibrates anything down to zero. Everyone dies, and because God's judgments are altogether righteous, this means that everyone is responsible at least to *that* extent.

We have noted before that the Apostle Paul loves *a fortiori* argument. He loves to think in terms of "how much more," and we do him a grave disservice when we translate this into terms that in effect mean "how much less." Earlier in chapter five, he used a standard "how much more" argument. If God did this for His enemies, what will He do for His friends? But in this place, it is a mind-boggling, ricochet kind of argument. Look at the worst that Adam's sons have been able to do, and use that, not to sink your faith, but rather to build it. The only problem of evil that we have here is actually evil's problem, which is that evil is going to be trampled to death by the goodness of God in human history. Measured against the reign of grace that is coming, the reign of death is puny and anemic. Life swallows up death. "Death, thou shalt *die*."[2]

The sufferings of the present time are not even worth comparing to the coming glory (Rom. 8:18). This means

---

2. John Donne, "Death, Be Not Proud."

the work of the last Adam does *not* exceed the devastation of the first by fifteen or twenty percent. It is not more extensive by half as much again. No—do you want to hear good news? All the murders, all the cruelties, all the poverty, all the pettiness, all the *sin* is all going to be swallowed up in an ocean of infinite kindness and glory. Take the one burning coal of human wickedness, fly it out over the middle of the Pacific somewhere, and throw it in. You don't need to worry about anything catching on fire.

Christians who have a divided system (this world/an upper-story spiritual world) can often take a stand against human wickedness. They do this because they care about their souls, as they should. But without forgetting that important consideration, we should also take a stand against it because *that is not where the human race is going.*

What is God up to then? Picture Adam as the headwaters of a great, enormous river. It is thousands of miles long, and for most of its length, it is several miles wide. Because of Adam's disobedience, the river is polluted and filthy. But several hundred miles downstream from the headwaters, God determined to establish a new font of water, pure this time. And from that point on, the water downstream got gradually cleaner and cleaner. By the time it reached the sea, it was like liquid crystal. *That* is what God is up to.

CHAPTER 6

HOW TO UNDERSTAND THE GOSPEL

Thus far in Romans we have learned of our universal plight in Adam, whether or not we are Jews or Gentiles (1–3). We have also learned of the universal salvation for the human race that has been accomplished in the second Adam (4–5), the salvation that was promised for the world through our father Abraham. But we now have to bring all this glory down to the individual level, and this can be tricky. For example, if "all" are condemned in Adam, and "all" are justified in Christ, then no more worries, right? Just do what you feel. Wrong. As we will see shortly, in chapters seven and eight, we *are* liberated to do what we most desire to do, but somebody has to die first.

What shall we say then? Shall we continue in sin, that grace may abound? God forbid. How shall we, that are dead to sin, live any longer therein? Know ye not, that so many of us as were baptized into Jesus Christ were baptized into his death? Therefore we are buried with him by baptism into death: that like as Christ was raised up from the dead by the glory of the Father, even so we also should walk in newness of life. For if we have been planted together in the likeness of his death, we shall be also in the likeness of his resurrection. (Rom. 6:1–5)

Paul begins here by setting up a false conclusion to what he has presented so far. What should our response to this glorious gospel be? Shall we continue our sinning so that God might continue with His gracious forgiveness (v. 1)? And of course the answer is *no*. God forbid. How can people who are dead to sin still live in it (v. 2)? But someone might come back at Paul—what do you mean, dead to sin? And Paul replies, "Don't you know what baptism means?" If you were baptized into Jesus, you were baptized into His death (v. 3). Not only were you killed in baptism, you were also buried (v. 4). But the whole point of this was so that you might participate in His resurrection as well (v. 4). Note that not only was Christ raised, He was raised from the dead *by the glory of the Father*. In the same way (by the glory of the Father), we should walk in newness of life (v. 4). This is because if you have been planted in the likeness of His death (which is what baptism is, the likeness of His death), you also participate in the likeness of His resurrection (v. 5).

The first thing we need to work through here is whether or not Paul is referring to baptism in water. And our first instinct is to say that he could not be referring to water because, as we evangelicals all know, water baptism doesn't do those things that are described here. Therefore, we must hunt around for a baptism that *does* do them, which would be baptism in the Spirit. This solves the problem, but perhaps it solves it a bit too handily. There is no contextual or grammatical reason to think that anything other than water baptism is meant. And at the same time, there is a way of taking this as water baptism that is nothing but religious superstition. How are we to deal with this?

The seed of the gospel is broadcast. It falls on good soil and hard, it falls on the asphalt parking lot and on the well-tilled ground. The thing that makes it germinate is faith. Faith is the catalyst, the only catalyst for anything of spiritual value. When the declaration of forgiveness is made, we find out who it was meant for by seeing who believes it. We don't test the declaration, sending it off to an objective lab somewhere in order to find out whether or not it is worthy of our belief so that we may then believe it. The gospel always brings its own credentials to those who are elect, to those who have genuine faith. Because of this there is therefore always a perfect correspondence between those people for whom the statement is true and those who believe it to be true.

The doctrine of definite atonement is certainly true. Jesus died in order to *secure* the salvation of His elect, and only His elect. But Jesus also died so that we might consistently *offer* salvation to every creature (Mark 16:15).

These two things harmonize wonderfully, and so we shouldn't worry about it. We are preaching the gospel to a raggetty-taggetty world, not doing clean little syllogisms about P's and Q's. So don't worry about it when your Arminian friends persist on telling people, "Jesus died for you." If it is true, that person will believe it. If it isn't, he won't. (Incidentally, many Calvinistic paedobaptists make the same kind of statement at the baptismal font. We say, in essence, "Jesus died for you," without having been given a clear copy of the electing decree with little Herbert's name on it. *We walk by faith, not by sight.*) But we want to be doctrinal fussers, saying that if it isn't true *and independently verified*, then we shouldn't even think about saying it. We should be reminded of Chesterton's comment about the poet who tries to get his head into the heavens, as opposed to the rationalist, who tries to get the heavens into his head—and it is his head that splits.[3]

The Westminster Confession rightly says that there is a sacrament *union* between sign and thing signified, such that it is appropriate to speak of one in terms of the other. So Saul of Tarsus was told to rise up in order to receive water baptism, washing away his sins (Acts 22:16), even though water doesn't really do that. And Peter preached the same way, preaching a baptism for the remission of sins (Acts 2:38). Someone with genuine faith sees Christ in his baptism, and in the Lord's Supper, in just the same way that he sees Christ on a tract made of paper and ink,

3. "The *poet* only asks to get his *head* into the *heavens*. It is the logician who seeks to get the *heavens* into his *head*. And it is his *head* that splits." G.K. Chesterton, *Orthodoxy* (1908; Moscow, ID: Canon Press, 2020), 13.

or he hears Christ in a sermon preached by a poorly edu-cated street preacher who breathes through his nose. God uses despised and weak things in order to humiliate the worldly-wise. Does the grace go in when the water goes on? No, of course not, no more than a tract left in a laun-dromat can zap you as you walk by. This is something we understand easily in other settings. When performing a wedding, I have never said, "Please repeat: 'with this ring I thee wed,'" only to have the bride stop me and say, "I didn't know that gold rings could do that!"

Follow the direction of Paul's argument. The direction of this argument, rightly understood, is always into newness of life. If you have a life of sin on the one hand, and a baptism into Christ's death on the other, which one should we follow? Which one is in charge? Paul says, "What are you doing *that* for? You're *baptized*." This is what it means to grab someone by their baptism. The logic is the same as a man rebuking a friend—"You can't go honky-tonking...you're *married* now." And when someone sees, really sees, that this is what their baptism *means*, then that is what their baptism *is*.

We have been planted together with, *united* with, Jesus Christ in baptism, this likeness of His death. We therefore have a covenanted obligation to be united with Him, *just as* united with Him, in His life. Let God be true and every man a liar. If there is an inconsistency between baptism and the sin, then it is the sin that must die—never the baptism.

THREE KINDS OF DEATH

As we continue to work through this great letter of the apostle, we can see in various ways how his mind works. We see it in how he answers objections—"One of you will say to me then..." We also see in this passage a typical Pauline move where he says, "These things are so, and you must therefore act as if they are so." This is something we must learn because it is how our sanctification progresses.

> Knowing this, that our old man is crucified with him, that the body of sin might be destroyed, that henceforth we should not serve sin. For he that is dead is freed from sin. Now if we be dead with Christ, we believe that we shall also live with him: knowing that Christ being raised from the dead dieth no more; death hath no more dominion over him. For in that he died, he died unto sin once: but in that he liveth, he liveth unto God. Likewise reckon ye also yourselves to be dead indeed unto sin, but alive unto God through Jesus Christ our Lord. Let not sin therefore reign in your mortal body, that ye should obey it in the lusts thereof. Neither yield ye your members as instruments of unrighteousness unto sin: but yield yourselves unto God, as those that are alive from the dead, and your members as instruments of righteousness unto God. For sin shall not have dominion over you: for ye are not under the law, but under grace. (Rom. 6:6–14)

As we build on what Paul has just said (vv. 1–5), we are, to use the language of the Puritans, "improving our baptism."

We do so "knowing this" (v. 6). Progress in godliness is not groping in the dark; it is the result of sound teaching. What do we know? That our "old man" was crucified in Jesus in order to destroy the "body of sin." This was so that we would cease to be slaves of sin (v. 6). The way out of sin-slavery is to *die* (v. 7). But there is no way to be united with Christ in His death without also being joined to His resurrection life (v. 8). When Jesus rose, He did so in a way that freed Him from death forever; death has absolutely no claim on Him (v. 9). Moreover, He died unto sin one time, at a specific point in time, but the life He lives is *continuous* and is before God (v. 10). All these things *are* so. How should we therefore act? We should therefore act as if they are so. "*Likewise* reckon ye also yourselves...." (v. 11). Jesus died at a point in history, and He lives forever before God. You should therefore reckon yourself to be dead to sin in a decisive way, and alive to God through Jesus (v. 11). What is included in such a reckoning? Refuse to let sin *reign* (key word) in your mortal body, which means obedience to the lusts of that mortal body (v. 12). Present or yield the members of your body as though you were raised from the dead (because you were), and make this presentation to God (v. 13). To present such resurrected members as instruments of unrighteousness is not just morally wrong, it is schizophrenic. It is a contradiction (v. 13). Sin is not to rule over you anymore because you are under grace, and not under law (v. 14).

In order to understand what Paul is teaching here, we have to sort something out first. There are three kinds of mortification. He is here describing a crucifixion, a death, a mortification. But this is not a concept that has only one application for the Christian life. There are different "deaths" that we must understand.

First is the death of the "old man," the old way of being human. This is equated with the overthrow of the rule and reign of sin, the dominion of sin (Rom. 6:6; Gal. 5:24; 6:14). The old man is dead—you don't have to keep killing him. This is something that is equally true of all who are genuine Christians. The old man is the way we all used to be in Adam.

A second kind of mortification occurs in the lives of Christians who have stumbled or fallen, and because of their backsliding, significant sin has grown up in their lives. This is what Paul addresses in his letter to the Colossians. "Mortify your members which are on the earth" (Col. 3:5). These are not trifles, because he goes on to define them as fornication, uncleanness, etc. But he is talking to *Christians,* who should have their affections set above, and the action he calls them to is a decisive action at a point in time.

The third kind of mortification is daily for each of us. As John Owen once put it, a man should not think he makes any progress in godliness "who walks not over the bellies of his lusts."[4] We will see this just a few chapters

4. "It is our duty to be 'perfecting holiness in the fear of God,' 2 Cor. vii. 1; to be 'growing in grace' every day, 1 Pet. ii. 2, 2 Pet. iii. 18; to be 'renewing our inward man day by day,' 2 Cor. iv. 16. Now, this cannot be done without the daily mortifying of sin. Sin sets its strength against every act of holiness, and against every degree we grow to. Let not that man think he makes any progress in holiness who walks not over the bellies of his lusts. He who doth not kill sin in this way takes no steps towards his journey's end. He who finds not opposition from it, and who sets not himself in every particular to its mortification, is at peace with it, not dying to it." John Owen, *On Temptation and the Mortification of Sin in Believers* (Philadelphia: Presbyterian Board of Publication, n.d.), 162.

from now—"if ye through the Spirit do *mortify* the deeds of the body, ye shall live" (Rom. 8:13, emphasis added). The verb here refers to an action that is continuous and ongoing. This mortification you will never get to walk away from on this side of glory. If you try to do that, then you will only be soon confronted with the duty mentioned to the Colossians—that of having to deal with sins that are far worse.

Picture a weed patch, not cultivated at all. When the first mortification happens, God plows the weed patch under and makes it a garden. It is now a garden, and not a weed patch. The old status is dead. The second mortification is what happens when that garden is untended for a week, and you come back to find weeds in it that are up to your thigh. Uproot them, pull them out. That is the second kind of mortification. The third kind is what any good gardener will tell you about. Get out there every morning and pull up the weeds that are the size of your thumbnail. They will always be there. That is the third kind of mortification.

We are not called to do good in order to impress God or to ingratiate ourselves with Him. We are not trying to *earn* anything. God has already reckoned the righteousness of Jesus Christ to you, and that is your justification. What is your sanctification? It is you reckoning the righteousness of Jesus Christ to yourself. Reckon (*logizomai* [λογιζομαι]) yourself to be dead to sin. So what is sanctification? It is acting as though you really believe what happened in your justification. It is acting as though the death, burial, and resurrection of Jesus Christ are really *yours*. Justification is what God does, and sanctification is us saying *amen*.

So the old man is dead. Don't worry about him. But the flesh, your mortal body, is *not* dead, and you should keep a wary eye on it. In verse 12, Paul cautions these Christians against letting sin "reign" in your mortal body (like back in the old days). He then equates this with obeying "it" in its lusts. What is the antecedent to "it"? As it happens, the antecedent is "mortal body," and not "sin." Your mortal body will make all kinds of suggestions to you all day long. Stop feeling like the lone pervert at church—there isn't a person there who doesn't deal with this. At the same time, there is a difference between godliness and backsliding. Pull up the thumbnail size weeds. Stay on top of it. Don't wait till the weed requires three shovels, two hands, and a backhoe.

We have drifted so far from the biblical understanding of the words *grace* and *law* that, to a certain extent, we have inverted them. We think that grace means "you get to sin," and that law means "you can't sin." But as Paul is describing it is here, being under law means that you can't stop sinning, and that you therefore cannot stop accumulating the condemnation for that sin. Grace liberates you from that sin trap, from that sin slavery. Notice what Paul says here. *Sin* shall not have dominion. And why? Because you are under *grace*. Grace is the liberty of the Spirit, not the slackness of lowered standards.

UGLY BABIES

We come now to Paul's treatment of the great theme of true liberty and freedom. What is the nature of freedom? We need to be especially careful with this because as Americans we are trained to believe that we understand liberty in some special way, while it appears that we have really lost an understanding of the foundation of all liberty.

> What then? Shall we sin, because we are not under the law, but under grace? God forbid. Know ye not, that to whom ye yield yourselves servants to obey, his servants ye are to whom ye obey; whether of sin unto death, or of obedience unto righteousness? But God be thanked, that ye were the servants of sin, but ye have obeyed from the heart that form of doctrine which was delivered you. Being then made free from sin, ye became the servants of righteousness. I speak after the manner of men because of the infirmity of your flesh: for as ye have yielded your members servants to uncleanness and to iniquity unto iniquity; even so now yield your members servants to righteousness unto holiness. For when ye were the servants of sin, ye were free from righteousness. What fruit had ye then in those things whereof ye are now ashamed? For the end of those things is death. But now being made free from sin, and become servants to God, ye have your fruit unto holiness, and the end everlasting life. For the wages of sin is death; but the gift of God is eternal life through Jesus Christ our Lord. (Rom. 6:15–23)

Paul begins by returning to the question that began this chapter (6:1). He asks if we should therefore sin because we are under grace. Is that what grace means (v. 15)? God forbid. Grace is liberation *from* sin, not liberation *in* sin, or *to* sin. Sin is a dungeon, and a set of chains bolted into the

wall. Paul then turns to instruct us so that we won't fall for
this elementary mistake. "Know ye not...?" he asks. The
word in this passage rendered *servant* is *doulos* (δουλος),
meaning "slave." The direction of obedience establishes the
nature of the servitude. You are either a slave of slavery,
leading to death, or a slave of righteousness (v. 16). Those
are the two options. But thanks to God, the Roman Christians, who used to be slaves of sin, had transferred their allegiance by *obeying* "the form of doctrine" they had heard
(v. 17). The gospel is obeyed. They were as a consequence
freed from one kind of slavery by means of enslavement
to another (v. 18). Paul is using a rudimentary illustration
because we are slow to get it (v. 19). Just as we used to
yield our bodies to iniquity, producing lots more iniquity,
so now we are to do the same thing to righteousness, producing more and more holiness (v. 19). Freedom from one
is attachment to the other. When the Romans were slaves
of sin, they were "free" from holiness (v. 20). But what was
the fruit of that other way? They were now ashamed of
what they used to feel free to do. And the result of all that
was death anyway (v. 21). But now they were free from sin
and were slaves of God—with the fruit being holy, and the
result everlasting life (v. 22). For wages of sin is death, and
the gift of God is eternal life through Jesus (v. 23).

The illustration of marriage does not become explicit for
a few more verses yet (7:1–5), but Paul appears to be anticipating something like this already. Even though he is
speaking of slaves and not wives, the language of verse
19 appears to have some sort of sexual connotation. A
verb form of the same word for fruit is found in 7:5, in the

context of marriage. So when you yield your members as slaves to uncleanness, the result is that iniquity produces more iniquity—a perverse kind of "increase and multiply."

You present your members to iniquity, and the result is lots of ugly babies. But when you leave that behind in repentance, the results of the gospel union are holy. In the spiritual realm, the babies always look like the father. If the unbelieving Jews had been children of Abraham, they would have *looked* like him (John 8:39). So keep in mind that tolerating sin in your life, especially hidden, secret sin, is like trying to be a little bit pregnant. The *reason* that your sin will find you out (Num. 32:23) is that sin grows and multiplies.

In our individualistic tradition, we have very unwisely truncated our definition of freedom. We tend to think of it as "freedom from" restraint, because this leaves room, as we like to imagine, for a pretended autonomy. But this definition is only *partially* true. And when it is taken for the whole truth, the results are routinely disastrous. A "freedom from" kind of liberty is entirely incapable of sustaining any concept of civil or political liberty unless we ground it in the Pauline concept of the "freedom to" be virtuous, which is nothing other than the freedom to obey Christ. Notice what Paul does here. If you are at the bottom of the sea, you are free from being dry. If you are in the desert, you are free from being wet. That, by itself, is as far as "freedom from" will get you.

This is because Paul takes it as axiomatic that you will be *someone's* servant. As Dylan put it in one of his moments of lucidity, "You're gonna have to serve somebody."[5] You will either be wet or dry. You will either serve iniquity or you will serve righteousness. If you are a slave to the wrong one, then the result is death—you will be a dead slave. If you become a slave to the righteous one, then the result is life, everlasting life, and at the end of the story, the slave will be adopted as a true son.

How does this matter? It matters because modern secularists want to pretend that they can establish a "freedom from tyranny" kind of liberty without serving Christ. But that is impossible. If you take that route, the result will only be an ever-increasing iniquity. But if we as a people "obey from the heart the form of doctrine" that faithful gospel preachers declare, the result will be holiness, righteousness, and *life*. Part of that fruit will be every legitimate kind of "freedom from" liberty. Spiritual freedom is the necessary precondition to every other kind of freedom (2 Cor. 3:17), and spiritual freedom always begins with slavery to Christ. Notice how Paul reasons from spiritual freedom to what we think is the only freedom (1 Cor. 7:22–23). Never forget that political and economic liberty is gospel fruit. Do you really think that God will permit us to grow that glorious fruit in our orchards of death?

Many Christians today, for the sake of what they call grace, react away from the word *obedience*. But Paul is not of their mind. Liberty *is* obedience. Grace and obedience are not contrary because grace demands to be obeyed. What was the form of doctrine that the Romans had delivered to

5. Bob Dylan, "Gotta Serve Somebody," 1979.

them? The book of Romans is as good a summary of that gospel as we could find anywhere. What did they do with it? They obeyed. In Paul's mind, we may obey in this direction or that one, but we are creatures and we *will* obey. The only question is whether we will obey words of life or words of death.

Life and death are opposite one another, but they are not symmetrical. Paul does not contrast the wages of sin and the wages of righteousness. Neither does he contrast the gift of death and the gift of life. These two destinations are not symmetrical at all. The death and the life are opposed, but so are the forms in which they come. One comes as a wage, a payment, a paycheck. The other comes as a present, as a *gift*. Connect this with everything that has gone before, and we see that the servitude that leads to death is a servitude of strict justice, and the servitude that brings liberty is a servitude of *grace*.

You are the people of God. Hear then the words of the gospel. "See, I have set before thee this day life and good, and death and evil" (Deut. 30:15). Which will you have?

CHAPTER 7

OUR SECOND HUSBAND

Remember that the apostle has laid out his gospel for us, and he is now in the midst of answering objections to that gospel. The universal problem is set forth in the first three chapters, and then the glorious gospel is laid out in chapters four and five.

Beginning in chapter six, he starts anticipating and answering objections. The first one is that if we are justified apart from the law, won't that result in moral chaos? No, Paul says, for we have died with Christ in our baptism. Now we come to the objection that is about the length of the Torah's dominion. Wasn't the law supposed to be permanent?

Know ye not, brethren, (for I speak to them that know the law,) how that the law hath dominion over a man as long as he liveth? For the woman which hath an husband is bound by the law to her husband so long as he liveth; but if the husband be dead, she is loosed from the law of her husband. So then if, while her husband liveth, she be married to another man, she shall be called an adulteress: but if her husband be dead, she is free from that law; so that she is no adulteress, though she be married to another man. Wherefore, my brethren, ye also are become dead to the law by the body of Christ; that ye should be married to another, even to him who is raised from the dead, that we should bring forth fruit unto God. For when we were in the flesh, the motions of sins, which were by the law, did work in our members to bring forth fruit unto death. But now we are delivered from the law, that being dead wherein we were held; that we should serve in newness of spirit, and not in the oldness of the letter. (Rom. 7:1–6)

Paul starts here by identifying who he is addressing—those who know and care about the Torah (v. 1). These are the people who would raise this particular objection. If we are justified by faith alone, then what was the role of the law supposed to be? The first question here has to do with the extent of the Torah's authority.

The second question, addressed through the rest of chapter seven, has to do with the point of the Torah. If it did not justify, then what was it *for*? Now Paul's point here is that the Torah does not have authority over men who have died (v. 1). We have to take care to follow him closely here because his illustration is a complex one. A woman is bound to her husband by the Torah as long as he is alive, but his death releases her (v. 2). She is guilty of adultery if she marries another man while her first husband is still alive, but if he has died, then she is free to remarry (v. 3). In a similar way, we are dead to the Torah because of the crucifixion of Christ's body (v. 4). This frees us to marry another—that one being Jesus, the one who rose from the dead. This was done so that we could be fruitful before God (v. 4). When we were "in the flesh," married to the old man, the Torah stirred up the "motions of sins," and the result was "fruit unto death" (v. 5). So now that we have remarried, we are delivered from that Torah, that condition in which we bore fruit to death (v. 6). The result is that we may now serve in the newness of the Spirit (v. 6), and not in the oldness of the letter (v. 6).

In order to grasp Paul's point here, we have to be careful to correctly identify the characters in his illustration. Who is *who* exactly? We are the woman, and our husband was the old Adam. He was the federal head of the entire human race (Rom. 5), and his sin meant that we, married to him, bore fruit to death. The Torah is *not* the husband in this illustration—the law is holy, righteousness, and good (Rom. 7:12). But a good law can bind a woman to a bad man.

The law holds people to their covenants, even when those covenants are destructive. A good law can insist that death must beget death (v. 5).

Note that in this illustration, the woman cannot just walk away from Adam, even if it is to marry Christ. Adam must die in order for her to be free (Rom. 6:5). Adam died in the new Adam, so that the human race could be married in the new resurrected Adam, walking in newness of life, while remaining truly human. The Torah faithfully required us to beget according to our marriage vows, and God in His grace enabled us to bear fruit in another way. This means that humanity is the woman, her first husband is Adam, and her second husband is Christ. The Torah held us fast to our first husband, which is not the same thing as approving of our first husband.

Note carefully how Paul discusses the issues of death here. Who dies? The first husband dies (v. 2). If the first husband dies, his wife is free to remarry (v. 3). Christ died, which is implied by the fact that He rose from the dead (v. 4). Because Christ died and rose, we are dead *to* the law (v. 4). A wife whose husband has died is not a dead woman, but as far as the laws of marriage are concerned, she is dead to the law, and the law is dead to her. The law that held us to our first husband is dead in that respect (v. 6).

As will become apparent shortly, Paul is *not* saying that the standards of righteousness are now waived or abrogated (Rom. 6:14; 13:8–10). He is talking about a particular aspect of Torah, that which regulates marriage unions and the issue born from such marriage unions.

The Jews who were still in Adam were bound to him by the Torah. The Gentiles who were in Adam were bound to him by the law of the heavens, seen in every clear night sky. The Jews were bound by Torah, the Gentiles by natural revelation, and the two of them together bore fruit to death. Now of course, the Jews of the Old Testament who walked by faith (Heb. 11) did not bear fruit to death—and that is because they were looking forward to Christ. And in the same way, the many Gentiles of the Old Testament who walked by faith did not bear fruit to death, either. Men like Melchizedek, Jethro, and Naaman walked before God.

It is too easy for us to caricature the "old man." The fact that our first marriage resulted in so much death and despair should not make us think that it was cartoon evil. Our first husband did not necessarily rampage through brothels and taverns, talking like a pirate.

This kind of thing of course happens in a fallen world, but the really serious temptations came from our first husband at his respectable best. The kingdoms that came from him were glorious enough to present a significant temptation to the second Adam (Matt. 4:8), and the angelic being who led the first Adam astray appears as an angel of light (2 Cor. 11:14). Recall that Paul is making this point over the objections of those who "knew the law." They were better than the unwashed Gentiles; that was a given. They were chosen. They were religious. They were respectable. But it was a respectable depravity. They were just as married to Adam as anybody else.

Notice that in this passage, Paul contrasts two husbands, death and life, fruit to death and fruit to life, and, right at the end, Spirit and letter (v. 6). He does this elsewhere, and we do well to understand it. He is not condemning letters as such, because he wrote this contrast of Spirit and letter *with letters*. But those who have those letters *only* are still married to the first Adam—and the fruit to death they consistently bear proves it.

But those who receive the letters of the New Testament (and the Old) in the power of the Spirit are not bibliolaters (John 5:39). When the Spirit is at work in you, you bear fruit organically. If, when you try to grow your apples, the trunk shakes and the branches clank and smoke, something is obviously wrong. We are to serve, that is true (v. 6), but we serve in newness of Spirit. This is life. This is regeneration. This is grace, and mercy, and peace. This is righteousness hanging heavy on the branches, *given* to you. We are talking about the fruit of the Spirit; we are not talking about crawling over the broken glass of rules for the Spirit. Our first marriage was full of turmoil. But now we are invited to be at peace.

TWO LINES

We are now on the threshold of a vexed portion of the book of Romans. Christians have long divided over whether Paul is describing his pre-Christian life or his post-conversion life in this section. Is the description of anguish in Romans 7 characteristic of the Christian life? Or is it a description of his experience prior to what happened on the Damascus road? If pre-conversion, then why the present tense? Why the delight in God's law (7:22)? And if post-conversion, then why does he describe himself as a slave to sin (7:14) when in the previous chapter he already insisted that this is precisely what Christian are *not*—slaves to sin? Fortunately, these are not the only two options.

What shall we say then? Is the law sin? God forbid. Nay, I had not known sin, but by the law: for I had not known lust, except the law had said, Thou shalt not covet. But sin, taking occasion by the commandment, wrought in me all manner of concupiscence. For without the law sin was dead. For I was alive without the law once: but when the commandment came, sin revived, and I died. And the commandment, which was ordained to life, I found to be unto death. For sin, taking occasion by the commandment, deceived me, and by it slew me. Wherefore the law is holy, and the commandment holy, and just, and good. (Rom. 7:7–12)

When we get bad news, a very common reaction is to blame the messenger. But the messenger did not create the bad situation; he has only told you about it. The doctor did not create your cancer; he just informed you of it. The law did not create sin in us; rather the law informs us of the presence of that sin (3:20) and inflames that tendency to sin (5:20; 7:5). But the law itself is not sin. This is the first misconception that Paul heads off (v. 7). God forbid that we say the problem is *in* the law. On the contrary, it was the law that informed us where the problem actually was. I would not have known what lust was had the law not revealed it by prohibiting it (v. 7). Sin is an opportunist, and it used the commandment to create in me all manner of concupiscence (v. 8). Without the law, sin has nothing to push against, nothing to rebel against (v. 8). Once I was alive before the law came, but in the human soul it is as though sin is simply dehydrated—just add the water of the law (v. 9). When sin lives, man dies (v. 10). The commandment, the Torah, bound me to the old man, to Adam, and I bore children of death (v. 10). Sin, using the Torah, lied to me, and through that lie, slew me (v. 11). But don't blame the law for any of this—the law is holy. The commandment is holy, just, and good (v. 12).

Now in the past when I have taught against individualism, this has not been done in order to reject the importance of *individuals*. Each one of us is fashioned in the image of God, and we go to Heaven or Hell by ones. There are no group rates. At the same time, when we are saved, one at a time, or we remain lost, one at a time, this is inseparable from an organic union with one of two *Adams*— the first Adam, or Christ, the second Adam.

This means that Paul is not giving what we would call a "personal testimony." This is not autobiographical, at least not primarily. He is speaking of himself as a representative unconverted Israelite. He is telling *Israel's* story, and he is explaining why Israel had such trouble under the Torah. At the same time, he is not telling Israel's story in such a way as to exonerate himself. He was typical—zealous for God, but without knowledge (Rom 10:2). We are not addressing here the problem of generic unconverted men (although there are some related issues involved in that), but rather are dealing with the problem of *Israel*, a problem that is woven throughout this entire letter.

Unregenerate Israel was a valley of dry bones, and the prophet Ezekiel had declared that one day the bones would all be brought to life again. God would make Israel to live again. This had begun to happen on the day of Pentecost, but to change the illustration, the first century was a time when the dead wood branches were going to be cut out, and the remnant of faithful Israel was going to welcome the believing Gentiles as they were grafted in alongside the believing Jews (Rom. 11:23–24). Paul has here selected himself (during his time of unbelief) as a personification of unbelieving Israel, and this is a remarkable identification. Paul had been an insolent man, a blasphemer, and persecutor of the Church, and he had done all this believing that God actually *wanted* this behavior from him.

So is this about unconverted Israel, or unconverted Paul? It is both, and has to be both, wrapped up together. For example, Paul says something about himself (v. 9) that was not applicable to Israel. He says he was personally alive before the commandment came, but when it came, sin revived, and he died. But before the law came into human history, we in the human race were *not* alive—death reigned from Adam to Moses (Rom. 5:14). That is a detail that has to be individual. But the overall picture cannot be separated from the themes of his larger argument.

If the Romans 7 experience is pointing to the unregenerate Israel, as I believe it is, there is no good reason not to take Saul of Tarsus as a marvelous representative of that Israel. And an argument can be made that Paul agreed, if he indeed used the first person singular pronoun as a way of describing the plight that Israel was in.

One of the things that Paul is doing in this book is demonstrating that God is righteous in His dealings with man. Circumcision is good, but unbelieving Israel has corrupted it by not being circumcised in their hearts

(Rom. 2:28–29). The Torah is good, and as a preacher of justifying faith, Paul is actually the one who upholds the law (Rom. 3:31). Christ is the end of the law for all who believe (Rom. 10:4), which means that those who do not believe in Christ, far from upholding the law, are actually *missing the whole point* of their precious law. The Torah prepared the way for Christ (Gal. 3:24; Rom. 5:20).

This description of an unregenerate Israel does not mean that all were unregenerate. Obviously not. This interpretation does not mean that David, and Samuel, and Isaiah, and Elizabeth, and John the Baptist, and Mary, the Lord's mother, were all "bearing fruit unto death." They were faithful Jews who lamented the condition of Israel generally, and who looked forward to the time when Israel as a whole would be renewed. They walked by faith, in line with their father Abraham, who is also our father. But prior to the Damascus road, Saul of Tarsus was *not* one of their number.

Paul teaches both in Romans and Galatians that once the covenant was established, *there were two lines within that covenant.* He makes this point multiple ways. Once Abraham is called, the sons of Abraham gather to take pride of place. But wait...Abraham had two sons, Isaac and Ishmael, and only Isaac was the child of promise. Very well then, let us gather to take pride of place in Isaac. But Isaac had two sons also—twins even—and they were named Jacob and Esau. Do you really want to start boasting of your lineage from *Jacob*? Those who do so are only demonstrating that they *don't get it.*

In Galatians, the same point is made by using the figures of Sarah and Hagar. These two women are two covenants. Hagar corresponds to Sinai, and Sarah corresponds to the heavenly Zion, the free woman, the free Jerusalem. Now as evangelical Christians we want to *heed* this warning. We do not want to define ourselves right out of any need for it. Paul teaches us two things that we must remember. The first is that the new Israel will not end up as the old Israel did. The second is that this will be true because we *heeded* the warnings, not because we didn't need to.

WRETCHED MAN

We have seen that the Apostle Paul continues to answer the questions created by the gospel of grace. There are a number of them. Gentiles are under sin. Jews are under sin. They are both under sin. God promised to remake the world through Abraham, and God did this by sending a final Adam. This glorious message can be twisted and distorted in various ways, so Paul has to answer objections to it. Won't this introduce moral chaos? No. Won't this render the Torah as a superfluous moral distraction? No, not at all. The Torah had a pivotal role to play in our salvation, as we will see.

> Was then that which is good made death unto me? God forbid. But sin, that it might appear sin, working death in me by that which is good; that sin by the commandment might become exceeding sinful. For we know that the law is spiritual: but I am carnal, sold under sin. For that which I do I allow not: for what

I would, that do I not; but what I hate, that do I. If
then I do that which I would not, I consent unto the
law that it is good. Now then it is no more I that do
it, but sin that dwelleth in me. For I know that in me
(that is, in my flesh,) dwelleth no good thing: for to
will is present with me; but how to perform that which
is good I find not. For the good that I would I do not:
but the evil which I would not, that I do. Now if I do
that I would not, it is no more I that do it, but sin that
dwelleth in me. I find then a law, that, when I would
do good, evil is present with me. For I delight in the
law of God after the inward man: But I see another law
in my members, warring against the law of my mind,
and bringing me into captivity to the law of sin which
is in my members. O wretched man that I am! who
shall deliver me from the body of this death? I thank
God through Jesus Christ our Lord. So then with the
mind I myself serve the law of God; but with the flesh
the law of sin. (Rom. 7:13–25)

Paul's purpose here is twofold. He intends to vindicate the
Torah (v. 12), and also to show how the Torah worked
within Israel to reveal and exacerbate the reality of sin
(3:20; 5:20; 7:13). Was the problem resident within the
Torah itself? God forbid (v. 13). The point was to have
sin use the Torah in order to grow up to its full wicked
maturity (v. 13). More on this shortly. Paul then continues to illustrate the problem of Israel in the vividness of a
first-person narrative—Israel's Torah is spiritual, but Israel
is not spiritual (v. 14). Israel was a slave—to sin, and then

to Rome because of her sin. The national ideals are good, but they don't really get upheld (v. 15). The hypocritical failure reveals the goodness of the standard (v. 16). The national conscience doesn't want to go that way, but the national "id" has other ideas (v. 17). So Paul comes to a conclusion—Israel is in the flesh, and cannot do what Israel knows is right (v. 18). The good remains undone; the evil is pursued and embraced (v. 19). Don't blame the Torah, and don't blame Israel's conscience—there is something deeper going on (v. 20). That deeper thing is a law deeper than Torah, responding to it (v. 21). Israel really does delight in the Torah "in the inward man" (v. 22). But that is not all; there is another law there as well—it is the law of sin, using the law of God, using it in order to plunge Israel into exile and captivity (v. 23). Wretched man! Who will deliver (v. 24)? Paul thanks God for the Messiah, the new Israel (v. 25), and then sums the whole thing up again. With the theological conscience, Israel was *right* to bind the Torah to itself (v. 25). And Israel was then *right* to be dismayed to find that this lawful binding resulted in spiritual disaster for Israel (v. 25).

There are three qualifications to make right away.

The first qualification is that Paul is not describing this problem as a detached theological spectator. He is certainly talking about Israel (because he is discussing Israel throughout the entire epistle). But he himself was right in the thick of this problem; he was not one of the glorious exceptions of grace that we find described elsewhere (Heb. 11). He was a Hebrew of Hebrews (Phil. 3:5), and to personify Israel's problems in his own unconverted voice was not at all a stretch. Because of this, we find that law and grace are *always* relevant categories.

Second, the Reformed doctrine of sanctification that includes a genuine internal moral struggle is correct. While it is my view that this particular struggle is not found here in Romans 7 (which way overstates the problem), that doctrine is found and well-grounded in Galatians 5. Too often, Reformed exegetes take this passage in Romans 7 as a description of the process of sanctification because those who deny it are usually theological perfectionists, which is clearly an error.

And third, to apply this to Israel in this way does not make this an irrelevant passage for us to meditate on. As Paul would say, God forbid. We are Christians, and in various places Paul tells us that as the new Israel we are called to learn the lessons that the old Israel failed to learn. We will see this quite clearly when we get to chapter eleven (cf. 1 Cor. 10). And, God willing, that lesson is one that we will in fact learn.

So Paul is simply digging deeper here. Romans 7 is simply the next pass at Romans 2:17–24. Romans 8 is the next pass at Romans 2:28–29, which explains why he needs to address the same question at the beginning of chapter three and at the beginning of chapter nine: "What is the point of being a Jew, then?"

Scripture contains many Adams. Israel received the Torah and then failed to keep it, meaning that Israel was another failed Adam. The fact that Christ was the *final* Adam should not blind us to the fact that Scripture shows us a series of Adams—founders who fail, founders who fall.

Think of Noah, for example, or Solomon. Think of Israel, adopted at Sinai and given the very words of life. What did they do with this? They did what every Adam still in the flesh must do—they rebelled against those words of life and turned them into instruments of death. So it was *not* the case that Israel successfully escaped from Adam while the Gentiles did not. Israel, just like the Gentiles, was in Adam. The only way to escape from him was through a *successful* Adam.

Now why did God want sin to grow to its full maturity? Why did God give a Torah that He knew sin would take full advantage of? Why did God deliberately grow sin up to its full height? He did this so that He could deal with sin *once and for all*. Israel was a greenhouse enclosed by Torah's glass and heated by the sun of God's holiness so that the most noxious weeds could grow up to their worst potential, in stark contrast to the sign outside that proclaimed it to be a greenhouse full of rare and exquisite orchids.

Paul could say that "with his mind" and in the "inner man" he delighted in the law, which was true enough. He could give enthusiastic assent to the rightness of the law. But he did not love it in another way, as indicated by the results. The fact that the law he stumbled over was the prohibition of covetousness perhaps gives us a hint. That is the one commandment out of ten that addresses heart issues only, and in the prohibition of coveting your neighbor's wife, there is a sexual element. This is a temptation and sin that illustrates the nature of this conflict for us very pointedly. A man can heartily disapprove of sexual uncleanness, and do so honestly, and yet find that on another level, he is helpless when the temptation comes.

God did this so that He could deal with sin *foundationally*. Just as He did not send Israel into Canaan until the iniquity of the Amorites was full (Gen. 15:16), so He did not send the new Israel into our Canaan until our evil had reached its full maturity. When Jesus collided with sin, He met it in full force. When Jesus took it all onto Himself, He took the full measure of it.

CHAPTER 8

NO CONDEMNATION

So what is the state of the "wretched man" now that he has been brought into Christ? What is the birthright of the new Israel? Throughout this chapter, we now see Paul begin to develop his teaching of the Holy Spirit's work and the glorious result of that work, which is found in the phrase *no condemnation*.

> There is therefore now no condemnation to them which are in Christ Jesus, who walk not after the flesh, but after the Spirit. For the law of the Spirit of life in Christ Jesus hath made me free from the law of sin and death. For what the law could not do, in that it was

weak through the flesh, God sending his own Son in the likeness of sinful flesh, and for sin, condemned sin in the flesh: that the righteousness of the law might be fulfilled in us, who walk not after the flesh, but after the Spirit. (Rom. 8:1–4)

Paul has given us a vision of the gospel, a vision with global sweep. The problem of sin is a deep and abiding one, for Jew and Gentile both (Rom. 1–3). God promised the salvation of the world through Abraham (Rom. 4:13), and He has fulfilled that promise by giving us *a new way of being human through Christ*, the last Adam (Rom. 5:14). Such a message is too good to be true; there must be a problem. So Paul starts answering objections. Won't this lead to moral licentiousness (Rom. 6:1)? No, because there is no way to receive Christ without also receiving His death, and all that such a death means and entails (Rom. 6:3). Doesn't this mean that God has cast aside His Torah, which He Himself had commanded Israel to treasure (Rom. 7:7)? No, He told them to treasure it, and also to understand what it was for. He gave the Torah so that sin might become utterly sinful, so that He might deal with it in the cross. Therefore, what do we find?

First, there is *no condemnation* for those who are in Christ Jesus (v. 1). How does Paul define those who are in Christ? He defines them as those *who walk* after the Spirit, not after the flesh (v. 1). Now the law of the Spirit of life (in Christ Jesus) has set us free from the law of sin and death (v. 2). Remember that the sin principle deep within every Jewish and Gentile heart is an opportunist. It takes advantage of the

Torah, or natural revelation, or both, and creates the law of sin and death. The law of the Spirit strikes off these chains. For what the Torah could not do (make us righteous), God did by sending His Son as a vicarious sin-substitute (v. 3). The Torah was unraveled by *our* weakness, not *its* weakness. God condemned sin in the flesh of Christ (v. 3). He did this so that the righteousness of the Torah (already vindicated by Paul) might be fulfilled in us who walk according to the Spirit, not according to the flesh (v. 4).

The word "law" admits of different uses, and there are four ways to think of "law" in these four verses. The first is the law of the Spirit of life (v. 2). The second is the law of sin and death (v. 2). The third is the Torah itself (v. 3). And the fourth is the law of love, the law that expresses the righteousness of the Torah (v. 4). Paul uses one word to describe all of them (*nomos*/νομος), and we must be careful not to be wooden in how we seek to understand him.

As we will see more clearly when we get to chapter eleven, Paul does not assume that every baptized Christian automatically understands these things. These things must be taught, insisted upon, and the body of Christ must be taught and discipled in terms of this gospel.

The way Paul is teaching, he is heading off a carnal Israelite approach to the Torah within the Christian Church. Notice that he uses *nomos* to refer to the objective, external presentation of something (like the Torah or, for us, the Bible), but he also readily uses it to describe an abstracted principle, taken from such objective gifts. This means that even the book of Romans (if the law of sin within us had its way) could be turned into a death-dealing Torah just like

Deuteronomy was. But if we read it *rightly*, it is crammed full of the words of life.

So we should make a point to describe this "right understanding" that is so important. What does it look like? What does it taste like? For those who have this grace, there are three things found in this passage. The first is that they are under *no condemnation*. The second is that they are *free* from the law of sin and death. And the third is that the *righteousness* of the law is fulfilled in them. That's it—guiltless, free, and holy. Not guilt-ridden, bound, and uptight.

But, we object, the rules that we find in Scripture, and which we derive from Scripture, are good. *Yes, they are.* And they should be descriptive of our lives. But sin remains the opportunist that it has always been. The libertine objects to the *rules* of the legalist, but often (not always) the legalist's rules can actually be pretty reasonable on paper. The legalist usually lives longer than the crackhead, and good for him. But does he *enjoy* his life? "If you eat these bran muffins made out of oak sawdust filler, you will live twenty years longer." But if that is what I have to eat, then why would I want to live for twenty more years? That's twenty additional years of eating those things.

The Spirit objects to the rules of the legalist not because that man is so holy, but because he isn't. He falls short of his own rules because there is an opportunist living in his heart, *just like everybody else's*. Nothing carved in stone or written on paper, not even by God, can deal with this. In order to deal with it, God had to give us His Spirit. And to make us fit to receive the Holy Spirit, His Son had to die.

Put this another way. There is no condemnation because there is condemnation. Paul begins by saying there is no condemnation for those in Christ. This is not because the need for condemnation was *waived*, but rather because the necessary condemnation is *past*. It has already occurred. God sent His Son "in the likeness of sinful flesh" (v. 3), and to deal with all of that sin, He condemned sin in the flesh (cf. 2 Cor. 5:21). The death of Jesus was the condemnation of sin—yours and mine. You are a desperate sinner on death row. If the governor puts off your day of execution, you still have a problem. "When shall I be executed then?" Temporary good news is, "The governor granted a stay, putting it off for six months."

But by way of contrast, this kind of gospel good news says that your day of execution was *yesterday*. "It's done. You are now free to go."

CHRISTIANS ON PAPER

So what is the difference between those who are simply called by God's name, and those who *really* belong to Him? This is a question that arises in both covenants, and it is answered (in principle) the same way for both. The Jews had drifted into the error of formal externalism, and Paul is here cautioning the new Israel against committing exactly the same error. The difference between formalism and the reality is the work of the Holy Spirit.

> For they that are after the flesh do mind the things of
> the flesh; but they that are after the Spirit the things
> of the Spirit. For to be carnally minded is death; but

to be spiritually minded is life and peace. Because the carnal mind is enmity against God: for it is not subject to the law of God, neither indeed can be. So then they that are in the flesh cannot please God. But ye are not in the flesh, but in the Spirit, if so be that the Spirit of God dwell in you. Now if any man have not the Spirit of Christ, he is none of his. And if Christ be in you, the body is dead because of sin; but the Spirit is life because of righteousness. But if the Spirit of him that raised up Jesus from the dead dwell in you, he that raised up Christ from the dead shall also quicken your mortal bodies by his Spirit that dwelleth in you. Therefore, brethren, we are debtors, not to the flesh, to live after the flesh. For if ye live after the flesh, ye shall die: but if ye through the Spirit do mortify the deeds of the body, ye shall live. For as many as are led by the Spirit of God, they are the sons of God. (Rom. 8:5–14)

The Spirit had obviously been at work in the times of the older covenant, but He had not been poured out so extensively. At the same time, the nature of the border between the Spirit's active work within the covenant and His absence within the covenant remains the same. Thus there were true Jews and Jews who only had the outside of the thing (Rom. 2:28). There are Christians just like that also.

You have the mind of the kind of person you are. The fleshly mind belongs to the flesh; the spiritual mind belongs to the Spirit (v. 5). To veer off to the left like that is death, while to be spiritually minded is life and peace (v. 6). The carnal mind is hostile to God and cannot help being hostile to God (v. 7). Notice that this hostility is evidenced through its refusal to be subject to the law of God (v. 7)—indeed, note its *inability* to be subject to it. This is why those who are in the flesh cannot please God (v. 8); they can't *want* to please God. But this is not the condition of the Roman Christians (v. 9), unless...Paul says that they are in the Spirit *if* the Spirit is in them. If the Spirit is missing from a man, that man does not (ultimately) belong to Christ. It does not matter how many times he has been baptized. Baptize him until he bubbles, but his carnal mind is still there, seething (v. 9). But if Christ is in a man, then the Spirit within him is life because of resurrection righteousness, justification righteousness (v. 10). This is true even though a true Christian's body will still die because of sin. But not to worry, even though we will die, we will be raised—*if* the Spirit that raised Jesus is in us (v. 11). Our obligations, therefore, are not to the flesh (v. 12). We owe the flesh *nothing*. If you live as though you owed the flesh something, you will die (v. 13). The contrast to this is to mortify the deeds of the body through the power of the (indwelling) Spirit. If you do that, you will live (v. 13). So who are the true sons of God? They are the ones in whom the Spirit is at work, leading them in mortifying the deeds of the body (v. 14).

Certain things are true independent of us. We are male or female, regardless of what we might think about it. These are objective realities. Our parents are our parents, whether or not we like it. We are baptized or we are not, and our baptism always means the same thing (union with Christ in His death) whether or not we approve of that meaning. These are objective realities. A Jew was a Jew whether or not he was a true Jew inwardly (Rom. 2:28).

In the same way, a Christian is a Christian, and he was baptized on a certain date with other people watching. The covenant, and all its attendant obligations, is an *objective* thing. Someone might say that if we have to be born again in the heart, then what value is there in being this kind of an external Christian? The Pauline answer is "much in every way."

This is not the answer given by those who like to float around in the invisible Church, like dust motes in a sunbeam. While rejecting their approach, we must also say that, when it comes to the *final* question, all these privileges (which are genuine and real) together with five bucks will get you a frappuccino.

Why is this? A man consists of more than his obligations and his covenantal identity. At the center, we are defined by our loves and our hates, and this is what Paul is addressing here. The flesh does what? It minds the flesh (v. 5), it seeks death through a carnal mind (v. 6), it hates God (v. 7), it chafes under the law of God (v. 7), it is uninterested in pleasing God (v. 8), and it rejects the ownership of Christ (v. 9). Those who are characterized by this fleshly mind, circumcised or not, baptized or not, church fixture or not, are those who *die*. Are they a kind of Christian? Sure...the kind that goes to Hell.

For the genuine believer, this flesh (*sarx*/σαρξ) is the seat of his remaining sin. It should not be confused with the mere fact of having a material or physical body. It is the fact of having a *fallen* physical body which is not yet fully redeemed.

So at the same time, we must not make the mistake of thinking that if we have *any* struggle with the flesh, we must be unconverted. Thinking you are completely above the fray means that you are actually deep in sin. Remember our earlier illustration—the weed patch, the true garden with three-foot weeds, and the true garden with weeds the size of your thumbnail. This last category is described here (v. 13). Mortify the deeds of the body—the sense of the verb is continuous, ongoing. This is something we are all called to daily, and the Spirit is the one accompanying us, leading us to those weeds, pointing them out. "There, now *that* one." The true sons of God are those who are *doing* this (v. 14). The Spirit's leading here is not directional (right or left), but rather moral (right or wrong). True sons will always have weeds to pull, and true sons will pull them.

If churchmen are not evangelicals, they will destroy the Church. Ironically, if evangelicals are not churchmen, they will destroy the Church also. We must insist upon being both. You must be baptized, and you must be born again. If you have true, evangelical faith, you don't set these things at odds with each other. You don't love the woman while refusing to put a ring on her finger. And you don't put a ring on her finger while refusing to love her. Here's a radical idea, kind of crazy when you think about it—why not both?

Why not have a beautiful ceremony *and* treat her right? You are more than a Christian on paper if the Spirit is in you.

COMING GLORY

We should always desire to *act* biblically, and not to *react* to the mistakes or abuses of others. Many of us came into the Reformed faith because we were trying to get away from all the relational goo. Well and good. But we still need to take care not to react mindlessly. There is no relational goo in a cemetery, either, but there should be more to what we want than that. We have something that contemporary evangelicals do not have—but remember that there is often something they have that we do not have.

> For ye have not received the spirit of bondage again to fear; but ye have received the Spirit of adoption, whereby we cry, Abba, Father. The Spirit itself beareth witness with our spirit, that we are the children of God: And if children, then heirs; heirs of God, and joint-heirs with Christ; if so be that we suffer with him, that we may be also glorified together. For I reckon that the sufferings of this present time are not worthy to be compared with the glory which shall be revealed in us. (Rom. 8:15–18)

Sin leads to death, as Paul has been pointing out, and so sin also leads to fear of death (v. 15; cf. Heb. 2:15). All liberation begins with liberation from sin, and all ungodly slavery begins with slavery to sin. The Spirit of adoption works two things in us. The first we have already covered—putting to death the deeds of the body (vv. 13–14)—and the second is here. He does this in the context of creating a sense of relationship and belonging. We cry out *Abba,*

Father (v. 15). The Spirit works in our works, testifying to others, and He works in our hearts, testifying to us as well (v. 16). He shows the world through our lives that we belong to Him and shows us in the Spirit that we genuinely do belong to Him.

But certain things follow from this. If we are children, true children, then we not only receive guidance, instruction and discipline now, but we also will receive an inheritance later (v. 17). If we are heirs, it is because we are inheriting *alongside* Christ. We are joint heirs together *with* Him (v. 17). If His suffering is ours, then His glorification is ours also (v. 17). And how does that shared suffering compare with that shared glory? The comparison, Paul says, is not even worth making (v. 18).

Our prayers are not to exhibit the professionalism of a well-run business meeting. We are *children* (v. 16), and we are children who *cry* (v. 15), and we are children who cry *Abba,* Father (v. 15). This is the Spirit we have been given, and this is the work that He does. He is at work in our hearts testifying, and because the Spirit is not a false witness, His testimony in our hearts lines up with His testimony in His Word, and His testimony in the character of our lives. And His testimony in these three places lines up and is consistent.

Abba is an Aramaic word, and the rendering *Father* is from the Greek. Why both? Paul echoes what Mark records for us in the example of the Lord (Mark 14:36). Now notice how the Spirit leads away from Himself and brings us to the Father. Jesus teaches us to pray, "Our Father" (Matt. 6:9). No man comes to the Father except through Him (John 14:6). For *to* Him (the Father), we both (Jew and Gentile) have access *through* Jesus *by* the Spirit (Eph. 2:18). The Father is the destination, the Son is the road, and the Spirit is the car. The direction of all biblical piety is toward the Father. That is what everything in the kingdom is straining toward (1 Cor. 15:24). And that is why it is so important for you men to be real *fathers*. You are testifying to something very large indeed.

Never consider Christ as just another individual. He is an Adam (Rom. 5:14). What happened to Him in judgment is reckoned and imputed as having happened to you (Rom. 6:3–5). We are united to Jesus, and this means that everything that happened to Him is also ours—His death, His burial, His resurrection, and His glorification. Further, the gulf across which imputation leaps is something we apprehend by faith now. But there is a grand convergence coming, when our union with Christ will become entirely visible.

Christ is our elder brother. When He comes into His final and complete inheritance, so shall we. We are joint heirs together with Him (v. 17).

Now the Apostle Paul knew what suffering was. He was no armchair theologian (2 Cor. 11:23–28). He was flogged at least five times and was in prison multiple times. He was beaten with rods at least three times. He was stoned once. He was shipwrecked once. There is much more than that, but you get the picture. He was no delicate flower, no apostolic buttercup. He knew suffering. He also knew the ultimate context of that suffering, which was the coming tsunami of glory. This is a very scarred man who said that our present sufferings are not worth comparing to the glory that will be revealed *from within us*.

What does he mean? Take all the sufferings of all God's elect throughout all history and place that fine dust on one side of the scale. Then take the one gold brick of five minutes in Heaven, and place it on the other side. That is what he means. "Not worth comparing" means that God is going to put everything into perspective, so we might as well start getting it into perspective now. God will dry every tear (Rev. 21:4), and they will not hurt or destroy in all His holy mountain. The former things will have passed away.

But Paul is getting the Romans on the edge of their seats with this. We are not yet talking about what is revealed in the latter half of this chapter, but we need to start craning our necks now. What is Paul about to tell us? Let us consider just one element of this now as a sort of trailer. He says here that this coming glory is going to be "revealed in us." That is the direction the glory tsunami is coming from. The creation is longing for *what*? The creation is looking out to sea, gazing earnestly for that tsunami. What is that sea? What is that ocean? Is it not *you* (8:19)?

TOO DEEP FOR WORDS

The glory welling up with us is the future of the creation, and it is the future of the entire creation. This is a much-neglected passage, perhaps because the view from here is so stupefying. We don't quite know how to take it in—but that is all right, because the Spirit will help us.

For the earnest expectation of the creature waiteth for the manifestation of the sons of God. For the creature was made subject to vanity, not willingly, but by reason of him who hath subjected the same in hope, Because the creature itself also shall be delivered from the bondage of corruption into the glorious liberty of the children of God. For we know that the whole creation groaneth and travaileth in pain together until now. And not only they, but ourselves also, which have the firstfruits of the Spirit, even we ourselves groan within ourselves, waiting for the adoption, to wit, the redemption of our body. For we are saved by hope: but hope that is seen is not hope: for what a man seeth, why doth he yet hope for? But if we hope for that we see not, then do we with patience wait for it. Likewise the Spirit also helpeth our infirmities: for we know not what we should pray for as we ought: but the Spirit itself maketh intercession for us with groanings which cannot be uttered. And he that searcheth the hearts knoweth what is the mind of the Spirit, because he maketh intercession for the saints according to the will of God. (Rom. 8:19–27)

The creation, meaning everything that has ever been made, is earnestly looking forward to something. That something is the manifestation (the unveiling, lit. the *apocalypse*) of the sons of God (v. 19). Remember, we have just defined the sons of God as those who are being led to put the old ways to death (vv. 13–14) and who hear the testimony of the Spirit being given to their own hearts (v. 16). When these sons come into their own, the creation will finally see what it is longing for.

The reason the creation longs for this is that it will signal the end of the creation's distress. The creation was not willingly subjected to vanity (v. 20), but God did it, intending from the beginning that this futility would look up in hope (v. 20). When that hope arrives, the creation will be delivered from its current bondage, and will share in the liberty of these newly manifested children of God (v. 21). Note Paul's striking image here—the whole creation is in labor (v. 22). Not only does the mother long to deliver, the baby also longs to be born (v. 23). By that I mean that we also groan, and Paul lets us know here what the day of "manifestation" is. It is our final adoption as sons, meaning the redemption of our body (v. 23). He is talking about the coming day of resurrection, the last day.

The creation was subjected to vanity in hope (v. 20). We were saved in hope (v. 24). But it wouldn't be hope if you could *see* it, right? Not seeing it enables us to cultivate patience in the groaning (v. 25). Because we can't see, we can hope. But also because we can't see, the Spirit has to help us in our infirmity (v. 26). We don't know what to pray for, because this is a baby that has never been born before. So the Spirit groans alongside us (v. 26), and His groans are deeper than words. In the meantime, Jesus searches our hearts and He also knows the mind of the Spirit. He is the one who prays for us constantly, and this means that *everything* is lining up (v. 27).

Paul says a few strange things in passing here. The creation was made "subject to vanity" (v. 20). The creation is currently struggling under the "bondage of corruption" (v. 21). The whole creation groans and travails (v. 22). But when you couple all this with false ideas of perfection, you could get the idea that any entropy at all is a sign of the Fall.

So we should ask (and answer) a few questions about the unfallen Adam. Could he have shuffled a deck of cards before the Fall, or would he have kept coming up with one royal flush after another? Did the leaves on the forest floor of Eden (*were* there leaves on the forest floor?) form perfect geometric patterns? When Adam ate the fruit he was explicitly allowed to eat, did that fruit get digested? In other words, the fact that the creation groans with longing now does not mean that it was made out of stainless steel before. *That* is not perfection. That was not the world God declared to be so good.

However, as we shall see in a moment, these pre-Fall examples of entropy did not include excruciating pain for any sentient animal. Neither was there any agonistic pain for humans. The Fall ushered in the era of that kind of *groaning*.

Never forget that this section of Romans is part of a larger, sustained argument. We need to be reminded of this because there are some memorable phrases here that tend to get quoted out of their context ("all things work together," "the Spirit groans," etc.). Paul is here driving toward the eschaton, the day of resurrection. That is his subject. The creation groans, looking forward to that manifestation. We share in that groaning, longing for the same thing. And the Spirit shares in our groaning, meaning that He is straining toward the same end. What is that end?

It is the apocalypse of the sons of God. That word apocalypse literally means an unveiling, or a revealing. That day will manifest our glorious liberty; it is our final adoption, the redemption of our body. This is the central meaning of predestination for Paul (Eph. 1:5), and of the famous predestination found in the next section. We are predestined to be conformed, and we groan in the direction of that predestination.

Those who truly affirm predestination *groan*. This is not a denial of a more general reality of foreordination; it rather depends on it. But they are not the same thing.

So the creation groans toward something. We groan toward that same thing. The Spirit sees us struggling, and He enters into the battle as well. And our great High Priest looks down on the whole thing and lifts it up to God with His intercession and *amen* (look ahead to v. 34).

When a baby is born, it is a manifestation. It is a revelation. In a positive sense, it is an apocalypse. It is the day of delivery.

The entire created order is heavily pregnant with power and glory, *and all the sons and daughters of God are the baby*. This means history is driven before the Holy Spirit of God, and the entire point of the whole narrative is to reveal the Church for who it is—the bride of Christ.

History is pregnant, and there can be no thought of an abortion, however much the devil would love to bring one about. Of course we know that our abortion culture is murderous, and it truly is. Blood does pollute the land. But there is something else going on here. The abortion culture that believes itself to be so powerful is actually a desperate and pathetic form of wishful thinking.

As early as Genesis, we knew that the seed of the woman *would* be born, and He would crush the serpent's head. In the same way, we know now that the sons of God will be revealed in all their glory.

This is not some horror flick where some chthonic monster will be born into the world. No, it will be power, light, glory, and radiance. And when we gaze into that resurrected radiance, we will see…one another.

WHAT SHALL WE THEN SAY?

We come now to the beating heart of what has been nicknamed Calvinism. But of course Calvin—that faithful servant of God—did not concoct these doctrines. He taught that where Scripture is silent, we ought not to pry (Deut. 29:29). But he also taught, following Augustine, that Scripture is always a safe guide. The same way that a mother stoops so that a toddler can keep up, so Scripture stoops for us. And if our mother leads us into certain topics, then we may assume that it is safe for us to go there.

> And we know that all things work together for good to them that love God, to them who are the called according to his purpose. For whom he did foreknow, he also did predestinate to be conformed to the image of his Son, that he might be the firstborn among many brethren. Moreover whom he did predestinate, them he also called: and whom he called, them he also justified: and whom he justified, them he also glorified.

> What shall we then say to these things? If God be for
> us, who can be against us? (Rom. 8:28–31)

We begin with the phrase "all things." Do not take this in a small or tiny way—Paul has just finished talking about how the entire created order is longing for the day of resurrection in the same way that a woman in deep labor longs for her delivery. When a woman is pregnant, her whole body is pregnant; *she* is pregnant. Every part of her is involved. So all things work together for good for those who love God, who are called according to His purpose (v. 28). Who are these people? These are the sons of God, who will soon be manifested. What is His purpose? We have just learned that it is the restoration of all things.

How does this work? Those whom God foreknew, He predestined to a particular end (v. 29). That end was full conformity to the image of His Son, which will obviously happen at the day of resurrection. Predestination here is to that final conformity. And when we get there, it will be manifested that Christ was the firstborn among many brothers (v. 29). We then come to what has been called the golden chain of redemption—those whom God foreknew, He predestined. Those He predestined, He called. Those He called, He justified. Those He justified, He also glorified. And note the past tense of that word *glorified* (v. 30). It is as good as done—the glorification is *predestined*, remember.

What is the appropriate response to these things? It is the kind of absolute confidence that comes from the knowledge that God is for you, despite your sins, and the resultant understanding that no one and nothing can effectively stand against you (v. 31).

FOREKNOWLEDGE

We must begin by dealing with a common evasion—the idea that God looks down the long corridors of time and history, sees you praying to receive Jesus, and on that basis predestines you to eternal salvation. This view is known as Arminianism, and goes back to the teacher Jacob Arminius (1560–1609), whose theology was condemned at the Synod of Dordt (1618–1619).

There are (at least) two problems here. The first is textual. It does not say on the basis of *what* God foreknew, it says *whom* He foreknew. The foreknowledge is of persons, not events. But of course, this takes the word *knowledge* into a different realm. God, speaking of Israel, said, "You only have I known of all the families of the earth: therefore I will punish you for all your iniquities" (Amos 3:2). Of course God (cognitively) knew all the families of the earth, not just Israel. His knowledge as mentioned here is relational, covenantal. The foreknowledge in this place is therefore a reference to those "upon whom God set His electing love." Those *whom* He knew and loved beforehand, He also predestined.

Second, the theological problem with the "corridors of time" approach is that it makes God a cosmic me-too-er, and it does this *without solving any of the problems*. If God looks forward in time and learns something, then this compromises His omniscience. This view argues that God loves us because we first loved Him, clean contrary to 1 John 4:19.

And these corridors of time—who created *them*? Who governs them? If God foreknew cognitively what would happen if He created the world, *and He created it anyway*, this constitutes a decision. Try as we might, there is no real way to have a Christian faith in which God is not God.

Notice how Paul ties everything together tightly. The people foreknown are the same group that is predestined "to be conformed to the image of his Son." This conformity, as we have just been noting, will occur as the day of the apocalypse of the sons of God, the day our adoption as sons is finalized. So those whom God foreknew, He predestined to be conformed to Christlikeness, which is their glorification. In between the predestination and the glorification (involving the same set of people), we find calling and justification. In between the foreknowledge and the glorification, *nobody gets off the train*. If it is possible to get off the train, this makes a complete hash out of the argument that Paul begins in the next verse.

Napoleon once said that he would rather meet ten thousand well-generalled and well-provisioned men than one Calvinist who thought he was doing the will of God. There is something about this doctrine that brings backbone along with it. And there is something about rejecting it, or sidling away from it, or nuancing the heck out of it, that promotes effeminacy.

But do not mistake this with fatalism—*que sera sera*. This is not an exhortation to just hunker down and take it. This is a chapter full of yearning, full of longing, and it is our task as the children of God to discover the work of the Holy Spirit in history and to groan in labor toward that end. History is not just one random thing after another. There is a *telos* here. The future is all glory. That glory will be revealed in us, and we are predestined to it. Everything that happens to those who love God is in line with that declared and stated purpose.

The universe is enormously complicated, and we should never minimize that. But we have been told the meaning of it—and we should always remember that the Spirit sticks to the agenda.

UNTOUCHABLE

The conclusion of this chapter of Romans ties in nicely with the way it began—it begins with *no condemnation*, and it ends with *no possible condemnation*. And the basis for this glorious and exalted grace is the entire argument of Romans up to this point—the free gift, justification, and the love of God. This is Paul coming to a *conclusion* of no condemnation; he is not offering it as a mere assertion. No condemnation is the conclusion of a very detailed argument.

> He that spared not his own Son, but delivered him up for us all, how shall he not with him also freely give us all things? Who shall lay any thing to the charge of God's elect? It is God that justifieth. Who is he that condemneth? It is Christ that died, yea rather, that is risen again, who is even at the right hand of God, who also maketh intercession for us. Who shall separate us from the love of Christ? shall tribulation, or distress, or persecution, or famine, or nakedness, or peril, or

sword? As it is written, For thy sake we are killed all the day long; we are accounted as sheep for the slaughter. Nay, in all these things we are more than conquerors through him that loved us. For I am persuaded, that neither death, nor life, nor angels, nor principalities, nor powers, nor things present, nor things to come, nor height, nor depth, nor any other creature, shall be able to separate us from the love of God, which is in Christ Jesus our Lord. (Rom. 8:32–39)

Paul resorts to a favorite form of argumentation here, offering a how-much-more argument. If God did not hold back His Son for our sake, why would He stint on anything else (v. 32)? Note the "freely give us all things." *All things* work together for good. And all things include the entire cosmos and all history. So who is going to be able to bring a successful charge against God's elect (v. 33)? *God* is the one who justifies them. Condemnation has no place to stand, because Christ died, and rose, and ascended, and is praying for us right now (v. 34). Christ prays for us because He loves us (vv. 34–35). And what can get in between us and that love? It is a rhetorical question, and the answer is *absolutely nothing* (v. 35). To drive the point home, Paul runs through a list of possible contenders, things that might attempt to drive a wedge between the believer and Christ in order to make some room for condemnation. Bring out your champions, Paul says. Tribulation? Distress? Persecution? Famine? Nakedness? Peril? Sword? The answer comes back, *of course not* (v. 35). *Of course not* to all of them.

These are not academic questions for the righteous, as a citation of Psalm 44:22 shows (v. 36). The great persecutions have not yet begun, but Paul is most certainly anticipating them. No, in all these things, Paul says, we are more than conquerors through Christ, who loved us (v. 37). Paul is convinced of this, and, fully persuaded, he works through another list of challengers, even more comprehensive than the first (v. 39). So get to the conclusion first.

Can *anything* separate us from the love of God which is in Christ Jesus our Lord (v. 39)? No. What sorts of things cannot bring about such a separation? Death cannot, and life cannot (v. 38). Angels are not up to it, and neither are principalities or powers (v. 38). Nothing that is happening right now can do it, and neither can anything that might happen in the future (v. 38). High things can't do it, and deep things can't do it (v. 39). And to fill out the list, nothing created can do it (v. 39). Did Paul forget anything? Did he leave anything out?

On the backside of the castle of your soul, is there an unlocked and unguarded gate, swinging on its hinges invitingly? Heh. Give Paul a little credit.

In order for this argument to work at all, we have to be talking about those people who are elect according to God's unalterable decree. Paul is being more pointed and specific here than he was, for example, in Colossians 3:12. I said in an earlier section that in between foreknowledge and glorification, no one gets off the train. If anybody can be forced, seduced, or tricked into getting off the train, then this wrecks Paul's argument completely. It does not slightly dilute the force of Paul's argument; it leaves it in a shambles.

What might persuade someone to use his "free will" to get off the train? Well, the sorts of things that are employed by the devil for this task are things like tribulation, distress, persecution, famine, nakedness, peril, sword, death, life, height, depth, angels, principalities, or powers. So other than *those* sorts of things that might sway you, you are quite secure. But if that is the case, then nobody is secure at all.

So Paul is not satisfied. Suppose someone wants to say that a person *himself* could make a series of choices to somehow interrupt the transition from foreknowledge to glory. Is my "free will" a thing present? A thing to come? Is it something in creation? Go back to the beginning. If someone is foreknown, then everything that follows is absolute security. And it is security found in the protection of *another*.

Paul quotes here from Psalm 44, and it is important to note that that psalm is not a prayer of confession. It is a lament from righteous martyrs. God had delivered them mightily in the past (Ps. 44:1–8), but now God had turned them over to their enemies, and so they are suffering terribly (9–16). However, where you would expect to then find a confession of sin, we find a protestation of innocence (17–26). These are Old Testament saints; these are righteous ones.

But the exaltation of Christ in history *has* made a difference. It is not a difference between unrighteousness and righteousness—but there is yet a difference between bewildered righteousness and triumphant righteousness. The Christ who reigns, and who prays for us, and who is at the right hand of God is the *same* Christ who was "delivered up." He is the one who "died." Now, in the light of *that* gospel, we have had it revealed to us that this thing called self-sacrifice is a weapon that completely undoes the machinery of the world. Those who are worldly-wise don't know what to do with it. They have no countermeasures.

So we are more than conquerors because Christ was more than a conqueror. Note that Paul has moved from a failure to *be* conquered to a success *in* conquering. The decrees of God are not just great on defense. What is it that overcomes the world? Is it not our faith? In and through the elect, the decrees of God will triumph in the world.

And please remember that Paul is not talking about an invisible, spiritual, seventeenth-dimension victory in some other place, a place that historians will never find. No. He is not seeing mystic visions about some other spiritual Neverland. No—we pray weekly for the kingdom to come, for God's will to be done...where?

Blessed are the meek, for they will inherit the *earth*.

CHAPTER 9

THE BAD ELECT

It may not be immediately obvious, but it may appear as though the Apostle Paul has painted himself into a corner. He began to wax a little too eloquent at the end of chapter eight, showing how absolutely *nothing* can separate the elect of God from the love of Christ. Who can lay a charge against God's elect? It is *God* who justifies. But the problem is that Israel was the elect nation of God, and the Jews had spent a great deal of time and energy chasing Paul around the Mediterranean, trying to kill him. What about that? Maybe something *can* separate us from the love of God? Couldn't it be whatever it was that separated the unbelieving Jews? *No*, Paul replies. As he will show in the coming passage, not only will unbelieving Israel be unable to undo or thwart God's purposes for the world, but in addition, God's purposes for the world will eventually gather up unbelieving Israel. Given all the grand themes that Paul has been propounding throughout this epistle, he is here developing a detailed answer to a most obvious question. What then, are we to make of Israel? What happens to Israel?

> I say the truth in Christ, I lie not, my conscience also bearing me witness in the Holy Ghost, that I have great heaviness and continual sorrow in my heart. For I could wish that myself were accursed from Christ for my brethren, my kinsmen according to the flesh: who are Israelites; to whom pertaineth the adoption, and the glory, and the covenants, and the giving of the law, and the service of God, and the promises; whose are the fathers, and of whom as concerning the flesh Christ came, who is over all, God blessed for ever. Amen. Not as though the word of God hath taken none effect. For they are not all Israel, which are of Israel. (Rom. 9:1–6)

Paul begins with a solemn oath. He is telling the truth in Christ, and not lying (v. 1). His conscience is also testifying (in the Holy Spirit) that he is speaking the truth (v. 1). The thing he testifies to is the fact that he is constantly burdened with sorrow (v. 2). And it is a *great* heaviness and a *continual* sorrow. He wishes that it were somehow possible for him to be accursed and separated from Christ for the sake of his kinsman, whom he calls his brethren (v.

3). More specifically, he is referencing the Israelites (v. 4). These Israelites have many privileges indeed—they have the adoption (v. 4), the (Shekinah) glory (v. 4), the covenants (v. 4), the giving of the law (v. 4), the service or worship of God (v. 4), the promises (v. 4), the fathers (v. 5), and the fact that they were the people from whom Christ came in the flesh (v. 5). This Christ is over all things and is the blessed God forever (v. 5). But Paul cautions us—don't draw the wrong conclusion from this. The conclusion that must *not* be drawn is that the Word of God was ineffectual (v. 6). And he gives the solution in brief summary, a solution to be developed at length in the argument that follows. Not all those who are *of* Israel *are* Israel. There is a two-tiered membership in Israel, just as there is a two-tiered membership in the new Israel.

We see here in Paul the heart of a true pastor. It is ironic that Paul is accused of being an enemy of the Torah, because he here shows himself to be animated by the same spirit as animated Moses. "Yet now, if thou wilt forgive their sin—; and if not, blot me, I pray thee, out of thy book which thou hast written" (Exod. 32:32). Paul wanted to be lost if that would save the Israelites, and Moses wanted to be lost along with the Israelites if God would not forgive them. The same spirit is very clearly there. Moses anticipated the Pauline spirit, and Paul reenacted the Mosaic heart.

There are two instructive things here. The first is that Paul knew for a fact that what he wanted was impossible. He has just finished teaching us that it was impossible. Nothing can separate us from the love of God in Christ—not even our desire for those who are outside to come in.

And second, it is crucial for us to see that Paul was no fatalist, surrendering limply to the decrees of God. He knows that God is sovereign, and he does not rail against that sovereignty. But he also knows *that he loves his kinsmen.* Belief in the sovereignty of God does not turn us into blocks of wood or stone.

We come now to a second pass on an earlier argument. Earlier in this letter to the Romans, Paul had outlined the great blessings that the Jews had (Rom. 3:1–2). He is doing it again here, and to much the same effect...

What value is there in being a Jew? Much in every way. All the things that Paul recites here are in the same vein as his earlier rehearsal of this reality. God values the objective gifts that He gave to His people, even if individuals within that people do not believe. These are true gifts, and the world is blessed through them—adoption, glory, covenants, the law, ministry, promises, and the fathers.

We learn from Paul not to set the gifts of God at odds with one another. They occupy different places—why *should* they be at odds? Objective grace and subjective reception of grace are both from God, and they each depend on one another. Possession of objective grace is not grounds for rejecting the need for subjective grace. Possession of subjective grace is not grounds for rejecting the need for objective grace. Are you saved? Praise and thank God for it, but *you still need the Church*, the sacraments, the ministry, the covenant, the preaching of the Word. Are you a Church member, the fifteenth generation in a line of Christians going way back? Well and good, but you still must be born again.

It is not possible to read the Old Testament without coming to the conclusion that there were Jews and then there were faithful Jews. There were the people who were kept by the covenant, and then there was the group within that first group who kept the covenant they were kept by. Paul divides them in this way—he says there is one group that is *of Israel*, and another group that *is Israel*. Harkening back to his earlier statement of this in Romans, a true Jew is one who is one inwardly, and circumcision is of the heart, by the Spirit.

Now it is freely acknowledged that there are many differences between the administration of God's grace in the Old Testament and New, *but this is not one of them.* It is astounding how many interpreters of Scripture can read the plain statements of the apostles in a way that is 180 degrees out from *what it actually says.* This must be emphasized here because if we don't get it, we are going to be absolutely lost in chapters nine through eleven. And here is the problem. We tend to draw contrasts between the old Israel and the new Israel *at just the point where the apostles are drawing parallels.* Consider, for example, the warnings of 1 Corinthians 10:6, 11–12, and Hebrews 3:7–14ff.

And so we take the lesson. Not all who are of the Church are the Church—even though they are.

JACOB HAVE I LOVED

We come now to the central lesson of all evangelical religion. We come now to the glorious revelation of the sovereign grace of God, as revealed in the gospel, and only through the gospel. We come now to the promises, which are great and precious.

> Neither, because they are the seed of Abraham, are they all children: but, In Isaac shall thy seed be called. That is, they which are the children of the flesh, these are not the children of God: but the children of the promise are counted for the seed. For this is the word of promise, At this time will I come, and Sara shall have a son. And not only this; but when Rebecca also had conceived by one, even by our father Isaac; (for the children being not yet born, neither having done any good or evil, that the purpose of God according to election might stand, not of works, but of him that calleth;) it was said unto her, The elder shall serve the younger. As it is written, Jacob have I loved, but Esau have I hated. (Rom. 9:7–13)

We have seen that not everyone who is *of* Israel is to be counted *as* Israel. This answers the objection that God's word has somehow failed (v. 6). But how does this work out in the course of scriptural history? For example, in order to be a "child of Abraham" it is necessary to be more than a child of Abraham. The promise was given to the line of Isaac (v. 7). Paul quotes Genesis 21:12 here. He then says that Abraham had two kinds of children—children of the *flesh* and children of the *promise*. The children of the promise are the ones considered to be his seed (v. 8). Quoting Genesis 18:10, 14, Paul cites the promise directly. Not only that, but the same thing is repeated over again in the next generation. Rebecca conceived twins by one man, the patriarch Isaac (v. 10). And then, Paul says, before these twins were born, and so that God's prerogatives in election would stand unchallenged (v. 11), God declared through a prophecy that the elder would serve the younger (v. 12). This is found in Genesis 25:23. And, finishing the thought, the apostle quotes from Malachi 1:2–3. Jacob was loved by God, and Esau was hated and rejected by Him (v. 13).

In debates between Calvinists and Arminians, a point is often made about that inflammatory quote—"Esau I hated"—and it is a point we should readily grant, but only to a point. The quotation is not from the book of Genesis, like the others here, but is rather from the last book of the Old Testament (Mal. 1:2–3). Malachi in context is talking about the nations of Israel and Edom. It is the word of the Lord to *Israel* (Mal. 1:1), and His hatred of Esau is why *Edom* is referred to as judged (v. 4). If we are following Paul's argument here in Romans, the corporate love that God showed to Israel did not mean that every Israelite was saved. Neither did His hatred of Esau mean that every Edomite was lost. Job was one of the godliest men ever to live (Ezek. 14:14), and he was almost certainly an Edomite (Job 1:1), and quite possibly the second king of Edom (Gen. 36:33). So the fact that Esau was hated by God did not mean that every Edomite was reprobate. At the same time, it does mean something. If God's sovereign dispensing of grace apart from works extends to entire *nations*, why would He balk in applying it to individuals?

The unbelieving Jews of Paul's day drew themselves up to their full height. "*We* are children of Abraham," they

said. "Oh," he replied, "Ishmaelites then?" "No," they re-
torted. "*We* are descended from *Isaac*." "Oh," he replied.
"Edomites then?" They had the generations of the patriarchs to learn the lesson, but their unbelief had blinded
them. Every generation must learn the same lesson over
again, and it can only be learned by the sovereign grace of
God. Learning this lesson is the gift of God.

The unbelieving heart always wants to trap God in the
fine print. Paul's point here is that we are not nearly so
adept at reading that fine print as we think we are. We
say that God promised salvation to the seed of Abraham,
and there, we have Him. Paul points out, in the fine print,
that Ishmael is the seed of Abraham in a certain sense.
Right? We retreat—God promised salvation to the seed of
Isaac. Surely He can't wriggle out of that. Paul points to
the next paragraph down. What about Esau? Is he part of
this salvation? The point is that when God reveals, at the
culmination of history, that the *seed* of Abraham are all
those who share the *faith* of Abraham (Gal. 3:28–29), this
is not moving the goalposts. This is not a fourth-quarter
rule change. God has been doing this from the very beginning. It has *always* been for the children of the promise,
and it has never been for the children of the flesh alone.

Related to this, the fundamental contrast for Paul is always between grace and works, and note that the allure of
works here is centuries before the Torah was given. Jacob
had the position he did by grace, and it was *not* of works
(v. 11). Jacob was given something apart from works long
before his great-great-grandson Moses, giver of the Torah,
was even born (Exod. 6:16–20). The Torah wasn't around,

but works were. Works are always around, and always whispering in your ear.

We know that God draws straight with crooked lines, but we sometimes rush to assign blame where the Bible does not. While she was pregnant, Rebecca inquired of the Lord and was told by God that the older twin would serve the younger (Gen. 25:23). Contrary to this word, Isaac favored Esau (Gen. 25:28) despite the fact that Jacob was a perfect man (Gen. 25:27). Rebecca believed in the Word of the Lord, and she favored her righteous son while Isaac favored the son who gave him the kind of food he liked (Gen. 25:28). Isaac was willing to give the blessing for the sake of food, and Esau was willing to sell his birthright for the sake of food. This is why the deception of Rebecca and Jacob saved Isaac from a spiritual disaster. Isaac tried to reject the Word of the Lord but was graciously prevented.

But the central issue here is the promise of God, and not the personal character of Jacob. God had given a prophetic word that the blessing was to go to the younger, and Isaac tried to disobey this. That is the great issue. But this does not make Jacob righteous in every respect. His name *means* supplanter, and he was this way from the womb as Hosea tells us, and God will punish him accordingly (Hos. 12:2–3). At the same time, in the next verse, we see that Jacob was truly converted to God (v. 4). And Jacob appears to have acknowledged his fault through the restitution that he offers to Esau when he returns home (Gen. 32:3ff). But with all that said, Isaac should have blessed Jacob on the basis of the prophecy alone.

So we need to embrace both sides of what Paul is saying. The children of the flesh are *of* the children of God in one sense (v. 6), but, as he says in verse 8, they are *not the children of God* in another. We are the children of God *by faith* (Gal. 3:26). Evangelists of Christ must never be shy about telling Christians that they aren't or telling evangelicals that they need to be born again. And pastors of Christ must never tire of telling Christians that they are accepted in the Beloved.

BAD PUPPET!

We now come to some hard words, whether they are hard to understand or simply hard to take. And as we seek to be faithful to what God has given us here, we have to be mindful of Peter's caution—there are places in Paul's epistles where it is not safe for ignorant or unstable people to go (2 Pet. 3:16). But if we receive the hard words the right way, the reward will be tender hearts. If we reject these hard words, then it will be our hearts that become hard—just like Pharaoh's.

> What shall we say then? Is there unrighteousness with God? God forbid. For he saith to Moses, I will have mercy on whom I will have mercy, and I will have compassion on whom I will have compassion. So then it is not of him that willeth, nor of him that runneth, but of God that sheweth mercy. For the scripture saith unto Pharaoh, Even for this same purpose have I raised thee up, that I might shew my power in thee, and that my name might be declared throughout all the earth.

> Therefore hath he mercy on whom he will have mercy,
> and whom he will he hardeneth. Thou wilt say then
> unto me, Why doth he yet find fault? For who hath
> resisted his will? Nay but, O man, who art thou that
> repliest against God? Shall the thing formed say to him
> that formed it, Why hast thou made me thus? Hath
> not the potter power over the clay, of the same lump
> to make one vessel unto honour, and another unto
> dishonour? What if God, willing to shew his wrath,
> and to make his power known, endured with much
> longsuffering the vessels of wrath fitted to destruction:
> And that he might make known the riches of his glory
> on the vessels of mercy, which he had afore prepared
> unto glory, even us, whom he hath called, not of the
> Jews only, but also of the Gentiles? (Rom. 9:14–24)

We have already seen that Paul refuses to let us draw the
conclusion that God's word is ineffectual (v. 6). Here he
refuses the implication that God Himself is unrighteous (v.
14). This means that he rejects the ancient Epicurean co-
nundrum on the problem of evil—wherein God must either
be incompetent or malevolent. Paul rejects both options.
Paul vindicates God from charges of unrighteousness by
citing the divine prerogative as it was spoken to Moses (v.
15). God will have mercy on those He will have mercy on,
and He will show compassion to those He wants to show
compassion to. Note that we are talking about mercy and
compassion here, not justice. It does not depend on the one
who wills or runs, but rather upon the mercy of God (v.
16). The flip side of this (not showing mercy) is evidenced

in God's treatment of Pharaoh (v. 17). Paul repeats the principle again, this time with both mercy and hardening stated (v. 18). Then the obvious objection is raised—if God makes us do these things, how can He judge us for them (v. 19)? Paul's answer looks like a nonanswer to us—as in, "*Shut up*, he explained" (vv. 20–21). But there is far more to it than that. What if God, who wanted to display His wrath, needed vessels of wrath in order to do it (v. 22)? What if He, in order to display His mercy, needed vessels of mercy (v. 23)? And those vessels of mercy, as it turned out, were selected not only from the Jewish race, but also from all the nations (v. 24).

The biblical position on this issue is concerned to reject the either-or fallacy of ascribing either impotence or malevolence to God. The biblical position begins by asserting the prerogatives of God, not the rights of man. As it turns out, that is the only way to preserve anything for man. And the biblical position always provokes the objection of verse 19. Just as preaching the gospel of grace will provoke the objection that this leads to "sinning that grace may abound" (6:1), so the preaching of sovereign grace will provoke *this* objection—and nothing else will provoke it.

When Paul summarizes the objection that is mounted against what he is saying, our initial reaction to it is, "*Yeah*! What about that?" If God hardens some and has mercy on others, where does He get off blaming us for being hard? It is as though God commands the little wooden puppet to avoid certain evil dances, then makes the puppet dance them, and then smashes the puppet to smithereens. "*Bad* puppet!" Before answering the objection, we have to ask, if your sympathies are there, whose side are you on? Paul's, or the apostolic critic?

Paul's answer does two things. First, it assumes the absolute right of the Creator to dispose of His creation as He pleases. God is the Potter, and we are the clay (Isa. 64:8). Remember that Paul is steeped in the Old Testament Scriptures, and Isaiah pronounces a woe on anyone who would strive with his Maker (Is. 45:9–13). Paul was thoroughly familiar with the fact that this was Jeremiah's image (Jer. 18:1–6; 19:11).

But second, notice that he also presupposes genuine moral responsibility on the part of the clay. He *blames* the clay for thinking a certain way, and for "replying against God." The point of his illustration is to display relationship and not to claim that men are inert substances like clay. They are subject to authority like clay. In some respects, we are nothing like clay, being much greater than clay— but of course, God is infinitely greater than a potter. We are more like clay than God is like a potter.

We are more like fictional characters in a Shakespeare play than God is like Shakespeare.

When Paul reminds you that God is the Potter, don't try to get satisfaction by making Him just ten times bigger than we are. God is not a big creature, like Zeus was. When one creature forces another, his exercise of freedom displaces the freedom of the one acted upon. If we conceive of God like that, simply bigger than anything else, we cannot escape the idea that He is actually a bully. But remember the Creator-creature divide.

So I have a question. In the scene where Hamlet is decid-
ing whether to kill his uncle while he is at his prayers—how
much of that was Shakespeare, and how much of it was
Hamlet? Whatever else it is, it is not a zero-sum question.
The God who ordains all that comes to pass is infinite,
ineffable, and transcendent. This means He is not locked
down inside the system with us, such that if He causes us to
do something, that causal action necessarily displaces our
free agency—the way one billiard ball would displace another. It is much more like Shakespeare writing the entire
scene, such that we can say that it was "all Shakespeare,"
while at the same time acknowledging that the entire
speech was spoken by Hamlet—it was also "all Hamlet."
And if someone objects by saying that we are true, living
beings, and not two-dimensional fictional characters, the
first reply is that God is far greater than Shakespeare also.
The distance between God and Shakespeare is infinite, and
the distance between Hamlet and us is finite. That's the
first thing. The second is that there is no objection to this
illustration that can be made that could not be made with
much greater force against Paul's earlier illustration of the
Potter and the pottery. We are much greater than pots also.

So why is there sin and evil in the world? This is the ancient question—why would an omnipotent, omni-righteous
God create a world that would go off the rails the way it
has? Paul does not assert anything here, but he does indicate a direction—what if? If this were the answer, Paul
would have no problem with it.

In a world without sin and evil, two attributes of God
would go unmanifested. And since their manifestation

glorifies God, we should want to see God glorified. In a world without sin, we would not see God's fierce wrath and His great power. But it glorifies Him for us to see that wrath and power. That is the first reason. The second is that, in a world without sin, we would not see the greatness of His mercy. In order for Him to forgive sinners, we must have them.

Before you react against these suggestions in anger, take a moment to compare this answer to the typical free-will theodicy. And by this phrase *free-will theodicy*, I mean the very common reaction of saying that God is not entailed in the problem of evil because He thought it necessary to give us free will. But the evil is still *there*—to which god is it offered? Why are we offended when the offering is made to the glory of God, and not offended when it is made to the glory of man, on the altar of free will?

It is strange that a passage so full of mercy could generate so much anger and distress. God offers His mercy through Christ, and we don't want to take it, because mercy presupposes our wickedness (Isa. 64:8). If there are ten inmates on death row, and the governor pardons seven of them, what is that? If it is mercy, then how is it construed as injustice to the remaining three?

SAVING THE REMNANT

In order to understand Scripture rightly, we have to understand the flow of redemptive history. God's revelation to us is progressive, and it unfolds over centuries. If we treat the Bible as the book that fell out of the sky, we are going to have a terrible time comprehending it rightly. The works of God's judgments and deliverances are *sequential*.

> As he saith also in Osee, I will call them my people, which were not my people; and her beloved, which was not beloved. And it shall come to pass, that in the place where it was said unto them, Ye are not my people; there shall they be called the children of the living God. Esaias also crieth concerning Israel, Though the number of the children of Israel be as the sand of the sea, a remnant shall be saved: for he will finish the work, and cut it short in righteousness: because a short work will the Lord make upon the earth. And as Esaias said before, Except the Lord of Sabaoth had left us a seed, we had been as Sodoma, and been made like unto Gomorrha. (Rom. 9:25–29)

In this short passage, we have four quotations—two from Hosea and two from Isaiah. And this is a very good place to let the apostle instruct us on what the two prophets were talking about.

We have just learned in the previous verse that the vessels of mercy included the Gentiles (v. 24). Paul then confirms this by saying that Hosea predicted it when he said that God will take those who were not His people and make them His people (v. 25; Hos. 2:23). He follows it up with another citation. Those who were called "not the people of God" would be accepted as children (v. 26; Hos. 1:10). Isaiah cries out concerning Israel—even though the children of Israel were as the sand of the seashore, only a remnant would be saved (vv. 27–28; Isa. 10:22–23). Isaiah had made the previous point that unless God saved a remnant, the Jews would have been wiped out just like Sodom and Gomorrah had been (v. 29; Isa. 1:9).

Let us begin with a summary of the citations. If you read carefully through the first two chapters of Hosea, this is what you will find. God takes Israel as a bride, and just as Hosea found Gomer unfaithful, so God found Israel unfaithful. Because of this, God put Israel away entirely (Hos. 1:6) but will have limited mercy on Judah (Hos. 1:7). Then those who were put away for their apostasy (and called "not God's people") will again be called God's people. This is the doctrine of the remnant followed by the full restoration. Paul also quotes Hosea on this restoration in a way that includes the Gentiles in it (Hos. 2:23). The restoration of Israel, after being utterly put away, means that other nations can come to the Lord also. Note the phrase comparing Israel to the sands of the sea (Hos. 1:10).

Isaiah uses the same expression—the sand of the sea—and says that even though Israel be of that great number, a remnant shall return to the Lord (Isa. 10:22). The Lord will make short work of it in a decisive judgment (Isa. 10:23). Paul is not dragging the Gentiles into this without warrant because just a few verses later, Isaiah himself includes the Gentiles (Isa. 11:9–10). This is not conjecture on our part, because Paul himself quotes this verse later in Romans while justifying the mission to the Gentiles (Rom. 15:12). In short, Paul is not proof texting here in some wooden way—he is appealing to a sustained vision from the Old Testament. And then of course we see what a great *mercy* that gift of a remnant was (Isa. 1:9).

Put all this together, and what do we have? The nation of Israel was called out from the nations to be a light for the nations. Though they grew and flourished numerically (sand of the sea), they consistently went astray, again and again, as anyone who has read their Old Testament knows. We have a history of cyclic apostasies and restorations. This typological pattern climaxed when the Messiah came. The vast majority of Israel fell away, and God spared a remnant. That remnant was to be used in such a way that the Gentiles would come to the Messiah, and then all Israel would eventually return, resulting in a huge blessing for the entire world (Rom. 11:15).

Now take what this means at the simplest level. It means that the ratio of saved to lost varies widely based on what moment in redemptive history we are dealing with. We cannot take particular passages like "many are saved but few are chosen," universalize them for all time, and make them a permanent fixture. It is not playing fast and loose with the text to contextualize it.

For example, if you were to say to someone that you believed that the vast majority of the human race will be saved (as you should believe), the first thing you will hear is that the Bible says that the way is narrow, and only a few find it (Matt. 7:13–14). But remember the remnant. Who are the remnant? The few who find it. But what else are they? They are *first-century Jews*. Consider it this way— with comments interspersed.

Then said one unto him, Lord, are there few that be saved? And he said unto them, Strive to enter in at the strait gate [*through which the remnant enters*]: for many, I say unto you, will seek to enter in, and shall not be able [*the majority of unbelieving Israel falls away*]. When once the master of the house is risen up, and hath shut to the door, and ye begin to stand without, and to knock at the door, saying, Lord, Lord, open unto us; and he shall answer and say unto you, I know you not whence ye are: Then shall ye begin to say, We have eaten and drunk in thy presence, and thou hast taught in our streets [*the streets of first-century Israel, remember*]. But he shall say, I tell you, I know you not whence ye are; depart from me, all ye workers of iniquity. There shall be weeping and gnashing of teeth, when ye shall see Abraham, and Isaac, and Jacob, and all the prophets, in the kingdom of God, and you yourselves thrust out [*the kingdom is taken from the Jews and given to those who will bear the fruit of it* (Matt. 21:43)]. And they shall come from the east, and from the west, and from the north, and from the south, and shall sit down in the kingdom of God [*the Gentiles will flood in and sit down with the patriarchs and with the remnant*]. And, behold, there are last which shall be first, and there are first which shall be last. (Luke 13:23–30)

At the same time, even in the first century, the number of the remnant was not tiny. Remember that all of Judea had gone out to be baptized by John the Baptist (Matt.

3:5). The Jewish leaders had to be extraordinarily careful about how they interacted with Jesus because He was enormously popular with the people (Matt. 21:26). The crowd that welcomed Christ to Jerusalem (Luke 19:36–40) was genuinely enthusiastic (and from what they were saying, biblically literate)—and we have no reason whatever for assuming them to be the same crowd that was calling for His crucifixion a short time later.

If we are wondering if we can come up with an estimate for the size of that faithful remnant, I think the best answer comes from a prediction made by the prophet Zechariah. The remnant was about a third of the people. Right after the Shepherd is struck and the sheep scattered (Zech. 13:7-8), the prophet says this:

"And it shall come to pass, that in all the land, saith the LORD, two parts therein shall be cut off and die; but the third shall be left therein" (Zech. 13:8).

THE STUMBLING STONE

Why is the issue of faith and works so complicated? The answer to that question is that it is *not*—it is the sinful human heart that is complicated. Because of that, we take something straightforward—trust God in all things—and tie it up into knots. But the issues outside the heart are simple. They are binary. Either you will build your life on the cornerstone that is Jesus Christ, or that same stone will fall on you and crush you (Luke 20:17–18).

> What shall we say then? That the Gentiles, which
> followed not after righteousness, have attained to

righteousness, even the righteousness which is of faith. But Israel, which followed after the law of righteousness, hath not attained to the law of righteousness. Wherefore? Because they sought it not by faith, but as it were by the works of the law. For they stumbled at that stumblingstone; as it is written, Behold, I lay in Sion a stumblingstone and rock of offence: and whosoever believeth on him shall not be ashamed. (Rom. 9:30–33)

What do we say in response to the argument from Hosea and Isaiah? Our conclusion is that the Gentiles, who were not chasing righteousness, have nevertheless attained to that righteousness (v. 30). The righteousness they attained to is the righteousness that is "of faith" (v. 30). Israel, in the meantime, was chasing after righteousness and did not catch it (v. 31). The righteousness they did not catch was something they missed because they did not understand the "law of righteousness" (v. 31). The law of righteousness is faith. This is made plain in the next verse—why did they not attain what they were chasing? Because they did not chase by faith, but rather by works of the Torah (v. 32). They tripped over the stumbling stone, and this issue of faith and works was that stone (v. 32). The quotation is from both Isaiah 8:14 and 28:16.

In Isaiah 8, God sets the rock of stumbling (v. 14), and in verse 17 we see the right response to that stone, which is *trust*. Moreover, verse 17 is also quoted in Hebrews 2:13. And in Isaiah 28:16, we see that if someone *trusts* in the precious cornerstone, they will never be dismayed. This verse is also quoted in 1 Peter 2:6 and later in Romans

10:11. This is a stone of stumbling, and it is a stone in which we are to trust—see the flow of the argument in 1 Peter 2:6–8.

We know from the teaching of the New Testament that the stone of stumbling and the basic foundation stone are the same stone—Jesus Christ. The stone was rejected by the appointed builders, and so they in their turn were rejected. But we must pay attention not only to the fact of their rejection of Christ but also to the *nature* of their rejection of Christ.

In Isaiah 8, the stone is a stone of stumbling. In Isaiah 28, it is a cornerstone, one in which we are invited to trust. But there are some other things in Isaiah 28 as well. Isaiah rebukes the people for their sin (vv. 1–8). They react to him—who is Isaiah trying to teach? Sunday School kids who can't even read yet (vv. 8–9)? What they think is beneath them is actually way ahead of them. Verse 11 is quoted in 1 Corinthians 14:21, where Paul applies it to the gift of tongues (Deut. 28:49). So then, Isaiah says, you despise these childish ABCs? I'll give it to you that way (v. 13)—so that you will fall backward and be broken, snared, and captured. But the one who trusts in the stone will be blessed (v. 16). The gift of tongues was therefore a sign of judgment on unbelievers, particularly unbelieving *Jews* (1 Cor. 14:22). When the streets of your city are filled up with people speaking a foreign language, this is an indication that you have fallen under some kind of judgment. This is why Pentecost was a sign of the impending catastrophe of AD 70.

In religious affairs, there can be a vast difference between what you are doing and what you *think* you are doing. In our text, the Jews were "following after" the law of righteousness and, when they got there, they discovered it was actually the law of unrighteousness. The Gentiles who did not have a thought of righteousness at all found themselves tackled from behind by that righteousness. Found by God, they found they suddenly had faith in Him. Pursuing God with all their hearts, or so they thought, the Jews found that they did not have faith in God. They actually had faith in their way of having faith in God. The Torah was not intended for that use, but that is the use they put it to. So when Christ came, they could do nothing but stumble over Him. Faith in faith, faith in your way of having faith, is damnable.

Faith is a pair of eyes designed to look at Christ. If they don't see *Him*, then they are blind eyes.

What is the nature of stumbling? Take two men. One says that we are justified by faith in Jesus Christ alone, by faith alone, plus nothing or no one else. Is he right? Of course he is right. But suppose he *says* this for the wrong reason, not trusting in Jesus but rather trusting in his correct doctrinal formulation. He is lost, precisely because his formulation is correct. And flip it around. Another man can have a true heartfelt trust in Christ but have been taught a real mishmash of doctrinal incoherencies. Can he be saved? Yes, but only because what he was taught is *wrong*. Was the Torah false doctrine? No, as we will see in Romans 10:6. Did God know that men would get it backwards? Yes, and He planned to use this as a way of bringing men to real faith (Rom. 10:5).

You were lost in sin, and Jesus Christ was sent to die on the cross in such a way as to deal with all that sin. *All* of it. He was buried, and then raised to life again so that you could participate in that eternal life. Look to Him. That's it—the death, burial and resurrection of Jesus Christ for screwed up people. That's the gospel. Don't look to Him while holding your mouth just so. Don't trust in Him and in your church volunteer work. Don't believe in Him coupled with your mastery of the Westminster Confession. We are saved by grace, not law. We are saved by grace, not refined law, not doctrinal law, not the *law* of righteousness. No, we are justified by the law of *righteousness*, which is faith. Look to Christ, who is the only one who saves.

CHAPTER 10

THE END OF THE LAW

We have already seen that Christ is the foundation stone and the stumbling stone, depending. For the one who believes, He is the foundation of all. For the one who does not believe in Him, He is the rock of offense.

> Brethren, my heart's desire and prayer to God for Israel is, that they might be saved. For I bear them record that they have a zeal of God, but not according to knowledge. For they being ignorant of God's righteousness, and going about to establish their own righteousness, have not submitted themselves unto the righteousness of God. For Christ is the end of the law

for righteousness to every one that believeth. (Rom. 10:1–4)

Paul has already said that he could wish himself lost if that would benefit his kinsmen (Rom. 9:3). Here he repeats his heart's desire and prayer—that they would be saved (v. 1). He can testify on their behalf that they are zealous, and that it is a zeal for God. But it is not in accordance with knowledge—it is a false-hearted zeal at bottom (v. 2). Their problem is that they were ignorant of God's righteousness (v. 3), and they were "going about" to establish their own righteousness (v. 3). As a result, they had not submitted to God's righteousness (v. 3). Paul's conclusion is that Christ was the end (*telos*/τελος) of the law "for righteousness to" everyone who believes (v. 4).

When Paul says that Christ is the "end of the law," he does not mean that Christ is the abolition or limit of the law, as in the phrase the "end of the dock," or "end of the road." He means that Christ was the whole point of the law, as in "What is the chief end of man?" The word *end* here does not mean limit or boundary, but rather it means purpose or point. The law of God was therefore teleological, and the telos, the one it was driving toward, was Jesus Christ. He is the point of the whole Bible. But He is the point of the law as more than just a person or placeholder. He is the end of the law *in His own righteous obedience to it*. More on this shortly.

Remember the conclusion of chapter nine. There is a trap for sanctimonious saints, there is a pit for the pious there. There is something in the (religious) human heart that wants to be righteous *on its own*. In our own tradition, in our own teaching and preaching, we must be careful not to leave any room for this tendency whatever.

N.T. Wright and other commentators say that the "righteousness of God" refers only to God's own faithfulness in keeping His own promises.[6] It does not refer, the argument goes, to any righteousness of God that can be imputed to others. When held up next to this passage, this view of God's righteousness is deficient for four reasons.

First, if the righteousness of God refers to His own righteousness, then the Jews were *not* ignorant of it. Second, they were "going about" to establish their own righteousness. Instead of what? Instead of the antecedent, the righteousness of God. They wanted their own righteousness instead of the righteousness of *another*. Third, the righteousness of God was not something they were willing to submit themselves to. This submission, we have just learned, is by faith—and if it is the righteousness of another, it has to be a submission by faith, by definition. And fourth, consider closely the language of verse 4. Christ is the end of the law *for righteousness to* everyone that

6. "Paul always uses this phrase to denote, not the status which God's people have from him or in his presence, but the righteousness of God himself. This is not to say that there is no such thing as a righteous status held by believers. There is. It is to deny that this is the referent of Paul's phrase *dikaiosyne theou*. Here a Pauline exegesis rooted in Paul's own understanding of Jewish scripture and tradition must challenge fuzzy thinking that, listening to yesterday's papers, I discover characterized most of the great, but basically Latin-speaking theologians." *Pauline Perspectives: Essays on Paul, 1978–2013* (Minneapolis: Fortress Press, 2013), 279.

believes. This fourth point requires some more from us because grace is everywhere you look.

If Christ is the whole point of the Torah, and if Christ is a stone of stumbling and rock of offense, then it follows that *the whole point of the Torah* is a stone of stumbling and rock of offense. In Scripture there is grace everywhere you look, and if you don't want to see it, then you have to do some really strange things to the Scriptures.

The language of verse 4 is consistent with the doctrine of imputed righteousness and is consistent with nothing else. Everyone who believes receives something. What is that? They receive *righteousness*. We know that it cannot be their own righteousness because, if it were, they would not "receive" it, but would already have it. And we also would not have just been told that those who wanted their *own* righteousness were stumbling over the rock of offense. There would be nothing wrong with wanting your own righteousness if that were the way it was supposed to go.

I looked at multiple translations, and they all render it *for righteousness to*. Paraphrase this, and amplify it. "Christ is the whole point of the Torah, His life and work being the complete fulfillment of it, in order that His righteousness might come to everyone who believes in Him instead of continuing to trust in his own righteousness."

What is the kind of thing that would make someone stumble so egregiously over news this good? God in His covenant righteousness sends a righteous Messiah in order that the people of God might be gathered up, included in His righteousness, and reckoned as complete and perfect in Him. What would make someone *kick* against this?

The answer to that question is actually found in our text. Religiosity is the thing that hides the righteousness of God from us. But it does not hide the righteousness of God considered as a goal toward which we might strive—no, it *magnifies* the righteousness of God that way. And the higher the bar, the better. At least that is what ignorant saintlets think.

God offers us a salvation that is by His grace from first to last. But because the God who offers us grace is also fully and completely righteous, there must be a completion of His holy requirements. This means that we, if we are to be saved at all, must be content with the righteousness of *another*, imputed to us. And in order to be content with this, *we need to be willing to have all our good deeds despised by God*. We must be willing for God to put them away with loathing, holding them between His thumb and forefinger. We must be willing for God to laugh at all our pious striving. Beads of sweat have broken out on the forehead as we wrestle with lust, with covetousness, with pride, with anxiety, with sin...we fight against everything *except* our culpable ignorance of what God is like. Poor, ignorant *sap*. Christ is here. Believe in *Him*.

THE GOSPEL STONE

If Christ is the stone, then the message of Christ is the message stone. People confess with their mouth and are saved, and people stumble over the words of grace and are lost forever. Preaching the stone is therefore a preaching of a gospel stone, and not a gospel cushion or pillow. The stone, when it is good news, is a stone. The stone, when it offends, is also a stone.

> For Moses describeth the righteousness which is of the law, that the man which doeth those things shall live by them. But the righteousness which is of faith speaketh on this wise, Say not in thine heart, Who shall ascend into heaven? (that is, to bring Christ down from above:) Or, Who shall descend into the deep? (that is, to bring up Christ again from the dead.) But what saith it? The word is nigh thee, even in thy mouth, and in thy heart: that is, the word of faith, which we preach; that if thou shalt confess with thy mouth the Lord Jesus, and shalt believe in thine heart that God hath raised him from the dead, thou shalt be saved. For with the heart man believeth unto righteousness; and with the mouth confession is made unto salvation. For the scripture saith, Whosoever believeth on him shall not be ashamed. For there is no difference between the Jew and the Greek: for the same Lord over all is rich unto all that call upon him. For whosoever shall call upon the name of the Lord shall be saved. (Rom. 10:5–13)

Remember that we have *two* different responses to the *one* stone. For the one with faith, it is a cornerstone. For the unbeliever, it is a stone of stumbling and offense. The gospel stone works the same way. Moses describes one kind of man, the man who wants to go about to establish his own righteousness. He says that the man who *does* these things shall live by them (v. 5). This is a quotation from Leviticus

18:5. Interestingly, this is part of the preamble to a list of sexual prohibitions. But Moses also is the voice of the other kind of righteousness, the righteousness that is "of faith." *It* says (v. 6), quoting Deuteronomy 30:12, that men should not pretend that Christ is way up in Heaven, needing to be fetched and brought down. Don't pretend there was no Incarnation. And it also says that men should not pretend that Christ is beneath the sea (v. 7; Deut. 30:13), as though there had been no resurrection. No, Moses told the Israelites that the word was near them, in their hearts and in their mouths (v. 8; Deut. 30:14). So what was in their mouths and hearts? The Torah—that is, the word of faith that Paul says he was preaching (v. 8). Christ is the end of the law, remember (v. 4)?

The summary is this: if you confess with your mouth that Jesus is Lord (v. 9) and believe in your heart that God raised Him from the dead (v. 9), you will be saved. For men believe unto righteousness, and they confess unto salvation (v. 10). This is true because everyone who believes on the *stone* (Isa. 28:16) will never be put to shame. This is the cornerstone; who may build upon it? There is no difference between Jew or Gentile here (v. 12). The Lord is *rich* to all who call upon Him (v. 12). How do we know? Joel promises that whosoever shall call upon the name of the Lord shall be saved (v. 13; Joel 2:32). Who have we just confessed as Lord? Jesus. Who is Joel talking about? Yahweh. Jesus is Yahweh; Jesus is Jehovah.

In Leviticus 18, Moses tells the people first that they are not to do what is customary in Egypt, where they came from, or in Canaan, where they are going (18:3). They must obey the laws of God (v. 4), and the man who *obeys* them will live by them (v. 5). What follows is a prohibition of multiple forms of incest (vv. 6–18), sex during a woman's period (v. 19), adultery (v. 20), child sacrifice (v. 21), homosexuality (v. 22), or bestiality (v. 23).

Now if we have learned the gospel rightly, the man who sees *Christ* in this part of the Torah is living by faith. The man who sees *rules* is not. Flipped around, the man with faith sees Christ. The man in unbelief sees rules. The man of faith sees a sexual stone to build on. The man of unbelief is crushed by the sexual stone, crushed by his lust. How so?

At first glance, this list of rules looks pretty easy. A fairly low bar, right? Avoid sex with your sister, your aunt, and barnyard animals. Going to Heaven is a cakewalk, right? Not so fast.

First, note that these things were customary in Egypt and in Canaan. The underlying command here is not to "not have sex with," but "not to *imitate*." Judging from how easily modern Christians imitate the unbelieving culture around us, we ought not to pat ourselves on the back too readily.

Second, if you are not looking to Christ, then you have no choice but to reflect the image of that which is *not Christ*. And *not Christ* eventually looks like this list of perversions, whether or not it is studying the Torah, a scriptural devotional, or looking at hard-R raunch.

Third, this is because the law (pursued as *not Christ*) is law that provokes and stirs up sin (Rom. 3:20; 5:20), and the sexual element is never far away from that (Rom. 7:7). One of the things we are not to covet is our neighbor's wife, also mentioned here in this list (Lev. 18:20). This means that traditional values without Christ are nothing less than a perversion generator. And open immorality is no better. There is no salvation anywhere apart from Jesus.

But speaking of Jesus...so Jesus Christ is everywhere. He is in Heaven, and He came down from Heaven. He is beneath the sea, and He rose up from Sheol, just as Jonah did. He is pervasive throughout the Torah for those who have the eyes of faith to see. He is in the gospel declared and preached for those who respond in faith. For those without faith, He is God AWOL, and all that is left are the dry bones and dusty rags of moralism.

Now the confession of verse 9 is glorious—if you confess with your mouth that Jesus is Lord, and believe in your heart that God raised Jesus from the dead, raising Him out of the graveyard of your heart, then you shall be saved. If the Spirit has been teaching us, we should see that fulfilling what this verse is talking about is *not* like touching second base as you run by it. Christ is found in every word of verse 9—do you believe? Christ is found in every sexual prohibition of Leviticus 18—do you believe? And *Jesus is Lord* is just another phrase that Jesus himself can be missing from, if it is found in the mouth of a man with no faith.

Who will touch the eyes of the blind men? Who will speak to the ears of the deaf? Who will tell the lame to leap for joy? How will this be done? How will it happen? When Paul tells us that Moses is speaking about the word of faith that he, Paul, is preaching, he is not wrenching words out of context. "And the LORD thy God will circumcise thine heart, and the heart of thy seed, to love the LORD thy God with all thine heart, and with all thy soul, that thou mayest live" (Deut. 30:6). In short, *you must be born again.*

So when it comes to these issues, issues of life and death, there is a right way to cite Scripture and a wrong way of doing it. The right way is to able to taste that "the word is near you, in your mouth and in your heart" (10:8, NKJV). The righteousness that strives to earn all its own laurels in accordance with the law says, "the one who *does...*"

With this regenerate heart, which alone is capable of believing, what do you see brought down from Heaven? What do you see brought up from the depths of Jonah's sea? You see the good of the land. "See, I have set before thee this day life and good, and death and evil; In that I command thee this day to love the LORD thy God, to walk in his ways, and to keep his commandments and his statutes and his judgments, that thou mayest live and multiply: and the LORD thy God shall bless thee in the land whither thou goest to possess it" (Deut. 30:15–16).

This is the gospel stone. Build upon it, and live.

AND HEARING BY THE WORD OF GOD

In this portion of Romans, we start to see the intersection of two realities—decretal realities and covenantal realities. This will come to full flower in the next chapter, but we begin to see it here. God is *utterly sovereign*, and, rightly understood, this means that when He chooses to use created *instruments* to accomplish His purposes, we do not have the right to give Him any backchat about it.

God is utterly sovereign, but He is exercising that sovereignty in His intention to save the world. It is a saving sovereignty, not a damning one.

> How then shall they call on him in whom they have not believed? And how shall they believe in him of whom they have not heard? And how shall they hear without a preacher? And how shall they preach, except they be sent? as it is written, How beautiful are the feet of them that preach the gospel of peace, and bring glad tidings of good things! But they have not all obeyed the gospel. For Esaias saith, Lord, who hath believed our report? So then faith cometh by hearing, and hearing by the word of God. But I say, have they not heard? Yes verily, Their sound went into all the earth, and their words unto the ends of the world. But I say, did not Israel know? First Moses saith, I will provoke you to jealousy by them that are no people, and by a foolish nation I will anger you. But Esaias is very bold, and saith, I was found of them that sought me not; I was made manifest unto them that asked not after me. But to Israel he saith, All day long I have stretched forth my hands unto a disobedient and gainsaying people. (Rom. 10:14–21)

In chapter eight, we considered the golden chain of redemption at the divine level—predestined, called, justified, and glorified. Here we have another glorious and redemptive chain—sending, preaching, hearing, believing, and calling (vv. 14–15). The beautiful feet of the gospel messenger is an image that is taken from Isaiah 52:7. But the beautiful message is not always beautifully received— just a few verses later, Isaiah laments the lack of faith (v. 16; Isa. 53:1). Nevertheless, faith still comes by hearing, and hearing by the (sent and preached) Word of God (v. 17). But there are two kinds of hearing—the one that leads to believing and calling on the Lord, and the other that leads to hardening. Did not the *unbelieving* Israelites hear? Yes, after a fashion (v. 18; Ps. 19:4). Paul asks the question again—surely Israel did hear in *some* way (v. 19). Yes, of course (v. 19; Deut. 32:21). In contrast, Isaiah boldly prophesies that God would be found by Gentiles who weren't looking for Him (v. 20; Isa. 65:1). And at the same time, God was rejected by Israel (v. 21; Isa. 65:2), the Israel that was pretending to be pursuing Him.

We now have a line of quotations. In this brief passage, Paul quotes six passages from the Old Testament—four from Isaiah, one from Psalms, and one from Deuteronomy. The first shows a division in Israel (Isa. 52:7). In the chapter immediately before the glorious prophetic statement of Christ's substitutionary death, we see Israel divided between those who blaspheme (Isa. 52:5) and those who burst into songs of joy (Isa. 52:9). On the threshold of the greatest statement of the gospel in the Old Testament, Isaiah laments the fact that no one believes him (Isa. 53:1). This is quoted more fully in John 12:38 and is based on God striking Israel with a judicial blindness (John 12:39–41; Isa. 6:10). Isaiah sees the glory of God *in Christ*, and he is told to tell Israel that they do not and cannot see (John 12:39, 41). So did the Jews not see at *all?* No, they saw, but did so in the way all men see the general revelation of God—suppressing the truth about what they see even as they see (Rom. 1:20). The glory of God is revealed through the whole creation (Ps. 19:4), and this is explicitly compared to the Torah in that psalm (Ps. 19:7ff). Paul then appeals to the Song of Moses, in which Moses makes the Israelites include a song in their liturgy that prophesies that they will be provoked to envy by Gentiles (Deut. 32:21). In order to be provoked by Gentiles finding God, the Israelites would have to *see* those Gentiles finding God. Moses also made them sing an invitation to the Gentiles (Deut. 32:43), an invitation cited by Paul just a little bit later (Rom. 15:10). So did they see? Of course they did, but only enough to condemn themselves. Isaiah prophesies that the Gentiles will come (Isa. 65:1) and that the Jews would refuse to come, despite God's grace to them (Isa. 65:2).

There is no way successfully to avoid seeing Christ, but there are two ways to see Him. Envy has more twists and turns than simple faith does, and this is often because envy has a sharper eye, and sees *more*, even though it does not want to. The attitude we should have in looking to God and His Word for *our* direction (Ps. 123:2) is the kind of sharp eye for detail that drives the envious. The envious who hate Christ are often far more aware than we are of the import of Christ. But note: the energy that sinful envy provides is something that God is most willing to use (v. 19). God is made jealous by idolatry among His covenant people (Deut. 32:21), so He pours out His blessing where no one expected it. Everything is thrown into turmoil, all the religious fussers fuss, and the kingdom of God advances in glory.

The point in verse 14 is often missed because of a translation issue. When it says, "and how shall they believe in him *of whom* they have not heard," it creates the impression that faith is created when people hear preachers talking *about* Jesus. But while this is true as far as it goes, much more is involved than this. A better translation here would be "and how shall they believe in him *whom* they have not heard," with no *of*.

Men, women, and children do not come to faith because they hear *about* Christ, but rather because they hear and see Christ Himself. How does this happen? It happens in full accordance with the folly of God—preaching (1 Cor. 1:18–21). God's plan for the transformation of the world is this: sending, preaching, hearing, believing, calling. When we ordain evangelists, missionaries, and church planters, what are we doing? We are sending *Christ*. Those sent preach Christ. The people hear Christ and believe in Christ. What do they then do? They call upon Christ, and they are saved.

This is not a mantra or a magical incantation. It is the gospel. Jesus Christ was born of a woman, born under the law. He lived a perfect and sinless life and was broken on the cross for our sins. He was laid in a tomb in full accordance with the Scriptures, and He rose from the dead on the third day. He then ascended in glory to the right hand of God the Father, and what can all the assembled unbelievers *and* their parliaments, armies, and laws do about it?

Absolutely nothing, that's what. As the prophet Isaiah also says, speaking of the glory of the gospel's work in *this* world (Isa. 64:4; 1 Cor. 2:9). "For since the beginning of the world men have not heard, nor perceived by the ear, neither hath the eye seen, O God, beside thee, what he hath prepared for him that waiteth for him" (Isa. 64:4).

CHAPTER 11

SEVEN THOUSAND BY GRACE

In times of spiritual declension—which *we* are certainly in—it is very easy to fall into the trap that Elijah fell into. Flatterers and false teachers always tell us that things are far better than we think, but when we work our way past their lies, we often have to be reassured by God Himself that things are not nearly as bad as we think. This is not blind optimism; this is *faith*.

> I say then, hath God cast away his people? God forbid. For I also am an Israelite, of the seed of Abraham, of the tribe of Benjamin. God hath not cast away his people which he foreknew. Wot ye not what the scripture

saith of Elias? How he maketh intercession to God against Israel, saying, Lord, they have killed thy prophets, and digged down thine altars; and I am left alone, and they seek my life. But what saith the answer of God unto him? I have reserved to myself seven thousand men, who have not bowed the knee to the image of Baal. Even so then at this present time also there is a remnant according to the election of grace. And if by grace, then is it no more of works: otherwise grace is no more grace. But if it be of works, then is it no more grace: otherwise work is no more work. (Rom. 11:1–6)

If there are two ways of hearing, what conclusion may we draw? If there are two ways of being Israel, what conclusion may we not draw? We may *not* conclude that God has cast away His people (v. 1). Paul speaks as a member of the true remnant—he is a son of Abraham, an Israelite, of the tribe of Benjamin. Those whom God foreknew have not been cast off (v. 2); this means that the promises were fulfilled in and through that remnant. Elijah prayed against Israel (v. 2), but he was praying against one Israel when God had preserved another. Elijah's complaint was that they had killed God's prophets, they had thrown down His altars, and they were trying to kill Elijah, the one faithful man remaining (v. 3). How did God answer His prophet? Paul then quotes 1 Kings 19:18. God said that He had reserved to Himself seven thousand men that had not bent the knee to Baal (v. 4). Paul was arguing that the first century had a remnant according to the election of grace in the same way (v. 5). And if by grace, then the seven thousand were *not* preserved by their works (v. 6). He plainly says that self-righteous works and grace cannot abide together; one drives out the other (v. 6).

There is a profound question created by these two Israels, these two ways of hearing God. What are we to say when judgment falls on one way of being Israel because of that one Israel's apostasy? Has God cast away His people? *God forbid.* God reserved the faithful to Himself. God's Word will never return to Him void (Isa. 55:11). Note that God is the subject of the sentences. *God* has not cast off. *God* has reserved to Himself seven thousand faithful men. Paul anchors the point beyond all dispute. The remnant of Israel that remained was a "remnant according to the election of grace." There were seven thousand according to the sovereign and free determination of *God*. Reformations that are not grounded on the free and unalterable gift of God are not reformations at all. That is the foundational point that Paul is making here.

Note that Paul argues that the difference between grace and works is not one that admits of compromise. You cannot split the difference between these two. Introduce *any* element of works into the equation, and it drives out grace. True grace, faithfully preached, will drive all works of the law before it. And it is important to remember that we are not talking about grace on paper, but rather grace in action.

Elijah and Elisha were the leaders in a renewal movement in the midst of a wicked and apostate Israel. They did not constitute what we might call a "free church" movement, but neither were they lapdogs for the kings and

corrupt priesthood. The schools of the prophets were simultaneously part of and separate from the wicked nation
they prophesied to. They consequently provide encouragement for us in a type.

We live in comparable times. We do not live in a time
that would be typified by the conquests of Joshua, or the
rise of David, or the established glories of Solomon. We
live in a time when idolatry and syncretism are largely accepted, even within the evangelical Church. We live in a
time when other gods are exalted in the public square in
the name of diversity. We live in a time when wicked men
appear to be able to do as they please, egged on by the
Jezebels behind them. We live in a time when children (by
the million) are being caused to pass through the fire. And
we live in a time when, if we held a conference to protest
these monstrosities, we could get at least seven thousand
to come. Not very much, but our God can work by many or
by few (1 Sam. 14:6). Here then are three basic principles
for us to apply to our day:

First, if any "saving America" is to be done, then the true
God will do it through Jesus. He will not share His glory
with another, and we are not permitted to offer to share it
for the sake of building coalitions. *God* reserves the seven
thousand, and we must reserve the right of God to be God.

Second, worship is the key. Worship is the litmus test.
How does God identify the good guys? He speaks to Elijah
about what they did and did not do in *worship*. He didn't
say whether they were registered to vote, and He didn't
say whether they paid any of Ahab's taxes. The watershed
issue is always worship, and the downstream issues, while

important, are not the place to begin. They are not where we place our trust—even though we must get there as well. The thing God mentions to Elijah is where the seven thousand have not bowed, and what they have not kissed.

And third, the relationship between faithful communities and apostate larger communities is a complicated one. There is a delicate balance here that only the Spirit of God can enable us to achieve. The faithful communities are distinct but not detached. In our day, we have to struggle with the misunderstandings of Christians who fail to get this principle right. They are either "distinct and detached," which is an escapist religion, or they are "not distinct and not detached," which is muddle and compromise.

AND THE REST WERE BLINDED

We have learned that there are two Israels, formed as a result of two different ways of hearing the Word of God. One hears the Word in a way that quickens true faith, and the other hears (after a fashion) in a way that hardens the heart in a persistent but wrongheaded pursuit of God—because it is a pursuit of God on *our* terms instead of on His.

> What then? Israel hath not obtained that which he seeketh for; but the election hath obtained it, and the rest were blinded (According as it is written, God hath given them the spirit of slumber, eyes that they should not see, and ears that they should not hear;) unto this day. And David saith, Let their table be made a snare, and a trap, and a stumblingblock, and a recompence unto them: Let their eyes be darkened,

that they may not see, and bow down their back al-
way. I say then, Have they stumbled that they should
fall? God forbid: but rather through their fall salvation is come unto the Gentiles, for to provoke them to
jealousy. (Rom. 11:7–11)

What then is the result of God's exercise of His sovereign
grace? Israel has not obtained it (v. 7), but the election has
obtained it (v. 7). This means that the election here were
those Israelites who heard to the salvation of their souls.
Those who did not hear were Israel in the other sense, Israel according to the flesh. So the election (which included
Paul) obtained it, while the rest were blinded (v. 7). This
fulfilled the Word from two places—Deuteronomy 29:4
and Isaiah 29:10, quoted here in verse 8. David also points
to the same reality in Psalm 69:22–23, which is quoted here
in verses 9–10. This being the case, Paul asks if they have
stumbled past the point of no return (v. 11). Is the apostasy
final? His answer to this is his standard *may it never be*,
rendered in this place as *God forbid*. His answer sets up the
discussion to follow, where we learn how Israel according
to the flesh will eventually be brought back to be grafted
back in. In the meantime, they have stumbled for a time,
and that stumbling resulted in salvation coming to the Gentiles, which in its turn will provoke the Jews to jealousy and
cause them to return again to the true Israel (v. 11).

Israel was "going about" to establish her own righteousness, and they were ignorant of the righteousness of God.
This means that they were seeking something—righteousness—which they were not *really* seeking. To use the words

the Lord used, they already had their reward. They got what they were seeking, but they didn't get what they were seeking. This is because they heard without really hearing. They were sons of Sarah who were really sons of Hagar, sons of Abraham who were really sons of the devil. They were Jews who were not Jews. This is the dividing line that separates the believer from the unbeliever *in every age*.

So the election obtained it, and as Paul has just emphasized, they obtained it by grace. They were the remnant *chosen by grace*. This means that God was the one doing the choosing, and that they were not the ones doing the choosing. When men choose God, it is not really God they choose. When men choose righteousness, it is not really righteousness they choose. When men do the pursuing, they soon veer off in another direction entirely. Paul, and not another of his classmates in Gamaliel's school, was chosen by God entirely and solely because God determined to do it this way, and He made this determination according to "His good counsel and will" (Eph. 1:11).

Those who were not chosen were left to their own devices. Those who were not sought out by God were left to their own pseudo-seeking of God. The Bible calls this a *blinding*. When God lets men go, God is giving them something—He is allowing them to eat their own cooking. Remember that in chapter one, the wrath of God is described as God "giving them up." Here God is striking them with a judicial blindness, a spirit of stupor. And in that stupor, what do they see? They see exactly what they insisted upon seeing. God gives them over to their own vision of things. *They see what they want.*

In Deuteronomy 29:4, the Israelites had not been given a mind to understand, or eyes to see, or ears to hear, despite the fact that great miracles had been done for them (v. 3). Isaiah 29 is a chapter that is filled with this truth—God gave a stupor to their prophets and seers. And in Psalm 69, we see that the whole thing relates to Jesus. In Psalm 69:4, those who hate Christ hate Him without reason (v. 4; John 15:25). In verse 8, rejection by His brothers was prophesied (John 7:5). In verse 9, we see the zeal of the Lord for the temple (John 2:17), and Paul applies the latter half of this verse to Christ as well (Rom. 15:3). A prediction is made of the gall Christ was offered on the cross in verse 21 (Matt. 27:34). The context swirls around the treatment that the Jews gave to their Messiah, and in *that* context, David says, "Let their table become a snare before them" (Ps. 69:22). And verse 25 is applied by Peter to the fall of Judas (Acts 1:20).

So we should see that the counsel of God's will in this had been settled seven hundred years prior (Isaiah), a thousand years prior (Psalms), and fourteen hundred years prior (Deuteronomy). God's gifts and His refusal to give those gifts stand outside the give and take of history. History cascades from His decrees, not the other way around.

So how much of Israel was really Israel was in the palm of God's hand—so that grace might be really grace. And in every age of the Church, it has been the same. How much of the Church is really the Church is in the hand of God. So we must turn to Him.

SMOKE IN THE EYES

There are two dangers when it comes to the interpretation of biblical prophecy. The first, fairly common among evangelicals, is to picture the fulfillment in lurid and garish colors, filled out with a crass literalism, but fully retaining the right to be called *fantastical*. Such fulfillments, were they to happen, would be amazing. But the second error is to learn about the first error and then to retreat into an acceptance of the kind of biblical fulfillments that could conceivably escape the notice of virtually every historian. These things were "spiritually" fulfilled, you see, and you can't expect them to alter the flow of history in any visible way. But this is not how the Bible teaches us to think. We are not to give way to a wooden literalism when it comes to prophecy, but neither are we to dilute it all into a homeopathic nothingness. Eye has not seen, nor ear heard, what God has prepared for those who love Him (1 Cor. 2:9). Eye has not seen it now, but all eyes will see it then.

> Now if the fall of them be the riches of the world, and the diminishing of them the riches of the Gentiles; how much more their fulness? For I speak to you Gentiles, inasmuch as I am the apostle of the Gentiles, I magnify mine office: If by any means I may provoke to emulation them which are my flesh, and might save some of them. For if the casting away of them be the reconciling of the world, what shall the receiving of them be, but life from the dead? For if the firstfruit be holy, the lump is also holy: and if the root be holy, so are the branches. (Rom. 11:12–16)

Paul's argument here is that if the apostasy of most of the Jews was such a blessing to the Gentiles, how much greater a blessing (to the Gentiles) will the fullness of the Jews be (v. 12)? Paul is speaking to the Gentiles there at the church in Rome, and he makes a big deal out of the fact that he had been designated to be an apostle to the Gentiles (v. 13; Gal. 2:8; 1 Tim. 2:7; 2 Tim. 1:11). The reason he does this is that he wants to provoke his brothers the Jews, and he wants that to be provocation unto salvation (v. 14). And as it bends back around again, this provocation of the Jews will be a blessing for the whole world (to whom Paul was sent), resulting in "life from the dead" (v. 15). Paul then argues that if the firstfruits were holy, then the lump would also be holy. If the root were holy, then the branches would be also (v. 16).

This is how God works. This is how He plots His stories. When something negative happens, like the apostasy of the majority of first-century Judaism, this is because God is working on a great blessing for the world. And we need to note that this apostasy was not just an unfortunate series of events, or a big-time sad time. It was a disaster for the Jewish people, a cataclysm in which over a million people lost their lives. Jesus spoke of it as the very worst moment in the history of the world (Matt. 24:21). This was to be understood, in the words of Paul here, as the "reconciling of the world" (v. 15). Just as the death of Jesus, another and much greater disaster, was our salvation, so the destruction of the Jewish nation was designed to open the door for everyone else.

We *think* we get this, and we would reason that if that is true, then when blessing returns to the Jewish people, then that will mean that we have to seesaw back to a time when the Gentiles are excluded and cursed. Not at all, Paul says. If the Jewish fall was a great blessing for us, how much more will their restoration be an even greater blessing for us?

Just as the apostasy did not include the remnant (the one that Isaiah had prophesied, and that Paul had discussed a little earlier in Romans), so also it does not include the many Jews who have come to faith in Christ over the centuries. In the first few centuries of the Church, there appears to have been a large migration of Jews into the faith. But all of that notwithstanding, the Jewish people considered *as such* have not believed in the Messiah that all their sacred books talk about. Those Jews who have come to Christ have tended to lose, over the course of a few generations, their identity as Jews. For just one example, our family is a Gentile family, even though my wife's great-great-grandfather was a Jewish rabbi. Those Jews who have kept their cultural identity have been those who have kept their distance from Jesus Christ.

Paul is here talking about a Jewish return to Christ that would be as public and as visible as their rejection of Him was. This was not something that a number of individual Jews could just drift into. This prophecy will not be completed until we can say that Judaism is Christian. And when that happens, there will be no middle wall of partition between Jew and Gentile (Eph. 2:14).

The word Paul uses for "provoke to jealousy" in verse 11 is the same word he uses here in verse 14. He wanted to make much of the fact that Gentiles were coming into salvation, that they were coming into the inheritance of Abraham, so that Jews would be stirred up by this and respond by coming to Christ. This is *all in Deuteronomy*, and it demonstrates that we are talking about something that goes far beyond what we evangelicals consider to be a "good testimony" about how Jesus saved us. We are talking about cultures, and we are talking about cultural jealousy. This tactic of God's was predicted in the latter part of Deuteronomy, and it is the same way that God worked when He was blessing the Jewish nation during the times of the older covenant. This is how God works.

"Keep therefore and do them; for this is your wisdom and your understanding in the sight of the nations, which shall hear all these statutes, and say, Surely this great nation is a wise and understanding people. For what nation is there so great, who hath God so nigh unto them, as the Lord our God is in all things that we call upon him for?" (Deut. 4:6–7).

One of the great tragedies in the history of the Church thus far is that we have not understood the evangelistic potency of cultural identity and cohesion, rightly held and rightly understood. Instead of provoking the Jews to jealousy, which is God's game plan, we have been envious and jealous of *them*, falling into the anti-gospel of anti-Semitism. And then, when we are feeling bad about that (as we ought to) we as a result abandon all attempts at building biblical culture and cohesion, believing that this sort of thing results in things like the Holocaust. In all this, we are refusing to do what our Master told us to do. We are being like that servant in Proverbs, the one who is smoke in the eyes of the one who sent him (Prov. 10:26).

WARNING TO ROME

When we fall into the trap of thinking of the Bible as a book to aid us in our personal devotions, we often miss the larger context. We need to remember that this is a letter to a particular church in a particular city, and Paul gave the warning because he saw certain kinds of arrogance developing.

> And if some of the branches be broken off, and thou, being a wild olive tree, wert graffed in among them, and with them partakest of the root and fatness of the olive tree; boast not against the branches. But if thou boast, thou bearest not the root, but the root thee. Thou wilt say then, The branches were broken off, that I might be graffed in. Well; because of unbelief they were broken off, and thou standest by faith. Be not highminded, but fear: for if God spared not the natural branches, take heed lest he also spare not thee. Behold therefore the goodness and severity of God: on them which fell, severity; but toward thee, goodness, if thou continue in his goodness: otherwise thou also shalt be cut off. (Rom. 11:17–22)

Those Jews who had not believed in their Messiah had been broken off from the olive tree—which is the tree of covenant continuity (v. 17). But Gentiles, wild olive branches, were then grafted in (v. 17). These newcomers were then exhorted by Paul not to boast about it—they don't support the root (v. 18). They might suppose there is an answer to this—weren't they cut out to make room for us (v. 19)? Paul says that very well may be, but the Jews were broken off because of unbelief, and you stand by faith. Paul says that high-mindedness is out, and fear should be there instead (v. 20). If God did not spare natural branches, why on earth would He spare grafted in, wild olive branches (v. 21)? There are two attributes of God that must be kept in mind—severity for apostates and goodness for those who stand by faith (v. 22).

The image of Israel as an olive tree is a common one in the Old Testament (e.g., Hos. 14:5–7). The root is obviously the grace of God found in Christ (John 15:1–7), but the ancient manifestation of this root grace was found in Abraham (Gal. 3:29). The Jews had been cultivated for so long that they were considered the natural branches on this tree, and the Gentiles were considered to be the wild branches. Normally, the grafting practice was to graft a cultivated branch onto a wild root, but Paul reverses this. Here the blessing comes on the Gentile branches who were privileged to be joined to the ancient covenant promises.

Notice in this image that we find a biblical illustration that ties everything together in one unified covenant throughout the Scriptures. The apostle does not call the Jews an olive tree, and then say that with the Gentiles we have a newly planted peach tree. No, it is all one tree, with one glorious story. This illustration, by itself, overthrows many common ways of understanding the relationship of the Church to Israel. But in this analogy, the Church *is* the renewed Israel.

So this is not a letter written to generic Gentiles. These words are given to the saints in Rome. *"To all that be in Rome,* beloved of God, called *to be* saints" (Rom. 1:7, emphasis added). Why would he caution them against hubris? He did it because he saw the first stirrings of it. Remember that Paul characteristically argues, "One of you will say then...," and he does this because he knows how his Q and A sessions usually go. And what happens here? "God cut out the Jews to make way for us Romans" (v. 19).

Remember that this was the capital city of the most powerful empire in the world. Anyone who thinks that Christians don't get caught up by this kind of reflected glory needs to ask more pointed questions of their sinful hearts. The Lord spurned the devil's offer of all the kingdoms of men in their glory; His followers have not always been so successful.

Here is the problem. Classical Protestants, following Paul's teaching in Romans 8 have long held that nothing can separate the elect from the love of God which is in Christ Jesus (Rom. 8:38-39). We hold to the final and complete perseverance of the elect because God will not fail to complete what He has begun (Phil. 1:6). In contrast, the church at Rome has ignored and set aside the letter than Paul wrote to *them,* not only on the question of faith alone, but also on the question of whether their Church can fall away. The Roman church teaches that the salvation of no one individual is secure in this life—three popes in a row, and ten cardinals in succession, if they commit mortal sin, could all die and be condemned eternally. But they also teach that their *church* is incapable of falling away, that it is "unfailingly holy," to use the words of their catechism. Paul reverses this, and so must we. Any given church can fall away (Rev. 2:5), and the elect individuals of God cannot fall away (John 10:29). The olive tree is the visible covenant.

We must face up to our constant temptation to draw contrasts between our position as Christians and the Jews' position in the Old Testament. The New Testament consistently draws *parallels*, and we (for the sake of our traditions) want to draw *contrasts*.

But the way Israel fell into sin is set before us regularly (1 Cor. 10:1–11; Heb. 3:7ff; 4:11; Rom. 11:17ff), and we are consistently warned against doing *the very same thing*. This means that the fact that Rome received this letter two thousand years ago does not make the warning less relevant, but rather far *more* relevant. How long before Paul wrote these words had the Jews been called through Abraham? Two thousand years—that is what created the temptation for them. And we should take care as well. After all, the Westminster Confession will eventually be two thousand years old also.

DELIVERANCE FROM ZION

We now come to the place where Paul makes his dramatic statement about the future blessedness that awaits Israel. He has shown us that Israel according to the promises must receive the blessings (by definition), but here he is saying that Israel according to the flesh will be included in them as well. How so?

And they also, if they abide not still in unbelief, shall be graffed in: for God is able to graff them in again. For if thou wert cut out of the olive tree which is wild by nature, and wert graffed contrary to nature into a good olive tree: how much more shall these, which be the natural branches, be graffed into their own olive tree? For I would not, brethren, that ye should be ignorant of this mystery, lest ye should be wise in your own conceits; that blindness in part is happened to Israel, until the fulness of the Gentiles be come in. And so all Israel shall be saved: as it is written, There shall come out of Sion the Deliverer, and shall turn away ungodliness from Jacob: For this is my covenant unto them, when I shall take away their sins. As concerning the gospel, they are enemies for your sakes: but as touching the election, they are beloved for the fathers' sakes. For the gifts and calling of God are without repentance. For as ye in times past have not believed God, yet have now obtained mercy through their unbelief: even so have these also now not believed, that through your mercy they also may obtain mercy. For God hath concluded them all in unbelief, that he might have mercy upon all. (Rom. 11:23–32)

Paul begins with a conditional, at least on the human level. If Israel repents of its unbelief, then God is certainly able to graft them back into their native tree again (v. 23). Just consider the nature of the case. If wild olive branches can be grafted in, then how much more can severed natural branches be grafted in (v. 24)? But Paul then moves from the logical possibilities to the prophetic necessities. He does not want the Romans to be ignorant of this mystery (*mystery* being Paul's common word for something prophesied in the Old Testament and made manifest in the New (Eph. 3:4–6; Col. 1:26–27). The partial blindness of Israel (excluding the remnant) was predicted until the fullness of the Gentiles had been reached (v. 25). And knowing this would keep the Gentiles from getting conceited about it (v. 25).

Then Paul cites a couple of the places that tell us about this (vv. 26–27—which are from Isaiah 59:20–21 and 27:9). God's covenant with Israel was that He would take away their sins (v. 27). For the time being, the Jews were enemies of the Gentile Christians because of the gospel. But as concerns election, they are still beloved for their fathers' sake (v. 28). How long will this last? It is irrevocable, which is why the Jews will in fact return to Christ (v. 29). The Gentiles used to be in unbelief, and they were brought out of it by the unbelief of the Jews (v. 30). In a reverse twist, God will eventually bring the Jews out of unbelief through the mercy that was shown to the Gentiles (v. 31). Put this all together, and we see that wrapping the Jews up in unbelief (for now) was the first move in His plan to bring mercy to the whole world—Jews included (v. 32).

Paul says that this is a prophetic mystery, now revealed, and revealed so that Gentiles would not become conceited. Salvation is from the Jews (John 4:22), and always will be. Let's look at how it works.

The prophet Isaiah laments the condition of man. Our iniquities have separated us from God (Isa. 59:2). This detestable condition is applied by the Apostle Paul to all men, to Gentiles and Jews alike (Rom. 3:15–17; Isa. 59:7–8). Everything falters. Everything fails. There is no soundness anywhere. All men are in need of a Savior.

When God saw this, when He saw that there was no man, He sent a man—He sent a Deliverer (Isa. 59:16). This great warrior will put on His panoply—the armor of Jesus (Isa. 59:17). Remind you of anything? Of course—this is the whole armor of God (Eph. 6:11–17). Put on the whole armor of God therefore, which is another way of saying that we are to put on the Lord Jesus Christ. What does Jesus do in this armor, back in Isaiah? First, He judges the wicked (Isa. 59:18). As a result, the Gentiles stream to Him. They shall "fear the name of the Lord from the west, and his glory from the rising of the sun" (Isa. 59:19). The world will gather to Him, and He will save them.

And *then* the Redeemer shall come to Zion—this is the place Paul quotes with reference to his brethren in the flesh, collating it with Isaiah 27:9. The covenant is that Israel's sins will be forgiven, and this is equated with the Spirit never departing from the mouths of all their descendants (Isa. 59:21). And this ties Isaiah 27 into the mix, as well. "Jacob shall take root" and "Israel shall blossom and bud, and fill the face of the world with fruit" (Isa. 27:6). Glory to God, and may He hasten that day.

God has, in His wisdom and providence, tied the fortunes of the world to the fortunes of the Jews. The apostasy of the Jews opened wide the door of salvation for the Gentiles, and their eventual conversion will be a blessing for them (of course) along with the remainder of the

Gentiles. This is a decision that God will never repent of—this is the mystery that He has revealed and that we are charged to live out.

Now this means that it is not possible to be in sync with the purposes of God in this world without loving the Jewish people. Christians who fall prey to anti-Semitism are trying to disrupt the grace of God for the whole world. It is counterproductive; it is anti-gospel. At the same time, loving the Jews as God does, for the sake of their fathers, is not the same thing as approving of what the Jews do, or agreeing with Zionism, or agreeing with the present position of the current administration of the Israeli government. That is not the point. The point is that animus against the Jews as Jews is *out*, and to give way to it is to rebel against God's gospel strategy. One might say, "What about the Palestinian Christians that Israel has killed?" Look, this teaching comes from Paul, who was willing to be damned for the sake of the Jews (Rom. 9:3), and he maintained this attitude while outlining their hypocrisies throughout this book and while in full knowledge of the fact that they had spent a great deal of energy trying to kill *him*.

Mercy to the Gentiles has been God's game plan for bringing mercy to the Jews, and mercy to the Jews is what He is going to use to bring about "life from the dead" for all (Rom. 11:15). So what we are called to do is preach God's mercy in Christ to all the nations—with a view toward cultural transformation, remember—and to live it out in such a way that the Jews want to get themselves some of that. Personal conversion, certainly. Planting of churches, even more. But what we are doing is building Christendom, and we are doing so in a way that leaves the doors wide open for the Jews. One of the great failures of the first Christendom was at just this point, and it is something we must address. We are called to provoke emulation (11:14); we are not called to *be* envious.

THEOLOGY AND DOXOLOGY

Paul's response to the very dense theology he has been working through is to break out into a song. His theology bursts forth into doxology. These are not two unrelated things—rightly done, rightly understood, theology leads inexorably to this kind of praise. Let's consider why.

> O the depth of the riches both of the wisdom and knowledge of God! How unsearchable are his judgments, and his ways past finding out! For who hath known the mind of the Lord? Or who hath been his counsellor? Or who hath first given to him, and it shall be recompensed unto him again? For of him, and through him, and to him, are all things: to whom be glory for ever. Amen. (Rom. 11:33–36)

The wisdom and knowledge of God have deeps that cannot be comprehended (v. 33). His judgments and His ways are beyond finding out (v. 33). Who could begin to undertake such a search (v. 34)? Who has known the mind of the Lord (v. 34)? Who could dare to volunteer to walk into the throne room of God to give Him a bit of helpful advice (v. 34)? Who is able to give to God in such a way as that God would need to repay him? Who can place God in his debt (v. 35)? These are all rhetorical questions, the assumed answer to each of which is *no one*. And the reason the answer is *no one* is that all things are of Him, and through Him, and to Him (v. 36). He is the one responsible for all that is, and He is the one who receives glory for all that is, or ever could be (v. 36). And *amen*.

Take a glance at the number of stars revealed in a photograph from the Hubble telescope. The God we worship knows every one of those stars by name (Ps. 147:4). The hairs on every head are all numbered (Matt. 10:30)—about seven billion people are alive today, and the average number of hairs on a head range between 90,000 for redheads and 140,000 for blondes. God numbers them all. Not a sparrow falls to the ground apart from the will of the Father (Matt. 10:29). God simply spoke, and the vast expanse of heavens and earth came into being (Gen. 1:1; John 1:3). The human body contains somewhere between fifty and seventy-five trillion cells, each one an exquisitely made library, each one with the capacity to manufacture what the information in its library tells it to. Every last bird that hops from branch to branch in the deepest wilderness is known to God (Ps. 50:11). Every raindrop is prepared by God (Ps. 147:8) and does not hit your forehead accidentally. He gives food to ravens (Ps. 147:9) and uses ravens to give food to prophets (1 Kings 17:4). Galaxies, oceans, mountains, nations, planets, giant stars, and all such things added together are just dust on His scales (Isa. 40:15). "Thy righteousness is like the great mountains; thy judgments are a great deep: O Lord, thou preservest man and beast" (Ps. 36:6). His understanding is infinite (Ps. 147:5). It must be—for of Him and through, and to Him, are all things (Rom. 11:36). We must never forget the *Godness* of God.

Now this God—can He save the Jews along with the rest of the world? Of course He can (Rom. 11:23). God is clearly able to do this. But will He? If He is the one who cares for sparrows in the way He does, what should we conclude from this? We are worth more than many sparrows (Luke 12:7). The psalm that tells us a number of these glorious natural gifts is also the same psalm that tells us that He gathers the outcasts of Israel (Ps. 147:2). *The God who governs is the God who saves.* We do not divide up the world—the God of nature is the God of grace. The Creator is the Redeemer, and the Savior is the one who spoke all things into existence.

This is the doxological conclusion to a very densely reasoned passage of theology, chapter after chapter of it. But for many people, the chapters immediately prior can be summed up by "God can damn whoever He wants; deal with it." With regard to His authority and power, that is true enough (Rom. 9:18). We don't deserve His mercy. He has the strength to condemn us, and no injustice would be involved if He did that.

But this stretch of Romans deals with two fundamental issues. The first is the divine nature of His authority. God is God, and we shouldn't try to pretend otherwise. The second is that this is the power of the God who has determined to save the world. Two things must be remembered—His *power* and His *intent*. Can He destroy? Yes. Will He save? Emphatically, yes. We need to be humbled down to the ground, true enough. But this humbling is not the prelude to the world's damnation. It is the threshold of salvation for all men, for all who believe. And here is the kicker—that faithless world *will* believe.

When we emphasize (as we ought to) how strong the power of His right arm actually is, we can make the mistake of believing that He is going to use that strength in order to strike the world, and all the sinners in it, such that they are blown to smithereens. Christians who emphasize God's power tend to believe that He doesn't really want to save anybody but will save a few people reluctantly. Those who emphasize His love (forgetting His justice, holiness, and power) tend to veer off into a soupy sort of sentimentalism. We should insist upon both. God hates sin, and He will make short work of it on the earth. God loves the world, and He did not send His Son into the world to condemn the world (John 3:17), but rather that the world through Him might be saved.

Now, by "saved" we mean *saved*. You mean *saved* saved? Yes—Africa, South America, North America, Europe, Asia, Australia, and the weather stations in Antarctica. All those people? Yes—red and yellow, black and white. All those. As soon as the meaning of this sinks in, what do we want to do then? We set up shop to be His counselor. We tell Him that all this is eschatologically irresponsible. We search out His judgments and bring them under review. His ways, which are past finding out, we claim to have found out.

Nebuchadnezzar came to understand that God's hand of rule could not be stopped (Dan. 4:35). But neither can He be stopped when He stretches out His arm to save.

CHAPTER 12

A LIVING SACRIFICE

As we have worked through this epistle we have seen certain common characteristics of Paul's turn of mind. We now come to another one, very much in evidence throughout his letters. His pattern of teaching is this—doctrine precedes ethics and is foundational to it. He teaches us what we must believe (*credenda*, things to be believed), and then he moves on to teach us how we are to live in the light of that doctrine. He moves from what must be believed, to what must be done (*agenda*). But it is not possible to be faithful and go straight to the agenda. Whatever we do, we must *therefore* do. Although there have been ethical exhortations before this in Romans, we come to the place in the letter where Paul pivots and moves to a steady stream of exhortations. Over the remaining chapters, Paul makes it all very practical.

> I beseech you therefore, brethren, by the mercies of God, that ye present your bodies a living sacrifice, holy, acceptable unto God, which is your reasonable service. And be not conformed to this world: but be ye transformed by the renewing of your mind, that ye may prove what is that good, and acceptable, and perfect, will of God. For I say, through the grace given unto me, to every man that is among you, not to think of himself more highly than he ought to think; but to think soberly, according as God hath dealt to every man the measure of faith. (Rom. 12:1–3)

Paul moves from teaching to exhortation. In the light of what has been taught thus far (therefore), he beseeches them "by the mercies of God" (v. 1) which are so evident and spelled out in the first eleven chapters, to *do* something. He asks them to present their bodies a living sacrifice (v. 1), holy and acceptable to God, which is their reasonable worship (v. 1). In doing this, he wants them to be conformed to the gospel as he has laid it out and to not be conformed to "this world" (v. 2). The alternative to being conformed to the world is to be transformed in the mind, in order that they might prove what God actually wants (v. 2)—which is, that which is good, acceptable, and perfect (v. 2). He goes on to spell out what this transformation will look like, as distinguished from what the world does to your head—which is to say, swell it. Our task is not only to look to Christ in faith, but also to see ourselves and our abilities by faith (v. 3). This demeanor will be of central importance in the upcoming discussion of spiritual gifts and Church government.

Life is to be lived on an altar. The word translated as *service* here is actually the word for *worship*, which is not a problem, because service is what worship is. Paul tells the Romans here that their bodies are to be presented to God—this is what He requires of believers in our worship. Our bodies are to be living sacrifices, meaning that the sacrifice is ongoing and doesn't stop. You present your body to God in the formal worship service as you kneel with that body, listen with it, sing with it, eat and drink with it, and lift hands with it. But the benediction is not where that sacrifice stops—the sacrifice encompasses all the rest of your life. The car you drive in is an altar. The bed you sleep in is an altar. The dinner table you sit down to is an altar. The sidewalk you stand on is an altar. And when sin intrudes it is like trying to offer up pig meat to the God of Israel. And as the Church is now the fulfillment of the Torah in Christ, making her the spiritual Israel, we should take care not to offer up any spiritual pig meat to God either.

Notice that Paul says that we are not to be conformed, but rather that we are to be transformed. You are hot, right out of the microwave, and the world is a Jell-O mold. As much as we like to pretend that we are all one-off individuals living the Bohemian dream of autonomy, we are all actually conformists to the bone. The only question concerns *what* we will conform to, not *whether* we will conform. We will conform either to the world or to Christ, and there really are no other possibilities. Joining up with that sector of the world that *pretends* to be nonconformist doesn't really do the trick. Young people want to become screenwriters and filmmakers by growing their hair long and smoking cigarettes, and nobody notices the sheer conformity until there are over a million of them doing it. So it is not *whether* we will conform, but rather *which* pattern we will conform to—the pattern of the old man, or the pattern of the new. Christ came to bring us a new humanity, a new Heaven and earth. He did not come to us in order to fob off a battered repaint.

So we have to be very careful here. What does Paul give us in verse 3 that *shows* we are being transformed by the renewing of our minds? The way that he sets forth here is marked by an accurate humility about yourself. The new way of being human is not determined primarily by the landscape, but rather by what the people are doing there. Paul says that every man is to think of himself soberly, and not more highly of himself than he ought to. Now, can people have a faulty understanding of themselves in a pirate den or in a thieves' kitchen? Of course. But how about in a prayer meeting? How about in a seminary classroom? An elder meeting? An assembly at a classical Christian school? Yes, also of course. This is why, if we neglect Paul's astonishing teaching here, many spiritual activities that would never be censured by your Aunt Mildred are nevertheless every bit as worldly as a tattoo parlor.

When we present our bodies to God as a living sacrifice, this is an acceptable worship. And when we follow through on our formal worship at church on Sunday by presenting our bodies to Him late Wednesday afternoon, this is what validates and proves "what is the acceptable will of God." When we present our bodies to God, we are refusing to allow the world to press us into its mold. This is not because it is bad to be pressed into a mold—rather, it is bad to be pressed into the wrong one. When we are transformed, it is because we have been placed in the Christ mold. We are being grown up into a perfect man.

But this is not a gospel self-help manual. The issue is not really *what* you see—we are all different and will see different things, different abilities, different gifts, and different limitations. The issue is the *way* we see—soberly and not more highly than we ought. Conceited pride sees a lot more than is actually there. A *faux* humility—which is just conceit doing a crab walk—pretends to see a lot less than is there and takes enormous credit for it. True humility provides a peculiar clarity and is the only demeanor that imitates Christ rightly, and it therefore grows up into the new man.

TRUE MEMBERS

Paul now moves into a discussion of body life—a theme he also treats in great detail elsewhere (1 Cor. 12–14). This body life is organic and alive, and it is not to be confused with simple administrative organization, although it *is* organized. With living organisms, the organizational principle arises from below and is not imposed externally. A body forms in obedience to the mysterious instructions that arise from the double helix; a body does not form because someone pushed Play-Doh into a mold. This is just another way of noting the difference between conforming and transforming that we saw in the verses just prior to this.

> For as we have many members in one body, and all
> members have not the same office: so we, being many,
> are one body in Christ, and every one members one
> of another. Having then gifts differing according to
> the grace that is given to us, whether prophecy, let
> us prophesy according to the proportion of faith; or
> ministry, let us wait on our ministering: or he that
> teacheth, on teaching; or he that exhorteth, on exhor-
> tation: he that giveth, let him do it with simplicity;
> he that ruleth, with diligence; he that sheweth mercy,
> with cheerfulness. (Rom. 12:4–8)

Paul now outlines how the body works. He says first that the one body has many members (v. 4). Each distinct member is set apart by this—each does not have the same office or function as do the other members (v. 4). Their loyalties are the same, but their functions are different. So then, the many are one body in Christ, and this means that each member is a member of the other members also (v. 5). Different gifts have been assigned to different members (which is what *makes* them different members), and these gifts differ according to the grace given (v. 6). If God has given the prophetic gift, then prophesy—but only accord- ing to the proportion of faith (v. 6). More about this short- ly. If the gift is ministry, then minister; if teaching, then teach (v. 7). Exhorters should exhort (v. 8). Givers should give with simplicity and without guile (v. 8). Lungs should

stop trying to be ankles and just take in oxygen. Kidneys
should filter the blood and stop trying to listen to the music. Those who rule should be diligent in that rule (v. 8).
The one who is gifted to show mercy should take care to be
cheerful in his pursuit of that duty (v. 8).

We have made an unfortunate error in our modern
tendency to define membership as simple inclusion on a
roster of names. When we think of Church membership,
we tend to think of a list of names in the directory at the
church office, as so many units in a mathematical set. As
C.S. Lewis points out, this is "almost the reverse of what
St. Paul meant by *members*." He goes on: "By *members*...
he meant what we should call *organs*, things essentially
different from, and complementary to, one another: things
different not only in structure and function but also in
dignity."[7] A good illustration of membership would be a
household with a crotchety uncle, mom, dad, three kids, a
dog, and a cat. As Lewis points out, the whole point is that
not one of these members is interchangeable.

Now how many gifts are mentioned here? We know
from elsewhere in the New Testament that there are more
gifts than these listed, so this list is not exhaustive. At the
same time, in a certain way these gifts are representative
of all gifts. There are seven gifts mentioned here: prophesy, ministry, teaching, exhortation, generosity, rule, and
mercy. Some of those who are gifted here are exhorted to
simply discharge their office. Others are cautioned against

---

7. C.S. Lewis, "Membership," in *The Weight of Glory* (Grand Rapids, MI:
Eerdmans, 1975), 33.

a particular temptation they might encounter while they are discharging their office.

Prophesy—The prophetic gift can be immediate, as with the prophets of old who were inspired by God, or it can be mediated, as a man declares the Word of God as found in Scripture. The former would be a man like Isaiah; the latter, a man like John Knox. In the Reformed tradition, preaching is understood as a prophetic office, but only in this latter sense. So the one who prophesies must do so in accordance with his proportion of faith. It is noteworthy that faith was just mentioned previously (v. 3) as a bulwark against conceit.

Ministry—The Greek word here indicates the diaconal office (*diakonia*/διακονια). So the deacons should be given to diaconal ministry—service to the body.

Teaching—This is the explanation of God's Word as distinct from the authoritative declaration of it. Teachers should explain, making things clear, as in Bible studies and in classrooms.

Exhortation—The one who has the gift of exhortation should enjoin and encourage.

Generosity—Some are gifted in giving, and they should simply overflow. A generous spirit is one open-handed with everything that spirit possesses—whether money, or time, or counsel, or a meal. A generous spirit gives from whatever stores it has.

Rule—This applies to who we call the ruling elder, or parish elder. He is to have authority in the Church, and he is not to put things on cruise control. We know this because he is charged to be *diligent*.

Mercy—Those who are gifted in the showing of mercy are exhorted to do so with cheerfulness. It is a striking fact that mercy work can veer off very quickly into censoriousness and dour pride. After all, it was *Judas* who wondered why the expensive perfume was not sold and given to the poor. And elsewhere, Paul anticipated that it might be possible to give all your money to the poor, and yet to do it without love (1 Cor. 13:3).

Each member will tend to view the condition of the body at large through the interpretive lens of his own gifts. If it is engaged in being critical of others, Paul cuts off this tendency. We should use our gifts to identify what *we* should be doing, not what everybody else should be doing. The eye should not fault the elbow for being blind, and the elbow should not fault the backbone for not being a hinge. The deficiencies in the Church that *you* see should be used by you as a spur to pursue and develop your own gifts. If you see discouraged people, encourage them. If you see ignorance, teach. If you see hurting people, show mercy cheerfully. And at the same time, don't think of yourself more highly than you ought (back to v. 3). The toenail is not the brain, and the eye is not the back of the knee.

Gifts are cultivated from below, as already noted. And as we worship God (Here am I, Lord, send me), He knits us together as we are engaged in growing up together—patiently and joyfully.

COALS OF FIRE ON THE HEAD

Having discussed some of the gifts of the body, Paul moves on to exhort the Roman Christians in how the parts of the body should function together. What does it look like when the saints are being knit together in love, as they ought to be? Paul gives us a distinctively Pauline expression of a Sermon on the Mount ethic, but with a surprising twist at the end of it.

Let love be without dissimulation. Abhor that which is evil; cleave to that which is good. Be kindly affectioned one to another with brotherly love; in honour preferring one another; not slothful in business; fervent in spirit; serving the Lord; rejoicing in hope; patient in tribulation; continuing instant in prayer; distributing to the necessity of saints; given to hospitality. Bless them which persecute you: bless, and curse not. Rejoice with them that do rejoice, and weep with them that weep. Be of the same mind one toward another. Mind not high things, but condescend to men of low estate. Be not wise in your own conceits. Recompense to no man evil for evil. Provide things honest in the sight of all men. If it be possible, as much as lieth in you, live peaceably with all men. Dearly beloved, avenge not yourselves, but rather give place unto wrath: for it is written, Vengeance is mine; I will repay, saith the Lord. Therefore if thine enemy hunger, feed him; if he thirst, give him drink: for in so doing thou shalt heap coals of fire on his head. Be not overcome of evil, but overcome evil with good. (Rom. 12:9–21)

Love must not be hypocritical (v. 9). We should hate what is evil and cling to what is good (v. 9). We should be affectionately loyal to one another (v. 10), honoring others before ourselves (v. 10). We should work hard (v. 11), and we should serve the Lord with a fervent zeal (v. 11). We should rejoice in hope, be patient in affliction, and constant in prayer (v. 12). We should be quick with a helping hand for the saints (v. 13) and given to hospitality (v. 13).

If people persecute you, then bless them. Do not curse them (v. 14). The duty of sympathy is next—rejoice with those who rejoice, and weep with those who weep (v. 15). We should think of one another in the same way (v. 16). We should not be snobs, but rather be willing to associate with the lowly (v. 16). With a look back at verse 3, we are told not to be wise in our own conceits (v. 16). We are not to retaliate against others (v. 17). We are to live honestly in the sight of all (v. 17). To whatever extent it is up to you, you are to live in peace with all men (v. 18).

But then comes the twist.

We are not to avenge ourselves, *not because vengeance is wrong*, but because it is the Lord's (v. 19). We are not to avenge, but rather leave room for wrath. The Lord will repay (v. 19). As far as *you* are concerned, feed your hungry enemy, give a drink to your hungry enemy, and in doing this you will heap coals of fire on his head (v. 20). Do not be overcome by evil (v. 21). But it is not enough simply to fight off attacks. Go on the offensive; overcome evil with good (v. 21).

Love sincerely. Hate sin. Hold the good. Like each other. Defer to one another. Work hard. Stay zealous. Rejoice.

Endure. Pray constantly. Give to others. Open your home. Bless enemies; bless and do not curse. Identify in sympathy. Stoop low. Drop your conceits. Don't retaliate. Live honestly. Keep the peace. Live the Jesus way.

This is a description of character, and not a list of rules. This is a description of what it looks like when the Spirit is at work in a community of saints, building what is called *koinonia* (κοινωνια), true and living fellowship. This is not an invitation to you to labor for six months on having your love be without hypocrisy, after which you can move on to abhorring what is evil. Check that box, and on to the next thing. No. In contrast, the fruit of the Spirit hangs together in one cluster, like the grapes of Eschol (Num. 13:23). When we live together in triune community, this is what it is like. When it is not like this, we are doing something *else*—however religious we think we might be.

Now in this place, God does not tell us that vengeance is wrong, but rather He says that "Vengeance is *mine*." This statement comes from Deuteronomy 32:35, a chapter in which God details the future history of the Jews and how He was going to use the Gentiles to provoke the Jews to jealousy (Deut. 32:21; Rom. 10:19). In this same context, God promised that He was going to bring vengeance down on the Jews (Deut. 32:34–35; Rom. 12:19; Heb. 10:30). In the next breath, Moses says that God will judge His people (Deut. 32:36; Heb. 10:30; Ps. 135:14), in the sense of vindicating them. As Paul has taught us in the previous chapter, the Jews will be brought back. At the end of Moses's song, he (and Paul) invite the nations to rejoice together with the Jews (Deut. 32:43; Rom. 15:10).

This means that the archetypical vengeance has already happened. The first-century Christians, who lived through this great event, established a pattern for us to imitate if we live through anything that is comparable—as many generations of Christians have had to do. The persecutors in the first century were the Jews; in subsequent centuries they have adopted many other names, including names ransacked from the Bible, but they all kept the same spirit.

We must remember that the chapter markings were not in the letter as Paul wrote it. When he says here that we are not to avenge ourselves, he says that we should step aside to make room for wrath (12:19). This is just a few verses before Paul tells us how that wrath comes, and is all part of the same argument. The God to whom vengeance belongs has deputized rulers to act in His stead (13:4), in this case, the Romans. The Romans were the appointed instrument in the hand of the Lord of all vengeance, and they were the ones who were to destroy Jerusalem, as the Song of Moses had promised would happen.

Does this not apply to us then? Of course it does, once the necessary adjustments have been made. But we must remember the context here. When Paul cautions against rebellion (13:2), he is not giving us an abstract classroom lecture in rarified civics. He is writing just a few years before an actual rebellion broke out, one that concluded with the fulfillment of the prophecies that he, Paul, has just been citing. So we must read this on the alert for Paul's premises.

Verse 20 is a quotation from Proverbs 25:21–22. But the question of what those "coals of fire" might be has been much discussed. Is this a kind act, a helping hand that puts starter coals in somebody's basin that they carry home on their head? That has the feel of a Bible handbook answer. Are these coals of fire an image of judgment (Ps. 18:12–13)? Or perhaps conviction of sin? That is possible, but given what is said about overcoming evil in the next verse, I would take it as an act of consecration. Treat your enemy as if he is an altar (Lev. 16:12). When we return kindness for evil, we have every right to turn to ask God to receive the offering that we have just made. The unkindness done to us in the person who did is transformed into an altar, and the good we returned to our adversary is a sweet-smelling savor to God.

EXCURSUS: 21 PRINCIPLES A CHRISTIAN CITIZEN MUST KNOW

Because the teaching of the Apostle Paul on civil authority is widely misunderstood and misrepresented, we are going to take our time going through this section. And because the instructions here are to Christian citizens and subjects, we are going to begin with a scriptural introduction to this entire subject. And because of who is addressed here, it is important to remember something that Abraham Kuyper once said: "In any successful attack on freedom the state can only be an accomplice. The *chief* culprit is the citizen who forgets his duty, wastes away his strength in the sleep of sin and sensual pleasure, and so loses the power of his own initiative."[8] We are therefore going to consider 21 principles on civil government that the Christian must understand.

21 PRINCIPLES

Civil government and rule is a blessing from God, not a necessary evil. "The God of Israel said, the Rock of Israel spake to me, He that ruleth over men must be just, ruling in the fear of God. And *he shall be as the light of the morning, when the sun riseth*, even a morning without clouds; as the tender grass springing out of the earth by clear shining after rain" (2 Sam. 23:3–4, emphasis added). We are not anarchists.

God establishes a righteous throne with majesty. "It is an abomination to kings to commit wickedness: for *the throne is established by righteousness*" (Prov. 16:12, emphasis added). "And the LORD magnified Solomon exceedingly in the sight of all Israel, *and bestowed upon him such royal majesty* as had not been on any king before him in Israel" (1 Chron. 25:29; Dan. 4:36).

The law of God is the soul of a good ruler. "Moreover thou shalt provide out of all the people able men, *such as fear God*, men of truth, hating covetousness; and place such over them, to be rulers of thousands, and rulers of hundreds, rulers of fifties, and rulers of tens" (Exod. 18:21, emphasis added).

God requires true humility of His rulers. "That *his heart be not lifted up above his brethren*, and that he turn not aside

---

8. *Abraham Kuyper: A Centennial Reader*, ed. James Bratt (Grand Rapids: William B. Eerdmans, 1998), 473.

from the commandment, to the right hand, or to the left: to the end that he may prolong his days in his kingdom, he, and his children, in the midst of Israel" (Deut. 17:20, emphasis added).

Our basic demeanor toward civil rulers should be one of honor. "Honour all men. Love the brotherhood. Fear God. *Honour the king*" (1 Pet. 2:17, emphasis added). What the kings of the earth bring into the New Jerusalem is not a sham or a pretense (Rev. 21:24).

Tyrants love moral corruption and hate virtuous men. As Chesterton once put it, free love is the first and most obvious bribe to offer a slave.[9] Tyrants therefore love public entertainments and private vices because they love an enervated people. "But I have a few things against thee, because thou hast there them that hold the doctrine of Balaam, who taught Balac to cast a stumblingblock before the children of Israel, to eat things sacrificed unto idols, *and to commit fornication*" (Rev. 2:14, emphasis added). Porn is therefore politics, and it reveals your *true* political allegiances.

Absolute perfection in our rulers is not the point. "Cast me not away from thy presence; and *take not thy holy spirit from me*" (Ps. 51:11). David had forfeited his throne by his evil deed as Saul had, and he knew it. But God in His mercy allowed David to remain as the king. And it is said of a number of kings that they were good, like Asa, but that

---

9. "Free love is the direct enemy of freedom. It is the most obvious of all the bribes that can be offered by slavery." G.K. Chesterton, *Fancies Versus Fads* (New York: Dodd, Mead and Company, 1923) 150.

they did not remove the high places (1 Kings 15:14). We do not require absolute perfection.

Tyranny is a judgment from God for the sins of the people. "And he said, This will be the manner of the king that shall reign over you: He will *take*..." (1 Sam. 8:11, emphasis added). But remember that the God who sends tyrants to chastise us may also send a deliverer to save us

Every manner of civil government is under the authority of God. God rules in His own name, and princes rule by derivation. Civil rulers are the lieutenants of God. Here in Romans 13, the word for *deacons* is used of them several times (Rom. 13:4). The ruler is therefore an appointed, delegated, and deputized *servant*.

Civil disobedience is required when matters of worship and the gospel are concerned. "But if not, be it known unto thee, O king, that *we will not serve thy gods*, nor worship the golden image which thou hast set up" (Dan. 3:18, emphasis added). "Then Peter and the other apostles answered and said, *We ought to obey God rather than men*" (Acts 5:29, emphasis added).

Civil disobedience is lawful in other areas as well. David honored Saul (1 Sam. 24:5) but did not turn himself in (1 Sam. 24:22). Neither did Peter turn himself in (Acts 12:11) or Paul for that matter (2 Cor. 11:32–33). Examples could be multiplied.

Civil government is covenantal and has a double covenantal nature. It involves God, the magistrate, and the people (2 Chron. 23:16).

No human authority, civil magistrates included, can be absolute. God alone has absolute authority; man's authority is always limited and bounded. This is what Nebuchadnezzar confessed—after his sanity returned (Dan. 4:35).

Not everything that is legal is lawful (Rev. 13:17).

Faithful believers will often be accused of lawlessness and treason. Ahab was the troubler of Israel, so that is what he accused Elijah of being (1 Kings 18:17). But the cause of the trouble is the problem; the solution is not the problem (2 Chron. 23:13).

The Bible teaches the principle of the "consent of the governed." Rehoboam was *elected* to be king (1 Kings 12:1), and he was no anomaly.

The lot of the people and the character of their rulers is linked together. "When the righteous are in authority, the people rejoice: but when the wicked beareth rule, the people mourn" (Prov. 29:2).

Resistance of tyranny is not the same thing as resistance of the established civil order. Jehoiada defended the throne by removing someone from it (2 Chron. 23:11).

Lesser magistrates obeyed Jehoiada, and they were right to do so (2 Chron. 23:1–3).

We must care what company our rulers keep. Panderers, whores, flatterers and other "mushrooms of the court"[10] are to be despised. "Take away the wicked from before the

---

10. "Yea, they deposed some because of their idleness and want of judgment, who exposed the state in prey to panders, courtesans, flatterers, and other such unworthy mushrooms of the court, who governed all things at their pleasure; taking from such rash phaetons the bridle of government, lest the whole body of the state and people should be consumed through their unadvised folly." Stephen Junius Brutus, *Vindiciae Contra Tyrannos: A Defense of Liberty Against Tyrants* (Moscow, ID: Canon Press, 2020), 174.

king, and his throne shall be established in righteousness"
(Prov. 25:5).

And last, Christian history matters. Included in our definition of "the powers that be" (Rom. 13:1) must be things
like the Constitution, the will of the people, the lesser magistrates, and the balances of powers.

CHAPTER 13

CIVIL OBEDIENCE IN CONTEXT

As we begin the task of unpacking this crucial part of Romans, always remember the broader context. In the latter part of chapter twelve, we saw that Paul was arguing from Deuteronomy 32 that Moses had predicted that God would be avenged upon the Jews, and that He would use a nation that has no godly understanding to do it (Deut. 32:21, 35).

That nation was to be the Roman nation, and this is how Paul knew that the believers of the first century were to be in Jeremiah's position (e.g., accept the judgment), and not Hezekiah's (e.g., resist the enemy). On top of that, the Lord Himself had prophesied that Jerusalem would be flattened within one generation (Matt. 24:34). Jesus had said this around AD 30, and Paul is writing this letter almost thirty years later (AD 57). So the clock was ticking. The Jews erupted in open revolt in AD 66—just nine years after Romans was written. Paul's writing on this subject was *not* an academic exercise.

> Let every soul be subject unto the higher powers. For there is no power but of God: the powers that be are ordained of God. Whosoever therefore resisteth the power, resisteth the ordinance of God: and they that resist shall receive to themselves damnation. For rulers are not a terror to good works, but to the evil. Wilt thou then not be afraid of the power? Do that which is good, and thou shalt have praise of the same. (Rom 13:1–3)

Every soul is to be obedient to the higher powers (v. 1). There is no authority except what God has established (v. 1), and this would include Nero, who was the emperor at that time, despite his unbelief and paganism. Paul is arguing that the Roman control of Jerusalem was God-ordained and that those who tried to recruit Christians to join with the Jews in resisting Rome from the "holy city" were actually recruiting them to damnation and judgment (v. 2). Paul then gives his rationale for this, which is that rulers are a terror to evil works, not to good works. If you don't want to live in fear of those in power, then earn their praise by doing what is good (v. 3).

In this setting, it would be difficult to overemphasize the importance of historical context. Nero had become emperor in AD 54, and his first five years were known as his golden years. So when Paul wrote these words, the apostle was *not* living in some utopian fantasy land—the rule really was decent. Nero was at that time advised by a man named Burrus and the Roman Stoic philosopher Seneca. That golden period ended in AD 59, when Nero had his mother murdered, an act that appalled pretty much everybody.

Further, this man Seneca had published *De Clementia* (*On Clemency*) in AD 55. Interestingly, a commentary on this book was the first book that John Calvin ever had published. And if you compare Romans 13:1–7 and *De Clementia* 1:1–4, the chances will appear to you outstanding that Paul was acquainted with Seneca's work and was laboring to have the Christians do their part. Seneca did what he could to keep his foot on the brake, and Paul wanted Christians to be helpful in this. How necessary a foot on the brake was can be seen in the subsequent events. (Incidentally, Seneca was the brother of Gallio, who makes a brief appearance in Acts 18:17.)

Later, when the Jewish revolt broke out, it initially looked like it had a good chance of success. In the middle of that war, in AD 68, there was a coup against Nero, and he was forced to commit suicide. He was replaced by a rapid succession of emperors, each of whom reigned for a matter of mere months. There was to be no real consolidated rule in Rome (in the city where the recipients of this letter were to be living, remember). As you probably know, the temple in Jerusalem was finally burned in AD 70, but this was preceded by the burning of the Temple of *Jupiter* on the Capitoline Hill in Rome in AD 69 (this mean that AD 69 became known as the year of the four emperors—Galba, Otho, Vitellius and Vespasian).

Vespasian appears to have been the one adult in the lot—and he had to leave the siege of Jerusalem to save Rome, leaving his son Titus to finish up the conquest of the Jews. So the time between Paul's letter and these events in AD 68 was just over a decade—not a long time at all.

The reason Paul gives for obeying the existing authorities is that rulers punish evil deeds and reward good ones. When he wrote this, it was true. That was what the Roman authorities did.

But everything was about to come unstuck. Consider just *one* example from these years—what would it *mean* to subject yourself to the higher powers when Vitellius was (*very* temporarily) ruling in Rome, and Vespasian was marching on Rome with his legions? And further, let us say that Vitellius had already distinguished himself as a debauched thug, driving the city into economic chaos by means of triumphal parades and three orgiastic banquets a day, and then trying to solve the economic problems by executing anybody who had declared him to be their heir. What about then? If there is a riot in the streets, and somebody clambers up on the courthouse steps with a megaphone, and shouts to everybody that *he* is the king, do you have to obey him because of Romans 13:1? What about the second guy who shouts that? Just ten minutes of such conditions should show why Paul was as urgent in his exhortation here as he was. In this fallen world, sinful anarchy is far, far worse than a sinful stability.

This goes back to a foundational principle that Paul set down in the previous chapter—no one should think they are more important than they are (12:3). As the drama unfolds, who are *you* in that drama? Are you Vitellius or Vespasian? Seneca or Paul?

John Knox used the apt illustration of a father who lost his mind and tried to commit mayhem against his family. If a couple of his sons forcibly restrained him until the madness passed, would they be dutiful sons or rebellious sons? If they are one, might someone else *say* they were being the other? Certainly. So what is our duty? We must be steeped in the Scriptures, and we must not think of ourselves more highly than we ought. How? According to the measure of faith.

AN ARMED DEACON OF GOD

For at least two reasons, we are taking care to work through this particular passage of Scripture deliberately and slowly. First, the issues involved are complex and important, and they are even more complex and important in our day than they usually are. Second, for quite a number of reasons, the misunderstandings that surround this portion of Scripture are legion. We have to be very careful here.

> For he is the minister of God to thee for good. But if thou do that which is evil, be afraid; for he beareth not the sword in vain: for he is the minister of God, a revenger to execute wrath upon him that doeth evil. Wherefore ye must needs be subject, not only for wrath, but also for conscience sake. (Rom. 13:4–5)

Contextually, we are talking about civil rule, *civil* power. Paul has called the magistrate the "powers that be." The word here is the word for authority. All authorities whatever are from God (v. 1), and so it follows that civil authorities are from God (v. 1). The word is *authority* in verses 1–2, and in verse 3, Paul calls those we are dealing with here "rulers." What kind of rulers we are talking about becomes plain here in verses 4–5, given their tools and what they are assigned to do with them. For he (the ruler) is a minister of God, a deacon of God, and his assigned task is to do the Christian good (v. 4). If a person is an evildoer, then he should be worried and afraid, because the ruler does not bear the *sword* in vain (v. 4). He is once *again* called the deacon of God, and his job is to execute vengeance and wrath upon evildoers (v. 4). The Christian needs to be obedient to the law, not just because he is afraid of this wrath (v. 5), but also because he is being obedient to God—that is, for conscience's sake (v. 5).

God has given these rulers two things—a task and a tool. The assigned task is to administer an avenging justice to those who do evil, and the tool for this task is the sword, an instrument of lethal violence. The word for sword here is *machaira* (μαχαιρα), and it was an instrument of warfare. It was not used for spanking bad boys with the flat of it.

This was a double-edged sword, usually about eighteen inches long, and was commonly used by Roman soldiers. Peter used one to cut off an ear (Matt. 26:51); James the brother of John was executed with one (Acts 12:2); however sharp it might be, it is incapable of separating us from the love of Christ (Rom. 8:35); it provides us with a figure for the Word of God (Eph. 6:17; Heb. 4:12). It was not a toy, and God gave it to His civil deacons to kill bad people with.

However much our pacifist brothers might sweat over this passage, it says what it says, and it is not in the Old Testament.

But vengeance is still the Lord's. Remember that this book is written just a few years before a rebellion breaks out against the Romans. The Jews, who would erupt in that rebellion, were under a prophetic statement as old as Moses, a statement that said they would lose this battle and that God would humiliate them through a people of strange language—because vengeance for all their idolatries belonged to Him. The Christians were being instructed here that under *no circumstances* were they to join this revolt. If God is coming after a people with vengeance in His eye, don't *you* jump in between.

From this circumstance, we can and should render to a general principle by induction. After all the Romans and all the Jewish rebels were dead and gone, there were still evildoers in the world who would need to be restrained generally, and they would need to be restrained by force. One of the uses of the law is to give guidance to the magistrate as he considers what to do (1 Tim. 1:9–11). All we are doing here is distinguishing the first-century application from our own (necessary) applications—to muggers, terrorists, rapists, and so on. We won't need the sword anymore when we don't have crime anymore.

The state is God's deacon (Rom. 13:4), and God never leaves His deacons without instructions. A deacon is, by definition, under authority. We should measure his appropriations and expenditures over against what he was told to do. When servants use the master's resources for tasks unassigned by him (Luke 12:46–47), what is the result? When the Lord comes back to evaluate His deacons in the Congress, what will He do? He will not be indiscriminate; the punishments will fit the crimes. Some He will cut in sunder, and others will simply be beaten with many stripes.

This will not happen because our rulers are not His deacons; rather, it will happen because they *are*. By definition, the armed deacons in this passage of Romans are under authority. Their authority does not originate with them, as much as they would like it to. Whose authority are they under? *God's*. We obey them because God tells us to (for conscience' sake), and not simply because we fear their punishments for wrongdoing. And if they are levying punishments for righteousness, we are not to fear them at all—and conscience is still operative.

The Apostle Paul tells the believers of his day that he advises against marriage because of the "present distress" (1 Cor. 7:26). In a similar way, he is also telling believers here in our text to stand back and let the Romans do to Jerusalem what they are going to do to it (Rom. 12:19; 13:1ff). Many believers have abstracted his principle here in the latter instance and applied it to every conceivable situation throughout all time, which they haven't done to the first passage—which was just as contextually situated. And why is this? We grasp the importance of limiting context in 1 Corinthians because it is fun to get the girl. A lot more fun than, say, standing up to tyrants is.

TAX CHEATS

When considering the subject of our duty to pay taxes, the Bible seems plain enough. But a lot rides on where you place the emphasis—where do the italics go? Governments exist by covenant, and governments like ours explicitly *claim* to exist by covenant. The word federal comes from the Latin word *foedus*, which means covenant. But covenants have terms and stipulations. They have conditions, just as our text before us has conditions.

> For this cause pay ye tribute also: for they are God's ministers, attending continually upon this very thing. Render therefore to all their dues: tribute to whom tribute is due; custom to whom custom; fear to whom fear; honour to whom honour. (Rom. 13:6–7)

The payment of taxes is linked to the reason that went before—"for this cause." Your conscience is bound to pay taxes because the magistrate is serving as God's deacon or minister in the execution of His wrath (v. 4). This is the foremost reason given for paying tribute: *because* they are functioning as God's deacons. Paul mentions this for the third time, only this time His ministers are His *leitourgoi* ($\lambda\epsilon\iota\tau\upsilon\rho\gamma o\iota$) (v. 6), the word from which we get liturgy. Remember that liturgies are prescribed. Free-form interpretive dance is not a liturgy, even if you are waving a copy of the Constitution over your head. We pay tribute because the magistrate is "attending continually" to this very task (v. 6). Render your obligations, therefore (v. 7). Render tribute, render custom, render fear, and render honor (v. 7).

We are told twice here to render *tribute* (vv. 6–7). In the New Testament, the word is used elsewhere only in Luke. Jesus is asked if it is lawful to pay tribute to Caesar or not (Luke 20:22). He answers in the affirmative, but with a striking exclusion. Later, He is accused of teaching that it was unlawful to pay tribute to Caesar (Luke 23:2).

We are also told to render custom (*telos*/τελος) to whom custom is due. The other place where this word is used in Matthew 17:24–27, where Jesus interestingly pays a tax that He says is not really owed. The last two obligations that Paul mentions here are not monetary in nature. We are told to render fear to whom fear is due, and honor to whom honor is due. Remember that Paul is writing this when Nero is emperor—and even in his relatively good five years of rule, he was no believer.

We need to get the theology of this thing straight first. If governments can steal, as we see in the story of Ahab and Naboth, then they can obviously do so through the tax code. Tax codes can be passed illegally and unjustly. Legislators can be bribed to get them to vote for it. The agents charged with enforcement can throw aside all biblical rules of evidence, and so on. If this can in fact happen, as it clearly can, then there can be circumstances in which a tax dispute between the government and the citizenry is a dispute which exists because the *government* is the one cheating on your taxes.

In other words, we should not assume that whenever the government says that money is owed, and a blood-donating turnip says that it isn't, that it is the turnip who is cheating. In short, it is quite possible (and some would say likely) that the biggest tax cheat in America today is the federal government. If you say that this is not even possible, then you are missing a basic biblical truth about government, and you have forgotten the nature of man.

But if it *is* possible, then it becomes important to determine where the line is. There is taxation which is not theft (see our text), and there is taxation which is theft. Where is the line? In this text, Paul firmly anchors the lawful payment of taxes to the lawful functions of government

How then should we file? When the government is recognizably fulfilling the functions that God has assigned to it, paying taxes stands as a moral obligation before God. We should pay our taxes dutifully and with gratitude toward God, and we should do so "for conscience sake" (v. 5).

When it starts to become evident that the "powers that be" have corrupted the process, then another round of decisions must be made—and the criteria here would be pragmatic and tactical. But when this starts to become clear, we should not approach it in an autonomous way—"Every man to his tents, O Israel!" (2 Sam. 20:1). Remember Calvin's doctrine of the lesser magistrates. Calvin taught that when resistance finally becomes necessary, that we should seek to express that resistance through the "lesser magistrates." An example of this would have been if 30 or more governors had told the Supreme Court that they were going to disregard the *Roe v. Wade* decision. Citizens who agreed with this would be expressing their dissent in submission to their governor, a lesser magistrate.

It is also important to remember that "corrupted the process" does not refer to government expenditures that you might disagree with. Corruption is identified by the stench.

The old Chinese curse is "May you live in interesting times." Well, we do, and here we are.

You bear God's image and Christ's name. *That* cannot be rendered to Caesar lawfully.

Scripture teaches the appropriate boundaries of government and appropriate responses when they are transgressed. If you don't know what that teaching is, then set yourself to learn.

You are citizens, not subjects. Christian history matters.

You are members of a corporate body. Learning how lawful resistance functions is a question of social theology. Individual cussedness should never be confused with godly individuality. Obedience is rendered to God by ones, but it should be obedience rendered to God and His people, and not to your own opinions.

Worship God, you and your family, in Spirit and in truth every Lord's Day. This is the source of all true reformations.

THE HEART OF THE LAW

A very popular mistake among Christians is that of contrasting love and the law, as though we had to pick and choose. Will we live according to love or according to the law? But if we *must* love, isn't that a law, a great commandment? And if we keep the law truly, won't we realize that love permeates all of it? Love God and love your neighbor—this is the law and the prophets.

> Owe no man any thing, but to love one another: for
> he that loveth another hath fulfilled the law. For this,
> Thou shalt not commit adultery, Thou shalt not kill,
> Thou shalt not steal, Thou shalt not bear false witness,
> Thou shalt not covet; and if there be any other com-
> mandment, it is briefly comprehended in this saying,
> namely, Thou shalt love thy neighbour as thyself. Love
> worketh no ill to his neighbour: therefore love is the
> fulfilling of the law. (Rom. 13:8–10)

In the verse 7, we were told that we should render to all
their *due*. The word used there is the noun form of what we
have here in the verb of verse 8, where it says not to *owe*
anything. *Not to owe* here does not therefore mean that we
are never to have obligations. It means that we may have
no obligations inconsistent with the obligation to love (v.
8). If you love your neighbor, then you have fulfilled the
law with regard to him, which means that you have fulfilled your obligations (v. 8). The Apostle Paul then lists
five of the ten commandments, and includes all the others,
and says that they are all summed up in the commandment
to love your neighbor as yourself (v. 9). Love does no harm
to his neighbor (v. 10), which is why we know that love is
the fulfillment of the law (v. 10).

As with so many passages of Scripture, to take a snippet
out of its context and absolutize it is a good way to distort
the Bible. "Owe *no* man anything" has a nice ring to it,
and is right up there with "Neither a borrower nor a lend-
er be." Unfortunately, this absolutist view collides with
Scripture. Jesus commands us to lend, for example. "But

love ye your enemies, and do good, and lend, hoping for nothing again" (Luke 6:35). Not only does He command loans, He commands dumb loans to our enemies. The ability to lend is a profound covenantal blessing (Deut. 15:6–8). Charging interest for poverty-relief loans is lawful outside the covenant, and is prohibited within (Deut. 23:20). Moreover, the law presupposes the lawfulness of borrowing (Exod. 22:14). The law does not slam the person who is in need of a loan, but rather protects him (Lev. 25:35–36). At the same time, it is better to lend than to borrow, just as it is better to be warm and dry than cold and wet (Deut. 28:12). The borrower has the weaker hand (Prov. 22:7), which relates to our text here—unwise and unwanted debt interferes with the obligation to love.

There are different kinds of debt, and only one kind of love. So before considering some common problems with our obligations, we need to settle one other issue first. The biblical laws regarding loans and interest, brothers and nonbelievers, are laws that still apply to poverty-relief loans. They are not laws that apply to a business investment, for example. But, having said that, the obligation to love your neighbor applies as much to the neighbor with whom you are working a business deal as it does to the impoverished neighbor. If a poor man cannot pay back a loan and he avoids his benefactor, he is not loving him. And if a man has a business deal blow up on him and he does not return his investor's calls, he is not loving him. There *are* different kinds of debt, but there is only one kind of neighborly love.

When we understand love the way we ought, we must always begin with what our love should look like when extended to our brother, and not what his love extended toward *us* should look like. Perhaps it *should* look like that, and perhaps you are quite right, but that is also not your principal business.

First, don't abuse your family. "Whoso robbeth his father or his mother, and saith, It is no transgression; the same is the companion of a destroyer" (Prov. 28:24). The fact that you haven't paid back family members makes it worse, not better.

Second, don't abuse the Golden Rule. Just because you wouldn't mind if that were done to you doesn't mean they don't mind it. Don't exercise other people's generosity and forgiveness toward you on their behalf. That's another form of *taking*.

Third, don't refuse to pay what you *can* pay. Words are free, communication is free, even if you are flat broke. When love is there, the debtor initiates communications before the creditor needs to, and the debtor is persistent with it.

Fourth, don't abuse the passage of time. A poor memory is not the same thing as a good conscience.

And fifth, don't measure his love with the yardstick of your debts. Measure your own love with it.

The Lord Jesus teaches us (Matt. 22:40) that the entire law is summed up in these two commandments—love God (Deut. 6:5) and love your neighbor (Lev. 19:18). The Apostle Paul teaches the same principle here. He says that certain specific commands, and any others you might be able to find, are summed up or "comprehended" in this one command. The Decalogue sums up the whole law (Exod. 34:28), as do these two commandments, which means that these two sum up the Ten Commandments as well. This is the heart of the law.

Love does no harm to his neighbor. The great lesson for us here is that this harm is defined not by our intentions or motives, but by the law of God. Just as love fills out the law, so the law defines love. The law is the riverbed, and love is the water. If you have no riverbed but a lot of sentimental water, what you have is a swamp in which a lot of fornication occurs. If you have no water but a long riverbed, you just have something for the tumbleweed to blow down.

TIME FOR THE WORLD TO GET UP

The Incarnation of the Word and the resurrection of that Word from the dead have entirely remade the world. We fail to recognize this because we really don't understand history—or the way the world actually was before Christ came into it. But humanity lived through a long night indeed, and when Christ came, the sun rose. Men still sin, but the sun is up. We can still have cloudy days, and even storms, *but the sun is up*—and cannot be made to ever go down.

> And that, knowing the time, that now it is high time
> to awake out of sleep: for now is our salvation nearer
> than when we believed. The night is far spent, the
> day is at hand: let us therefore cast off the works of

> darkness, and let us put on the armour of light. Let
> us walk honestly, as in the day; not in rioting and
> drunkenness, not in chambering and wantonness, not
> in strife and envying. But put ye on the Lord Jesus
> Christ, and make not provision for the flesh, to fulfil
> the lusts thereof. (Rom. 13:11–14)

We have seen how the believers were to submit themselves to the old authorities. They were true authorities, but their rough governance of humanity was in the process of being replaced. We have also seen how believers were to treat one another lawfully from the heart, which is what love actually is. Then we come to some very interesting applications.

The Apostle Paul takes the Decalogue, the meaning of love, and pushes it into some very interesting corners. He says that the Roman Christians should *know the time* (v. 11). What time was it? Time to wake up, because salvation was nearer than when the first Christians first believed (v. 11). What *is* this approaching salvation? It is the cataclysm that Paul has been preparing the Roman Christians for—the conclusion of the Judaic aeon and the formal, unfettered commencement of the Christian aeon.

Note that the night is "far spent" (v. 12), and that the day is "at hand" (v. 12). Paul is not talking about the second coming, many thousands of years in the future. The response to this immediate eschatological reality is to cast off the works of darkness and put on the armor of light (v. 12). Once up, with that panoply on, what are these believers to do? They were to walk honestly, because it is

daytime (v. 13). This honest walk excludes six things—
riotous partying, drunkenness, fornication, wantonness,
strife, and envying. Put off the old man, and instead put
on the Lord Jesus (v. 14), making no provision for the flesh
or its lusts (v. 14).

How should someone act if they are dressed in the armor of light? What should their behavior be? Right away,
it excludes certain things. Orgies or riotous parties are out.
So is drunkenness. The next sin is translated *chambering*
in the KJV, but the word means sexual immorality. After
that is sensuality, lasciviousness, or filthiness. Then comes
strife or quarreling, and after that is envy. We are dressed
in the armor of light, and we are to walk as the children
of light (Eph. 5:8). We are to do this in a way that produces the fruit of the Spirit, the fruit of light—that which is
good, right, and true (Eph. 5:9). Set your minds on heavenly things (Col. 3:2). Whatever is pure, (Phil. 4:8), Paul
argues, think about *that*.

These instructions are given to Christians. When you
were first converted, you *put off* the old man, and you *put
on* the new man, Jesus. That was a fundamental action.
But it is not the kind of action that never needs to be repeated. We repeat this motion throughout the course of
our lives (although not at the foundational level). We put
off, and we put on. We put off the old, corrupt way of being a human being, and we put on the new and glorious
way of being a human being—the Lord Jesus.

An important part of what it means to put off the old
man concerns the way we speak. "Let *no corrupt communication* proceed out of your mouth, but that which is good

to the use of edifying, that it may minister grace unto the hearers" (Eph. 4:29, emphasis added). "And have no fellowship with the unfruitful works of darkness, but rather reprove them. For it is *a shame even to speak* of those things which are done of them in secret" (Eph. 5:11–12, emphasis added). Right after this, Paul uses the same image he uses in our passage here in Romans—the image of waking up from sleep so that Christ the sun could shine on us.

One of the disgraceful things in the modern Church is slack entertainment standards, being willing to be entertained in our homes by people that we wouldn't have in our homes. But digitizing a dirty joke doesn't clean it up any. And then Christians begin speaking and joking that way themselves—although the Bible plainly says not to. Wake *up*, sleepers. Scripture does not prohibit the confrontation of sin with blunt terms, but it does reject any accommodation with sin, whether that accommodation is subtle or overt.

The Bible calls us to holiness because of who we are— we are named as Christians in our baptism. But the Scriptures also summon us to purity because of *where we are in the story*. That is what is happening here.

The Roman Christians were told not to behave in a certain way because it was morning. Christ is the sun who rose, and this is why this contextualization does not make it inapplicable to us in our situation. The first Christians were staggering down for coffee at 5:30am. We are busy at work, mid-morning. Does this reasoning apply to us, less or more? We are still engaged in the work of the Great Commission, which consists of racking people out of their beds. As the morning progresses, this becomes even more of a necessity. As the day progresses, we must stay with it. Some lazy men have trouble getting up, which is what Paul was addressing. Other lazy men have trouble working through the day, which is what we are addressing—but the point is the same.

Don't be like that archbishop who once joked that he didn't get up early because it made him proud all morning and sleepy all afternoon.

CHAPTER 14

LOVE IS NOT RELATIVISM

We are the beta test for the new humanity, but this might require some explanation. Jesus Christ is the perfect man, but we are not yet grown up into that perfect man (Eph. 4:13). So, as far as *we* go, we are the working prototype of what God is up to. There are some significant bugs to work out yet, mostly having to do with our lack of love for one another. So let's work on that.

> Him that is weak in the faith receive ye, but not to doubtful disputations. For one believeth that he may eat all things: another, who is weak, eateth herbs. Let not him that eateth despise him that eateth not; and

let not him which eateth not judge him that eateth:
for God hath received him. Who art thou that judgest
another man's servant? To his own master he standeth
or falleth. Yea, he shall be holden up: for God is able
to make him stand. (Rom. 14:1–4)

Paul has been explaining the gospel, that message which
establishes a new race descended from the new Adam, designed by God to replace the corrupt mass of humanity
wrought by the old Adam. We are living in a time of great
transition, so we in the Church must live in a way that
displays to the outside world how this whole thing is supposed to work.

The first thing to understand is that the Church is not an
exclusive club for spiritually superior people. Receive the
one who is weak in faith (v. 1), we are told, and we are not
supposed to receive him in order to argue with him (v. 1).
For example, one Christian believes he can eat anything,
while a weaker brother with dietary scruples is a vegetarian (v. 2). Paul sets down the principle of love—do not despise or judge one another, and this is a principle that cuts
both ways. It goes from the strong to the weak and from
the weak to the strong (v. 3). If God has received someone,
don't you try to get more exclusive than God (v. 3). It is
bad to try to have higher standards than God does. It is
not our place to judge the workmanship that is submitted
to another (v. 4). To his own master a man stands or falls
(v. 4). And for Paul's money, he is going to stand—because
God is able to make him stand (v. 4).

Paul has already defined the bedrock of love for us, which is the law of God. He tells us what love looks like. Love does no harm to his neighbor, as defined by what *God* says harm is. *We* don't get to define it. In this area—the tangled debates Christians get themselves into—Paul says that love receives a brother without engaging in doubtful disputations. Paul says that the stronger brother must take care not to despise the weaker brother, and the weaker brother must not judge the stronger. These are different verbs, but they both have to do with "not receiving." The one who despises looks down on the one who tangles himself all up in unnecessary rules and complications, and thus his despising breaks the law of love. The one who judges does so according to his own made-up standards, substituting them in for God's actual standards. This means he has to judge uphill, which makes him cranky.

Both are forms of acting like a supervisor over people you weren't given any authority over. Your brother stands or falls before somebody else, and the one before whom he stands or falls loves him more than you do, and is not nearly as eager as you are to see him mess up.

This means that love—as *God* defines it—trumps everything. It is to be the governing demeanor in all our discussions, disputes, and debates, and it is this attitude of love that prevents us from becoming "faddists for Jesus." C.S. Lewis warned against the error of what he called "Christianity and..." Christianity and vitamins, Christianity and homebirthing, Christianity and no cheeseburgers, Christianity and the grunge aesthetic, and so on. Now of course, we must make our decisions in these other areas, but we must never do so in a way that links them to the faith *in the wrong way*. Neither may we leave them *un*linked—that would leave our fads without *any* regulating authority, which would be terrible.

So we must link them up intelligently and in love. In these other areas, we need to be fully convinced in our own minds—we don't float through life—our *ands* must be followed by something. But if we accept the duty to love others along with being fully convinced in our own minds, then we are protected against most forms of faddism. This is because fads are not very much fun without the added fun of recruiting for a movement. The substance of the fad is just the raw material. The real attraction lies in supervising people who don't answer to you, which is the very thing that Paul prohibits.

But Paul is no egalitarian. He does *not* say that any decision made by any Christian is just as good as any other. Love is not relativism. He most emphatically does not say that. In the first of his examples, he takes sides. The *weaker* brother is the "vegetarian." Keep in mind that use of the term vegetarian is likely anachronistic. This situation may have been caused by Jewish concerns about how meat was prepared, for example. In the modern era, a similar problem might occur because one brother thinks that kale tastes really good, and another brother dissents. But at the same time, if a modern day Pauline carnivore takes this verse and beats a veggie-brother over the head with it—"It says *weaker* brother here, el stupido..." the stronger brother clearly is not the stronger brother at all. He is right about the meat, but wrong about everything else. He is right about the meat, all except for the meat in his head.

Paul comes to other examples in this chapter, but he begins with the food. This is a perennial problem area for a certain religious type of man. Men have a deep desire to have God care about what they put in their mouths. The problem is that the triune God of Scripture doesn't care—bacon is fine, as are oysters, and refined sugar, and processed stuff made out of what used to be corn, and beer, and tofu, and wheat germ, and dirt cookies, and alfalfa sprouts from the co-op. God doesn't care...about *that*.

Within the Church, the imperialist for whatever fad it is struggles with Paul's acceptance of his option as a mere *option*. He doesn't want to define love the way Paul does—in terms of leaving your brother alone—and instead wants to say that it is only because of his deep *love* that he is urging his brother to start taking these pills "for what ails ya," $4.99 a bottle. Love is what makes a helpful sister tell a newly pregnant woman a bunch of hospital horror stories. Right. Love meddles, love bustles, love volunteers information, love won't shut up. Love refuses to listen to Paul, which can't be right somehow.

Love and wisdom go together. If everyone loves one another, disagreement is manageable—even when the consequences of being wrong can be significant. The less able you are to keep your crusade to yourself, in line with Paul's instruction here, the more likely it is that your wisdom on that issue is not really wisdom at all.

FULLY PERSUADED

As we work through this chapter of Romans, we will find ourselves reinforcing the same principle over and over—love your brother while keeping the big deals big, the middle deals middle, and the small deals small. Keep a sense of proportion—and as you monitor these things, look to your own sense of proportion *first*...not the other guy's.

> One man esteemeth one day above another: another esteemeth every day alike. Let every man be fully persuaded in his own mind. He that regardeth the day, regardeth it unto the Lord; and he that regardeth not the day, to the Lord he doth not regard it. He that eateth, eateth to the Lord, for he giveth God thanks; and he that eateth not, to the Lord he eateth not, and giveth God thanks. For none of us liveth to himself, and no man dieth to himself. For whether we live, we live unto the Lord; and whether we die, we die unto the Lord: whether we live therefore, or die, we are the Lord's. (Rom. 14:5–8)

Paul's first example was in the realm of diet, and he now moves on to calendar observance. One man thinks one day is more important than another, and another man doesn't think that (v. 5). Each one should be fully persuaded. The man who observes the day does so before the Lord, and the one who doesn't is rendering his *non*offering to the Lord (v. 6). Paul hearkens back to his point about eating, and he makes the same point there. One man says grace over what he eats, and the other man gives thanks for what he does not eat (v. 6). We are not individuals; we are interdividuals (v. 7). If we don't live or die to ourselves, then we don't mark a day or set a table to ourselves. Note the phrase "to himself," contrasted with the earlier (and later) phrase "unto the Lord." If we live, it is unto the Lord (v. 8). If we die, it is unto the Lord (v. 8). And therefore, whether we live or die, or do anything in between, we belong to the Lord (v. 8).

Let us reiterate the principle by coming at it from another angle. If you are loving your brother and are grateful to God, then you have the right to be fully persuaded in your own mind about *whatever*—whether home-birthing, cancer treatments, biblical diets, "green" concerns, or whatever might be the hot item two years from now.

On the other hand, if you are not loving your brother and are not giving a life of gratitude, then you do *not* have the right to be fully persuaded in your own mind. Any lack of charity and a lack of thanksgiving means that you have forfeited your right to your own opinion. If you reel it in again, then you do. Go ahead, now that you are walking in love, read that book or visit that website.

You love your brother by not judging or despising him (as we saw earlier in verses 1–4), and you render thanks to God in deep contentment, as we can see here. Opinions, of whatever stripe, must be built on the foundation of love for those who differ and gratitude to God for all things. By way of contrast, faddists ride roughshod over those who differ, and they are driven by discontent over what they are *rejecting* more than gratitude for what they are *receiving*.

Paul gives us another example from the first century, which is that of honoring one day over another. The apostle clearly teaches that (if the central principles are observed) one man has the right to esteem one day over another. He teaches just as plainly that another man has the right not to. Now in the first century, this would have meant Judaic calendar observance, with some Christians not honoring Yom Kippur and others doing so. Some would not have marked Passover, and others would have. Let it ride, Paul argues, and love each other.

Twenty centuries later, we would have an analogous situation with the observation of Christmas, Easter, Ascension, and Pentecost. The Bible does not require these days to be observed, and so *neither may we*.

The Old Testament festivals were God-ordained, but this was a time of transition. Other festivals were not demanded by the law (like Purim), but were God-honoring anyway. Neither may a man who does not observe Christmas demand that another man cease. If the law of love is remembered, then we may remember other things, or not. But always remember the nature of the human heart—the farther we get away from Scripture, the more likely it is that we will be neglecting the law of gratitude and love. The Church should therefore not establish any festival honoring the death of St. Frideswide's house cat.

But what about the Lord's Day? Does that fall under Paul's stricture here—is it okay for a man to consider all seven days exactly the same? Yes and no. To the extent that the Sabbath was part and parcel with the old covenant calendar (seventh day observance and one of the days of

Israel's convocation), that obligation (and the particular manner of its observance) has now ceased (Lev. 23:1–3). The law, and this part of the law was nailed to the cross (Col. 2:14). That weekly Sabbath died.

But when something dies in this way, in God's economy, it rises again (Heb. 4:9–10). This is why a Sabbath rest remains for God's people today. The Lord's Day is made new, just as all things have been made new. Mark the first day of the week in gospel rest; this is a glorified, resurrected Sabbath. So do not retreat to pharisaical corruptions of what was designed to be the lesser glory.

We are not individuals; we are interdividuals. We are *connected* to one another, and we are connected to one another precisely because we are connected to the Head, in whom we are being knit together (Col. 2:19). If we look to the Head, we are going to be coordinated one with another. If we look to ourselves and our own opinions, however right we insist they must be, we are living to ourselves.

But a part of the body that lives to itself is a part of the body that is seeking to make the body spastic. Love gives the body of Christ hand-eye coordination. Self-absorption makes the body gangly and spastic, and it is the source of one dispute after another. So do not let health diets, or home-birthing, or vitamin therapy, or partisan politics, or anything else you found on the internet become a basis for judging. And if you see somebody in the Church not heeding that exhortation, don't you despise them.

FOR TO THIS END...

We are continuing with the same theme so that we might remember the importance of loving our brothers and sisters in the faith, but we are doing so in a very spacious context. Learning the extent of that context will be what enables us to live rightly with one another in close quarters.

> For to this end Christ both died, and rose, and revived, that he might be Lord both of the dead and living. But why dost thou judge thy brother? Or why dost thou set at nought thy brother? For we shall all stand before the judgment seat of Christ. For it is written, As I live, saith the Lord, every knee shall bow to me, and every tongue shall confess to God. So then every one of us shall give account of himself to God. Let us not therefore judge one another any more: but judge this rather, that no man put a stumblingblock or an occasion to fall in his brother's way. I know, and am persuaded by the Lord Jesus, that there is nothing unclean of itself: but to him that esteemeth any thing to be unclean, to him it is unclean. But if thy brother be grieved with thy meat, now walkest thou not charitably. Destroy not him with thy meat, for whom Christ died. (Rom. 14:9–15)

Living and dying and everything in between are to be rendered to the Lord (v. 8). It was for this very purpose that Christ died and rose again—so that He might be Lord of both the dead and the living (v. 9). The ramifications here are enormous. In light of the fact that Christ is Lord of both the dead and the living, do not judge your brother (v. 10). Judging him is equated with setting him at nothing (v. 10) and zeroing him out. This is identified by Paul as a really bad idea, given that we will all appear before the judgment seat of Christ (v. 10).

We know that we will all appear before Christ because of what was prophesied in a collation of Isaiah 49:18 and 45:23 (v. 11). Every knee will bow. Standing before the judgment seat of Christ is identified with each one of us giving an account of himself to God (v. 12). As we are doing so, nobody else will be craning their necks trying to hear how we are going to explain our peculiar beliefs about food allergies. Everybody will have something else on their minds. In the light of that coming judgment, our judgments of one another (on issues like this) should be set aside, with the exception of judging that we ought not to stumble one another (v. 13). Jesus Christ Himself persuaded Paul that nothing is inherently unclean, but Jesus also taught Paul that someone's scruples about some things being unclean *ought to be respected nonetheless* (v. 14). If Christ died for a man, that man being your brother, then you are not to take your liberty concerning meat (or whatever) and destroy him with it. To do so is to refuse to walk in charity (v. 15).

We have been considering some of our modern disputes and practices in the light of what Paul is teaching here. We have our debates over food, birth control, home education or day school, conventional medicine or alternative, home-birthing, and so on. What should we think about these things? Again, Paul is not relativistic here. Read your

Bible. Study it through. In his example of food, he is fully persuaded by Jesus Himself that no food is *inherently* unclean. Jesus taught him that, but Jesus also taught him that He is willing to let people be wrong and that we should be willing to do the same. But remember—the person who *must* be right probably isn't.

Revelation 20:11 talks about a great white throne of judgment, one that is based on the Book of Life and the Book of Deeds. Matthew 25:32–33 addresses a judgment that will separate the sheep from the goats. This judgment separates those who are in Christ from those who are not in Christ. In order to stand in this judgment, it is not necessary to have anything covering you but the righteousness of another, the righteousness of Jesus. No one could stand otherwise.

But do not conclude from this that genuine Christians will not be judged in the particulars. You are accepted into life on the basis of the obedience of Jesus Christ. But what happens in this passage? Paul says that *"we shall all stand before the judgment seat of Christ,"* and he further adds that *"every one of us* shall give an account of himself to God."* (emphasis added). The central thing we will have to give an accounting for will be our petty judgments of our fellow believers—so (the Pauline advice would be) knock it off. The judgment with which you judge will be the judgment by which you shall be judged (Matt. 7:1–3). If each one of us remembers that each one of us will have to stand before God to give an accounting for how much we pestered the saints over insignificant issues, life in the body would be much improved.

And so now just imagine yourself approaching the throne of Christ to explain to Him how Suzy over there used to use *way* too much eye liner.

"For we must all appear before the judgment seat of Christ, so that each one may receive what is due for what he has done in the body, whether good or evil" (2 Cor. 5:10, ESV).

If Jesus is the Lord of both the dead and the living, then He is the absolute Lord of all history. Earthly kings rule over those who are alive, and once a man dies, he passes out of their jurisdiction and realm altogether. But Jesus died and rose *to this end*, for *this* purpose (v. 9, emphasis added). He died and rose so that He might be Lord (Paul does not say *Savior* here), and He died and rose so that He might be Lord of those who have died and those who are alive. His universal lordship is precisely the conclusion that Paul draws here. This is what makes Him Lord of history.

The section of Isaiah exults in the Lord's sovereignty over all the earth, and in His intention to save the entire world. The promise that Paul quotes is Isaiah 45:23. The verse immediately before that says, "Look unto me, and be ye saved, all the ends of the earth: for I am God, and there is none else" (Isa. 45:22). Paul ties this entire section together by introducing the quote with a phrase from Isaiah 49:18. God swears by *Himself*, and He swears that He will not forget Zion (v. 15). That would be impossible—He has graven them on the palms of His hands, which He did in a singularly bloody way (v. 16). God's purposes are glorious.

RIGHTEOUSNESS, PEACE, AND JOY

The Apostle spends quite a bit of time and energy on this question of "things Christians disagree about," and this is why we are doing the same thing. What will distract us from those things on which God places great value? It will be those things on which *we* try to place high value, and all on our own authority or in our own name. But we are creatures—we need to submit to God's set of values and stop trying to generate our own.

> Let not then your good be evil spoken of: For the kingdom of God is not meat and drink; but righteousness, and peace, and joy in the Holy Ghost. For he that in these things serveth Christ is acceptable to God, and approved of men. Let us therefore follow after the things which make for peace, and things wherewith one may edify another. For meat destroy not the work of God. All things indeed are pure; but it is evil for that man who eateth with offence. It is good neither to eat flesh, nor to drink wine, nor any thing whereby thy brother stumbleth, or is offended, or is made weak. Hast thou faith? Have it to thyself before God. Happy is he that condemneth not himself in that thing which he alloweth. And he that doubteth is damned if he eat, because he eateth not of faith: for whatsoever is not of faith is sin. (Rom. 14:16–23)

Do you believe that this thing of yours is the very greatest? Then don't behave in a way that makes people speak ill of it (v. 16). The reason is that the heart of all kingdom values can be found in righteousness, peace, and joy in the Holy Spirit (v. 17). The kingdom is not about food and drink—God doesn't care what you eat. In these things—whether eating or not, drinking or not—a man who serves Christ is acceptable to God and should not be a pain in the neck to other men (v. 18). So let us adjust our values and follow the things which make for peace, and things which build up our brothers and sisters (v. 19). Important note: your particular hobbyhorse is not what Paul is referring to with his insistence upon edification. Your calling it edifying doesn't *make* it edifying. The work of God is not to be destroyed for the sake of meat (v. 20). This means that your brother is the work of God, and your dinner fetishes are not. Paul reiterates the correct position again (all things are pure), but another man can still stumble in his conscience (v. 20). Should his conscience be stronger? Sure. So give it some time to *get* stronger. Stop kicking it. Don't swing your liberty around on the end of a rope (v. 21). Are you the strong-faith-boy? Great. Prove it by shutting up about it (v. 22). The man is happy who does not choke on his own liberty (v. 22). And the weaker brother should be careful not to try to rush how quickly he grows stronger (v. 23). Whatever does not proceed from faith is sin (v. 23). The Christian life can be described by rule, but it is lived by *faith*—not by rule.

We have already noted that there is a deeper right than being right. Paul is teaching this principle here, but he is also taking it a step or two further. Often those who are in the right are that right's greatest and most tenacious adversaries. Who better to give Sabbath-keeping a bad name than gnat-strangling Sabbatarians? Who better to give sexual decency a bad name than censorious prigs? Who better to give liberty a bad name than the libertines? Pretended friends are often far worse than staunch adversaries. *Do not let your good be evil spoken of.* We can misrepresent in this way our own standards of good, and we can even do the same thing (slanderously) to God's standards of good.

When someone is in the right and is willing to destroy a weaker brother for the sake of that right, then not only is he missing the deeper right, he is actually embracing a deeper wrong. "Happy is he that condemneth not himself in that thing which he alloweth" (v. 22). Do you allow it? Well and good. Are you correct to allow it? Good and even better. Allow away. But to stop there is to condemn yourself, and to condemn yourself with something that is perfectly fine in itself. There are a great many twists and turns involved when the righteous ones choke on righteousness. It is a terrible thing to choke on.

What is the kingdom about? It is not about food and drink. God doesn't care. It is not about robes and candles. God doesn't care. It is not about music with a back beat. God doesn't care. It is not about buying things from corporations or not. God doesn't care. It is not about meat offered to idols. God doesn't care. It *is* about your brother and sister—God does care, and He cares a great deal.

The center of kingdom life is righteousness, peace, and joy. This triad of blessings is not something that we gin up to present to God. It is God's work in us—note that Paul says righteousness, peace, and joy "in the Holy Ghost." This is the environment that the Holy Spirit creates in order to work in. If it is any other kind of environment, the Holy Spirit's work is limited to conviction of sin—sin, righteousness and judgment (John 16:8).

God is the only one who gets to define righteousness. Righteousness is an expression of His holy character and is described in His law. Sin is therefore lawlessness (1 John 3:4) and nothing else. We don't get to take away, like the libertines, and we don't get to add or substitute like the legalists. When we let God define what sin is (righteousness), and we pursue peace, just as He instructed here (v. 19), the end result is joy.

This joy is the work of God. It is not the joy of being right. It is not the joy of persuading people to adopt your dietary regimen. It is not the joy of seeing others proven wrong. It the joy of your salvation—your citizenship papers in the kingdom of God.

Paul concludes this section by noting that if it doesn't proceed from faith, then it is a sin. It is sin to eat, and it is a sin to not eat. Faith relates to a person. We cannot stay out of sin by relating all our behavior to an external rule alone. We must live in the *presence* of God.

CHAPTER 15

TRUE LIKEMINDEDNESS

The Apostle Paul has been piling one argument on top of another in his attempt to urge these Christians to simply get along with each other. He has appealed to the judgment seat of Christ, the sacrifice of Christ bestowed on the person you are at odds with, and the folly of slandering the very thing that you think is so good. And then he points to the example of Jesus Christ—He who was strong bore with us, though we were weak.

> We then that are strong ought to bear the infirmities
> of the weak, and not to please ourselves. Let every one
> of us please his neighbour for his good to edification.

> For even Christ pleased not himself; but, as it is writ-
> ten, The reproaches of them that reproached thee fell
> on me. For whatsoever things were written aforetime
> were written for our learning, that we through pa-
> tience and comfort of the scriptures might have hope.
> Now the God of patience and consolation grant you to
> be likeminded one toward another according to Christ
> Jesus: That ye may with one mind and one mouth
> glorify God, even the Father of our Lord Jesus Christ.
> Wherefore receive ye one another, as Christ also re-
> ceived us to the glory of God. (Rom. 15:1–7)

Strength should be used *for* the weak (v. 1), not *on* the
weak. Strength is not a gift that was given to you in order
that you might waste it on yourself (v. 1). Every one of us
(and not just some of us) should therefore use whatever
strength we have been given in order to please our neighbor, such that he is edified (v. 2). Why? We are Christians,
and we follow the example of Jesus Christ. Christ did not
please Himself (v. 3). Paul then quotes Psalm 69:9, making the point that Jesus was willing to suffer insult for the
sake of God (v. 3) and of course on our behalf as well.
That which was written down beforehand in Scripture was
written so that through patience and comfort in them we
might have hope. Hope in what? Hope that we might learn
this lesson, the thing Paul is talking about right now (v. 4).
God is the God of patience and consolation, so He is the
one to give us patience and comfort. The God of patience
and consolation can bless us by making us likeminded toward one another (v. 5) "according to Christ Jesus." This

likemindedness is exhibited by means of one mind and one mouth in glorifying God, who is the Father of Jesus (v. 6). Receiving one another, as Christ received us, is therefore the way to tune up the orchestra so that we might glorify God with it (v. 7).

As already noted, Paul quotes Psalm 69 in the course of his discussion here. This psalm contains quite a cluster of references that are cited throughout the New Testament. "They that hate me without cause" (Ps. 69:4; John 15:25); "zeal for your house consumes me" (Ps. 69:9; John 2:17); the reproaches of those who hate God fell on Christ (Ps. 69:9; Rom. 15:3); they gave the Lord vinegar for His thirst (Ps. 69:21; John 19:29–30); the rebellious Jews will have backs that will be bent forever (Ps. 69:22–23; Rom. 11:9); and Judas would lose his position among the apostles (Ps. 69:25; Acts 1:20). Jesus is the Messiah, and the Messiah lives among His *people*. But people mean differences, and differences mean conflict, and what are we supposed to do?

As the Bible teaches us to work and live together, it tells us to make sure to strive for true like-mindedness (Rom. 15:5; Phil. 2:2; 2:20). This, interestingly, is not what our culture tells us to do—*it* tells us not to drink the Kool-Aid and tells us further that we should make sure to stack every committee with divergent opinions. That is because we have come to believe that determining truth is a matter of taking averages or statistical analysis. But it isn't. If we consider Paul's teaching on the body and the members of the body, this like-mindedness is not the same thing as birds-of-a-featherness. Christians are to have a like mind

the same way that knees and elbows and tendons do—
they express a common desire by doing completely different things, *toward the same end.*

Think of different instruments in the same orchestra.
You could have different instruments playing different
songs entirely—cacophony. You could have the same instruments playing different music entirely—cacophony of
a different timbre. You could have the same instruments
playing the same music—boring. Or you could have different instruments playing the same music—glory.

So two counterfeits we have to deal with are common-
ality without distinction and distinction without common-
ality. But the Spirit unites disparate elements. If we have
a duty to be like-minded, and we do, and we have another
duty to pull in various directions, according to our various
gifts, and we do, then what could go wrong? If we are to be
striving toward the same goal, and we are to do so differ-
ently, then what problems might arise? The most obvious
thing would be counterfeits of each duty. The counterfeit
of like-mindedness is being a yes-man, and the counterfeit of exhibiting different gifts is being a contrarian. And
each counterfeit is poised to denounce the genuine article
across the way as a counterfeit.

Think *endurance* and *encouragement.* God gave us the
Scriptures so that we might have hope. God has created
us in such a way that we are able to draw strength and
comfort from examples that are recorded in a story. The
culmination of all such stories, of course, is the victory of
Christ over sin and death. In addition, the God who wrote
those stories down is the same God who is called the God

of *endurance* and *encouragement*. What He wrote into the stories He is in the process of writing into us. And what does the God who is called by these attributes do exactly? Well, He grants like-mindedness.

This is a narrative, a story. Imitate the Christ of the narrative, not the Christ of a snapshot. We serve the living Christ, not a frozen Christ. As Christ received you, receive the others. As Christ continues to receive you, so you also— receive them. Your receiving them is part of the story.

IN THAT DAY...

Our views of evangelism are far too tiny, too anemic, and too weak. Evangelism is not a matter of recruiting enough people so that your church can pay its bills. Evangelism is not a matter of getting market share. Evangelism is not a matter of the Israelite army settling for a portion of Canaan. Evangelism is about the salvation of the whole world. The entire thing.

Now remember that the book of Romans is a fundraising letter. Paul wanted to enlist the help of the Romans in his mission to Spain. But an essential part of that mission would involve preaching to the Gentiles there, and so it is necessary for Paul to explain and defend his role in the Gentiles' world mission, a part of which would include Spain. Paul has set forth his gospel, he has defended it against standard objections, and has applied it to the basic ethical issues that confront Christians. He is now circling back around to his reason for having written any of this.

> Now I say that Jesus Christ was a minister of the cir-
> cumcision for the truth of God, to confirm the promis-
> es made unto the fathers: And that the Gentiles might
> glorify God for his mercy; as it is written, For this
> cause I will confess to thee among the Gentiles, and
> sing unto thy name. And again he saith, Rejoice, ye
> Gentiles, with his people. And again, Praise the Lord,
> all ye Gentiles; and laud him, all ye people. And again,
> Esaias saith, There shall be a root of Jesse, and he that
> shall rise to reign over the Gentiles; in him shall the
> Gentiles trust. (Rom. 15:8–12)

Jesus Christ was a minister of the Jews, a minister of the
circumcision, in order that the promises that God made to
the patriarchs might be confirmed (v. 8). Jesus was a rabbi
of Israel. But He was not just a rabbi of Israel, He was also
the desire of the nations. He came in such a way that the
Gentiles might glorify God for His mercy to them (v. 9).
In support of this, Paul cites 2 Samuel 22:50 and Psalm
18:49—confession is to be made among the Gentiles, and
songs of praise sung in *their* midst (v. 9).

Then he quotes Deuteronomy 32:43, where the Gentiles
are invited to join in the praise (v. 10), and Psalm 117:1,
where all the nations are called upon to sing praise to the
Lord (v. 11). And he tops it off with a most instructive quotation from Isaiah 11:10, where the prophet tells us that the
root of Jesse will spring up, that He will rule over the nations, and that the Gentiles will in fact hope in Him (v. 12).

Jesus Christ came to the Jews, and He came to them as a
servant, as a deacon. He is described here as a minister or

servant of the circumcision in order to accomplish two things. The first was to fulfill the promises that had been made to Abraham, Isaac, and Jacob. The second was based on the first, and it was something that the physical descendants of Abraham, Isaac and Jacob had not understood rightly.

The promises made to the patriarchs of the Jews were not exclusive promises, but rather promises that encompassed the whole world. The confirmation of these promises therefore overflowed into the Gentile world as well—Jesus was a minister of the circumcision *so that* the uncircumcision would be able to glorify God for His mercy. This was not an esoteric aspect of the promises given to the fathers. It was not hidden in the fine print. Abraham was told, remember, that *all the families* of the earth would be blessed through him (Gen. 12:3). The Lord had pointed to the stars and had said, "So shall your descendants be."

And as Paul argued earlier in Romans, Abraham believed God in this matter *before* he was circumcised, making him the archetypical Gentile. And he was then circumcised, making him the archetypical Jew. He truly is Father Abraham.

As the great King David was on his death bed, he sang about how he would praise the Lord in the presence of the Gentiles (2 Sam. 22:50). A variation of this is found in Psalm 18:49. The Gentiles watched while David praised the Lord. But they were destined to be more than just spectators. So let the Gentiles sing.

Remember that Deuteronomy 32 has been a key to understanding Paul's view of Israel's apostasy. In that verse, the Gentiles were invited to praise the Lord together with His people, for the Lord will avenge the blood of His servants. The Gentiles are now invited to sing and rejoice in the context of the coming demolition of Jerusalem (Deut. 32:43). Then Paul cites the very short psalm, where the nations are invited simply to praise the Lord—His merciful kindness is great toward us (Ps. 117). The salvation that the Lord is bringing upon the earth is by no means limited to the Jews. This salvation is for all the world, all the nations, all the peoples, and all the tribes.

The Church needs to stop preaching to the devil's stragglers and start preaching to the *world*.

The next quotation, the one from Isaiah 11, is quite instructive. Let's look from the beginning of that chapter.

> And there shall come forth a rod out of the stem of Jesse, and a Branch shall grow out of his roots: And the spirit of the LORD shall rest upon him, the spirit of wisdom and understanding, the spirit of counsel and might, the spirit of knowledge and of the fear of the LORD; And shall make him of quick understanding in the fear of the LORD: and he shall not judge after the sight of his eyes, neither reprove after the hearing of his ears: But with righteousness shall he judge the poor, and reprove with equity for the meek of the earth: and he shall smite the earth with the rod of his mouth, and with the breath of his lips shall he slay the wicked. And righteousness shall be the girdle of his loins, and faithfulness the girdle of his reins. The wolf also shall dwell with the lamb, and the leopard shall lie down with the kid; and the calf and the

young lion and the fatling together; and a little child shall lead them. And the cow and the bear shall feed; their young ones shall lie down together: and the lion shall eat straw like the ox. And the sucking child shall play on the hole of the asp, and the weaned child shall put his hand on the cockatrice' den. They shall not hurt nor destroy in all my holy mountain: for the earth shall be full of the knowledge of the LORD, as the waters cover the sea. *And in that day* there shall be a root of Jesse, which shall stand for an ensign of the people; to it shall the Gentiles seek: and his rest shall be glorious. (vv. 1–10, emphasis added)

What is Paul doing? He is citing this passage, along with all the others, in order to justify *his* mission to the Gentiles, which he began two thousand years ago. There are two things we must remember in this regard. The first is that these days of glory do not arrive, wham, overnight. The leaven works through the loaf, and the mustard seed grows. But the second is that Isaiah tells us what the loaf looks like fully risen, and Paul tells us that the leaven was at work in the loaf in his day. So is Isaiah out of his mind?

No, not at all. But we who call ourselves Christians are frequently out of ours. Why do we not believe what the prophets have spoken?

THE PRIESTLY WORK OF EVANGELISM

We have seen that we should not have lethargic or anemic views of evangelism. God is in the processing of saving the entire world, and that has ramifications for the town in which we live. But we must also be careful to not have irreligious views of evangelism. Evangelism is not mere recruitment; in this text, the Apostle Paul gives us a striking image for our evangelistic work.

> Now the God of hope fill you with all joy and peace in believing, that ye may abound in hope, through the power of the Holy Ghost. And I myself also am persuaded of you, my brethren, that ye also are full of goodness, filled with all knowledge, able also to admonish one another. Nevertheless, brethren, I have written the more boldly unto you in some sort, as putting you in mind, because of the grace that is given to me of God, that I should be the minister of Jesus Christ to the Gentiles, ministering the gospel of God, that the offering up of the Gentiles might be acceptable, being sanctified by the Holy Ghost. I have therefore whereof I may glory through Jesus Christ in those things which pertain to God. For I will not dare to speak of any of those things which Christ hath not wrought by me, to make the Gentiles obedient, by word and deed, Through mighty signs and wonders, by the power of the Spirit of God; so that from Jerusalem, and round about unto Illyricum, I have fully preached the gospel of Christ. Yea, so have I strived to preach the gospel, not where Christ was named, lest I should build upon another man's foundation: but as it is written, To whom he was not spoken of, they shall see: and they that have not heard shall understand. (Rom. 15:13–21)

God is the God of hope, and He creates hope in us a particular way. He fills us with all joy and peace in our believing, and He does this through the Spirit, so that we might abound in hope (v. 13). Paul is convinced that the Roman believers are filled with goodness and filled with knowledge, with the result that they are able to admonish one another (v. 14). He wrote to them boldly, not because he did not think this of them, but simply to remind them of what they knew (v. 15), according to the grace that had been given to him.

God gave this grace to Paul in order that he might be a minister of God to the Gentiles, in the priestly office of the gospel, in order that the sacrificial offering of the Gentiles might be sanctified and acceptable to God (v. 16). As a result, he glories in what Christ has done through him (v. 17), and he refuses to take any credit for work he did *not* do in the labor of making the Gentiles obedient (v. 18), while at the same time saying that God did indeed accomplish some marvelous things through him in the power of the Spirit (v. 19). Thus far, he had preached from Jerusalem in the east through Illyricum to the northwest (in the region of modern Croatia, Serbia, and Albania). He has been careful to avoid building on another man's foundation (v. 20), an important courtesy. Paul must have preferred building from scratch. One likely reason is that it helped to avoid turf wars. Even if the apostles themselves remained in fellowship, the same could not always be said of their followers—I am of Paul, I am of Cephas, and so on.

In support of this approach, Paul then cites Isaiah 52:15—the verse right before the great gospel declaration of Isaiah 53 and right after the promise that many nations would be sprinkled.

When God does a work in our hearts, He does not do it simply by zapping us, with the result that we are simply happy in some generic spiritual sense. God is an architect, and He builds His graces in us. Certain things come first, and others follow after, and it is all done by the wisdom and power of the Holy Spirit. In this case, the God of hope fills us with something else—joy and peace—so that hope may follow abundantly. Without the joy and peace, the hope will be a vain hope and will collapse in on itself. This is the pattern that the Holy Spirit follows. If you are agitated, for example, and you *hope* that your emotional agitation will cease, this is not the same kind of hope that Paul is talking about here. If you are solemn and grim, and you hope that all these frothy fellows cavorting about you will get a real job sometime, that is not the right kind of *hope* either. Real peace, real joy, leads to abundant hope. This is the Spirit's way.

Paul assumes that a lot of pastoral work is going to be done within the congregation. As the leaven of gospel teaching grows and spreads within the congregation, so does the ability of members of that congregation to admonish one another rightly. But notice what the two preconditions are. The first is that the one delivering admonition be full of goodness, and the second is that he be full of knowledge.

Goodness without knowledge leads to well-intentioned mayhem in the admonition. Knowledge without goodness leads to censorious priggishness, and certain self-appointed fellows with the "gift of rebuking" start letting other people have it.

When a man is *full* of goodness and *full* of knowledge, then and only then is the beam out of his eye. But when these conditions pertain across a congregation, a *lot* of pastoral ministry occurs that the church leadership never even hears about.

The language Paul uses to describe his evangelistic efforts is quite striking. In verse 15, he says that the grace of God was given to him to make him a minister of Jesus Christ (v. 16). The word for minister here is *leitourgos* (λειτουργος), a word used for priestly ministers in a temple. We get the word *liturgy* from it.

He then says that he ministers the gospel of God. The word here is *hierourgeo* (ιερουργεω), which means "to minister as a priest." To preach or declare the blood of Christ shed for sinners is to conduct a priestly work. It is not priestly in the old typical sense—clouds of incense and blood on the altar—but it is the antitype. This makes it the *real* priestly work, of which the older forms of priestly work were just shadows and smoke. We must appropriate the reality here by faith and by faith alone. This is not a way of spiritualizing it away—evangelists and ministers really are priests of the gospel. Note that the converts are an offering made to God. This too is sacrificial language, and it is quite striking. The Gentiles, symbolized by unclean animals, are now sanctified by the Holy Spirit and are to be offered up as an acceptable offering. *Acceptable* is even more sacrificial language (Rom. 12:1–2; Isa. 60:5–7). If we think of this rightly, it is not worship *and* evangelism, or worship *or* evangelism. It is that worship *is* evangelism. In learning this, we must not skew it.

Priests served in an orderly fashion (Luke 1:8). The work of God is conducted in a manner that is consistent with order and good government (1 Pet. 5:3). Just as the land of Canaan was apportioned among the tribes, so also the ministry of worship/evangelism is apportioned. Paul says in this passage that he had been assigned the Gentiles, and this is why he was very careful in his ministry to the Jews. This is part of the reason why I believe that Paul was very careful when it came to "turf concerns."

We must take care to distinguish works from obedience. Our understanding of obedience is based on whatever the commandment was. If the command was to believe, then obedience is to have faith alone. If the command was to climb this greasy pole all the way to Heaven, then obedience would be works. So which is it? This is the work of God, that you believe in the one God has sent (John 6:29). Obedience is something rendered to the gospel; obedience is a *gospel* duty (Acts 6:7; Rom. 6:16; Rom. 15:18; Rom. 16:26, and more).

THE MINISTRY OF FUNDRAISING

We have noted earlier than this that the book of Romans is a fundraising letter. The fact that it is so strikingly different from modern Christian fundraising letters tells us all we need to know about the attitude of the modern Church to money...and to the gospel.

For which cause also I have been much hindered from coming to you. But now having no more place in these parts, and having a great desire these many years to come unto you; whensoever I take my journey into Spain, I will come to you: for I trust to see you in my journey, and to be brought on my way thitherward by you, if first I be somewhat filled with your company. But now I go unto Jerusalem to minister unto the saints. For it hath pleased them of Macedonia and Achaia to make a certain contribution for the poor saints which are at Jerusalem. It hath pleased them verily; and their debtors they are. For if the Gentiles have been made partakers of their spiritual things, their duty is also to minister unto them in carnal things. When therefore I have performed this, and have sealed to them this fruit, I will come by you into Spain. And I am sure that, when I come unto you, I shall come in the fulness of the blessing of the gospel of Christ. Now I beseech you, brethren, for the Lord Jesus Christ's sake, and for the love of the Spirit, that ye strive together with me in your prayers to God for me; that I may be delivered from them that do not believe in Judaea; and that my service which I have for Jerusalem may be accepted of the saints; that I may come unto you with joy by the will of God, and may with you be refreshed. Now the God of peace be with you all. Amen. (Rom. 15:22–33)

Since Paul did not plant the church in Rome, his desire not to meddle with another man's foundation had kept him from visiting the Roman church (v. 22). But now, since he was done with his current work and since he could hit Rome on the way to Spain, he thought to indulge a desire of many years and visit them (vv. 23–24). Before heading west, Paul was going to go to Jerusalem first (v. 25). His ministry there was a financial one, delivering a contribution from Macedonia and Achaia (v. 26). The Gentiles of Greece had an obligation to do this because they were beneficiaries of the spiritual inheritance of the Jews (v. 27). After Paul had performed this duty, what he called a "sealing of fruit," he intended to visit Rome on his way to Spain (v. 28; *cf.* Rom. 1:8–15). By bringing this up, he is returning to a significant theme of the book, which is the theme of Jews and Gentiles. In addition, just a short time before, he said that the only debt we should be willing to owe is the debt of love—and in this case, it was a debt that the Gentiles clearly owed to the Jewish believers.

He clearly would love the support of the Romans in this endeavor. When he comes, he is sure that he will do so in the fullness of the blessing of the gospel (v. 29). Paul then beseeches their prayer support (v. 30) for his pending trip to Judea. He asks them to pray for three things. The first is that he would be spared from the unbelievers of Judea (v. 31). The second is that his financial ministry would be acceptable to the saints there (v. 31). The third is that his subsequent trip to Rome would result in mutual refreshment and joy in the will of God (v. 32). Paul then finishes with a benediction (v. 33).

We have already noted that this letter was written in the mid-fifties. As we can read in the book of Acts, this trip that Paul was requesting prayer for was a trip that in fact needed a great deal of prayer. He was received by the saints gladly (Acts 21:17), meaning one of his requests was answered. But the unbelievers he mentioned here successfully got a tumult going (Acts 21:27–28), with the result that Paul was arrested/rescued by a centurion. Held for a time by Felix and then by Festus, Paul eventually appealed to Caesar and was shipped off to Rome (Acts 27:1). The book of Acts ends with Paul under house arrest (Acts 28:30–31), and we are still in the fifties.

According to Clement of Rome, who was a friend of Paul's, the apostle "taught righteousness to the whole world, having traveled to the limits of the west" (1 Clement 5:7).[11] This most likely refers to Spain, but possibly to Britain. Paul wasn't executed by Nero until the persecution that broke out in AD 64, so it is safe to presume that Paul was released after the end of Acts, made his way west, and was subsequently rearrested.

Paul knows the necessity of fundraising. He also knows and fully understands the necessity of not doing it in any way that discredits the gospel. Indeed, the gospel is to be honored and spread by this means, and Paul knows that in order for the Romans to support his work with a clean conscience, he needed to set the gospel he preached before them, and he does so by means of the full synopsis that we find in this book.

Unlike so many, Paul says, he is not a huckster peddling the Word of God (2 Cor. 2:17). So many? That is a telling indictment, and we still need to be reminded of it today. At the same time, to walk away from the responsibility of

11. Robert M. Grant and Holt H. Graham, ed., *The Apostolic Fathers, A New Translation and Commentary, Vol. 2: First and Second Clement* (New York: Thomas Nelson, 2020), 26.

raising money is to be negligent in ministry. The people of God need to be taught these financial principles. Consider how often Paul addresses it. The one taught should share all good things with the one who teaches (Gal. 6:6–9). The spiritual nature of ministry does not mean that it runs on air (1 Cor. 9:7, 14). Generosity in financial matters is a spiritual form of farming (2 Cor. 9:6–7). At the same time, it is important to avoid any appearance of impropriety (2 Cor. 8:20). Paul is exceptionally sensitive at this point (Phil. 4:17), but not so sensitive that he withholds the truth from Christians (Phil. 4:10).

The word used for *contribution* in Romans 15:26 is the word for fellowship, *koinonia* (κοινωνια). Paul is talking about a fellowship in money. A verb form of the same root is used in Philippians 4:14, when he says that the Philippians shared with him in his trouble. He does the same in Galatians 6:6. When Paul takes the gift from Greece to Jerusalem, he does so in order to minister to them. The word is related to *diakonos* (διακονος), and refers to service ministry. And the word for the Gentiles ministering in verse 27 is another word we discussed before—*leitourgos* (λειτουργος). This whole subject of finances has to do with religious and priestly service.

As believers devoted to generosity, we don't want to save up our guilt-edged securities. *Gilt* is superficial, but *guilt* goes all the way down and contaminates everything. You have heard many times that guilt is a poor motivator in giving. But notice what happens when we move this whole subject into the sanctuary. At our church, we confess our sins at the beginning of the service, and we hear the words of peace spoken over us from God. That means that when the offering is brought forward at the end of the service, the whole thing should be a delight. The offering is part of the consecration offering, and is *not* part of the guilt offering. Jesus made *that* offering for us.

CHAPTER 16

PHOEBE OUR SISTER

In this last chapter of Romans, Paul says his farewells, gives various greetings, and does so in a way as to teach us many invaluable things. Some might wonder what kind of message we might get out of a passage in which Paul basically says *hi* to everyone the Roman church phone directory, but we have to remember that all Scripture is profitable.

> I commend unto you Phebe our sister, which is a servant of the church which is at Cenchrea: that ye receive her in the Lord, as becometh saints, and that ye assist her in whatsoever business she hath need of you: for she hath been a succourer of many, and of myself also.

Greet Priscilla and Aquila my helpers in Christ Jesus: who have for my life laid down their own necks: unto whom not only I give thanks, but also all the churches of the Gentiles. Likewise greet the church that is in their house. Salute my wellbeloved Epaenetus, who is the firstfruits of Achaia unto Christ. Greet Mary, who bestowed much labour on us. Salute Andronicus and Junia, my kinsmen, and my fellowprisoners, who are of note among the apostles, who also were in Christ before me. Greet Amplias my beloved in the Lord. Salute Urbane, our helper in Christ, and Stachys my beloved. Salute Apelles approved in Christ. Salute them which are of Aristobulus' household. Salute Herodion my kinsman. Greet them that be of the household of Narcissus, which are in the Lord. Salute Tryphena and Tryphosa, who labour in the Lord. Salute the beloved Persis, which laboured much in the Lord. Salute Rufus chosen in the Lord, and his mother and mine. Salute Asyncritus, Phlegon, Hermas, Patrobas, Hermes, and the brethren which are with them. Salute Philologus, and Julia, Nereus, and his sister, and Olympas, and all the saints which are with them. Salute one another with an holy kiss. The churches of Christ salute you. (Rom. 16:1–16)

Paul commends to the Romans a woman named Phoebe, who was probably the messenger who carried the letter to the Romans. As valuable trusts go, this was probably one of the most important missions in the history of the Church. She is called a sister and is identified as a servant of the church at Cenchreae (v. 1). In the next verse, Paul urges them to give her a saint's welcome and to assist her in whatever business she might need. She had been a great help to many, Paul included (v. 2). Greet Priscilla and Aquila, Paul's helpers in Christ (v. 3), who risked their lives for Paul (v. 4). Greet their house church (v. 5), along with Epaenetus, the first convert in Achaia (v. 5). The greetings are then extended to Mary (v. 6); Androni-cus and Junia (v. 7); Amplias (v. 8); Urbane and Stachys (v. 9); Apelles and the household of Aristobulus (v. 10), Herodion and the household of Narcissus (v. 11); Tryphe-na, Tryphosa, and Persis (v. 12); Rufus and his mother (v. 13); Asyncritus, Phlegon, Hermas, Patrobas, Hermes, and the brothers with them (v. 14); and finally Philologus and Julia, Nereus and his sister, Olympas, and all the saints with them (v. 15). Paul then tells them to greet one an-other with a holy kiss (v. 16) and says that the churches of Christ salute them (v. 16).

Paul is greeting a number of the saints who are there at Rome, and it is striking how many of them he knows—a number of them apparently quite well. I take verse 7 as say-ing "notable among the apostles" as opposed to "notable apostles," as Junia is a woman's name. These saints were converts out of paganism, as most had common names for that culture and others had the sorts of names that a Chris-tian mom would not have given—such as Hermes or Olym-pas. Paul refers several times to kinsmen (vv. 7, 11), and that he and Rufus had the same (unnamed) mother. These are most likely *like* kin, and not actual relatives. But who knows? After all, a nephew shows up in Paul's life around this time (Acts 23:16).

We can see how close Paul is to these people. We can also see *how* he got close to them—for Paul, labor and sacrifice were right at the center of his value system. Phoebe was a great help to many (v. 2). Priscilla and Aquila put their necks on the line (v. 4). Mary was a hard worker (v. 6). Urbane was a helper in the Lord (v. 9). Tryphena and Tryphosa labored in the Lord (v. 12). Persis labored much in the Lord (v. 12)

We were created for work. The fall into sin makes that work harder, true enough, but it also gives us more to do. We should gather up the kind of friends that Paul was attracted to and get to work.

The church at Rome was actually a cluster of churches. One of the assemblies met at the home of Priscilla and Aquila (v. 5). It is possible that a couple of others met at the homes of Narcissus and Aristobulus, who may have been unbelievers since they were not greeted directly by name. Two other groups are mentioned in verses 14 and 15. At this point in history, there were no church buildings, and so the singular church at Rome (to which Paul could write *one* letter) was actually a collection of home churches. Paul could write to them, give a number of greetings to the saints in different gatherings, and expect that they would see one another in order to pass on those greetings. Geographical separation, whether it was with Paul across the ocean or with the other Roman saints who were across town meeting with the household of Demetrius, is not a separation in fellowship.

Phoebe is called a number of things, from which we learn a great deal. She is "our sister" (v. 1), she is a servant (*diakonos*/διακονος) of the church at Cenchreae, clearly serving that church in some sort of official capacity. Phoebe was the one who delivered the letter to the Romans, and Paul instructs them to help her out now that she is in Rome (v. 2). The word translated in the KJV as *succourer* is a word that means "benefactress" or "patroness." She was clearly wealthy, and she came from the eastern port of Corinth (Cenchreae), a place that had been about six miles east of Corinth and is today underwater.

The word *diakonos* as it is used here can either denote a formal office, or it can simply mean a generic helper or servant. Given Phoebe's prominence, and the importance of the help, it seems that the former is meant. But it does not follow from this that the church at Cenchreae had a deacon board and that women were on it. To reason that way is anachronistic. We are likely talking about official women helpers in the church, women who held a distinct office from the male deacons, but who were on the church staff, nonetheless. I explain in my commentary on the pastoral epistles my reasons for believing that these deaconesses were the enrolled widows.[12]

And speaking of anachronism, some Christians take Paul's reference to the kiss here to mean that Christians are required to greet each other in some special liturgical fashion, i.e., with a liturgical kiss, or a holy kiss. Others, like myself, would want to say that your greetings, such

---

12. Douglas Wilson, *The Pillar of the Truth: A Commentary on the Pastoral Epistles*, (Moscow, ID: Canon Press, 2016). 42–43.

as they are and how they function, should be *holy*. Your kiss, or your handshake, or your Christian side hug, should be *holy*. They would want to point out that Paul has just finished a long list of ordinary greetings, and he then urges them to greet one another (using the same word)—and to do so in holiness. Applying scriptural principles to widows is another place we must think about cultural context. A modern woman could be eligible to be enrolled as a widow, even if she had never, ever literally washed any of the saints' feet (1 Tim. 5:10), but we understand from this the kind of service she was characterized by. As we make cultural transpositions, we must always remember the difference between principles and methods.

THE GOD OF PEACE WHO CRUSHES

In this small portion of the last chapter of Romans, the apostle arranges a number of profound and important truths. If we have eyes to see the sweep of redemptive history, we will get it. If we do not, then we are missing some crucial aspects of the gospel.

> Now I beseech you, brethren, mark them which cause divisions and offences contrary to the doctrine which ye have learned; and avoid them. For they that are such serve not our Lord Jesus Christ, but their own belly; and by good words and fair speeches deceive the hearts of the simple. For your obedience is come abroad unto all men. I am glad therefore on your behalf: but yet I would have you wise unto that which is good, and simple concerning evil. And the God of peace shall bruise Satan

under your feet shortly. The grace of our Lord Jesus
Christ be with you. Amen. (Rom. 16:17–20)

Paul pleads with the Romans, and what he asks them to
do is identify those who are schismatic and have nothing
to do with them (v. 17). These are men who, despite their
presence within the Church, do not serve Jesus Christ but
rather worship their own belly (v. 18). They are deceptive
and dangerous (v. 18). Paul knows that the obedience of
the Roman church is known to all men (v. 19), and he is
glad for this. But at the same time, he has a caution for
them—they should be good-wise and evil-simple (v. 19).
If they are, then the God of peace will fulfill His glorious
promise through them (Gen. 3:15) and bruise Satan under
their feet shortly (v. 20). Paul then pronounces a benediction over them (v. 20).

There is a kind of simplistic liberalism that wants to
evaluate everything as though right and wrong were not
real categories. So if you strike a child, they say, you are
simply teaching them violence. Actually, if you spank with
a sense of love and justice, then when you spank, you are
actually teaching your son not to clock his little sister over
the head with his plastic firetruck.

They say that if you follow what the apostle says here
and you divide from those who cause divisions, then have
you not *joined* them? Hmmm? But in the world God made,
the antithesis is inescapable. This means that you must
divide the way God says, or you will divide in another,
destructive way. We do not have the option of not dividing. We will either divide from the schismatics, or we will

divide from those who love Christian unity. There are no other options. There is no way to love the wolves without hating the sheep, and vice versa.

Note the character of these schismatics. First, *they* cause divisions and offenses. Right and wrong—some are guilty, and some are innocent. We are responsible to know which are which. Second, God has given us a way to do this. The measuring rod is the doctrine that we have learned. What does the *Bible* say? Third, though these people are *in* the Church they are not *of* the Church. They do not worship Jesus Christ. They do not serve Christ, but rather they serve their own bellies. The rumbling of those bellies gives unction to their eloquence, and with smooth flatteries, they deceive the hearts of the simple. Anyone who believes that these bellygods have disappeared from the Church since Paul's day is not paying close attention...or is one of them.

Paul says that these smooth talkers deceive the hearts of the simple. Yet in the next breath, he wants our hearts to be a certain kind of simple—simple with regard to evil. We must be the right kind of simple. We are to be wise in what is good, and simple in the convolutions of evil. Keep it simple. Love God; hate sin. Read your Bible; love your neighbor. Trust in Jesus. Love the good people; fight the bad people. Enroll in the graduate schools of goodness, and repeatedly flunk out of the kindergartens of sin.

Remember that the God of peace is a great warrior. The glorious promise of verse 20 is packed with implications that we must draw out. First, we conquer evil, crushing it, bruising it, because the God of *peace* enables us to do so. Remember the earlier point about dividing from division.

There is no contradiction when the God of peace crushes the serpent head of all discord. Peace is brought into this sorry world by means of *conquest*, and not with a group hug.

Second, notice how Paul shows that the Messianic promise that the seed of the woman would bruise the serpent's head is a promise that is not limited to Jesus Himself. It is partially fulfilled by means of the body of Christ—it is *your* feet.

Third, Paul says that this will happen shortly. The Roman Christians he was writing to did not have to wait for the Day of Judgment for this to happen.

Fourth, we see here how *Satan* is connected by the New Testament writers with the events in the Garden of Eden. Genesis doesn't mention Satan by name, but Paul places him there. Other writers do the same (1 John 3:10, 12; Rev. 20:2).

And fifth, the fulfillment of this promise is connected to the instructions he has just given. If we mark and identify the sowers of discord, pursuing goodness with deep and profound wisdom and avoiding evil with a very simple revulsion, then what? Then the God of peace is at work in our midst, and He will use *our* feet to crush the serpent's head. Dividing from the schismatic is to crush the serpentine head of discord.

Emissaries of Hell don't show up at your door like they were straight out of a zombie movie. They don't say, "Hello, I am here from the devil to lead you astray. Come with me to the hellish inferno." Satanism is not characterized by severed goats' heads, pentagrams on the floor, and guttering candles. *Jesus* was once tempted to become a Satan worshipper (Matt. 4:8), and He was tempted by something *glorious*. The Apostle Paul tells us that Satan is an angel of light (2 Cor. 11:14), and it is no wonder if his ministers come off looking like ministers of righteousness (2 Cor. 11:15). So what does *not* crush disturbances in the church? It is the conviction held by certain people that their wants and desires are always righteous, true, and holy. They don't want that deeper right than being right. The only serpent they want to be crushed is out there.

But the godly plea is this one—bruise in *us* the serpent's head.

THE COMMANDMENT OF THE EVERLASTING GOD

We now come to the final blessing, the final benediction. In this letter, Paul has given us a mere synopsis of his gospel, and that synopsis is overwhelming. If the entire gospel were to be laid out for us all at once, we would be crushed by the glory of it. Never forget that God is in the *universe* business; we are not servants of some local baal or tribal deity. As Thomas Chalmers once put it, "Regardless of how large, your vision is too small." Far too small.

> Timotheus my workfellow, and Lucius, and Jason, and Sosipater, my kinsmen, salute you. I Tertius, who wrote this epistle, salute you in the Lord. Gaius mine host, and of the whole church, saluteth you. Erastus the chamberlain of the city saluteth you, and Quartus a brother. The grace of our Lord Jesus Christ be with you all. Amen. Now to him that is of power to stablish

> you according to my gospel, and the preaching of Jesus
> Christ, according to the revelation of the mystery,
> which was kept secret since the world began, but now
> is made manifest, and by the scriptures of the proph-
> ets, according to the commandment of the everlasting
> God, made known to all nations for the obedience of
> faith: to God only wise, be glory through Jesus Christ
> for ever. Amen. (Rom. 16:21–27)

Paul has sent his greetings to his friends in Rome, and he now sends greetings from those who are with him. He begins with Timothy, Lucius, Jason, and Sosipater (v. 21). Paul's secretary, the man who did the actual writing of Romans, a man named Tertius, sent his greetings (v. 22). Gaius, the host of this apostolic entourage, and the whole church as well, sent his greetings (v. 23). Erastus, a city official, presumably of Corinth, sent his greetings, as did a brother named Quartus (v. 23).

Paul appends a benediction to this set of greetings (v. 24). He then turns to deliver a powerful benediction that encompasses all of them in accordance with all that he has said thus far (v. 24). He commends everything to Him who has the power to establish the Romans according to Paul's gospel and the preaching of Jesus Christ, and this in accordance with the revealing of the mystery, a mystery kept secret from the beginning of the world (v. 25). But that which had been hidden is now made manifest (v. 26). That which was secret is now made known to all nations (so that they might obey) by the Scriptures of the prophets, according to the commandment of the everlasting God (v.

26). We render glory to the only wise God, and we do so through Jesus Christ, and we will do so forever (v. 27). And amen (v. 27).

You can learn a lot about the center by looking at the group standing around it. You can learn a lot about Paul by looking at the kind of men he collects to work with him. What was the apostolic entourage like? Just as Jesus gathered disparate characters—like Levi the collaborating IRS agent and Simon the John Bircher—so also with Paul. Timothy had been his co-laborer for many years. We don't know much about Lucius, Jason, and Sosipater. All we know about Tertius is that he worked as a secretary taking dictation, and that the Apostle Paul dictated this letter to him. Paul was hosted by Gaius, but he was a most hospitable man—he hosted the whole church. There was Quartus, another man we know nothing about, and Erastus, a city official. His position is described as, literally, city economist, probably the treasurer. Archaeologists have unearthed a stone at Corinth with the inscription "Erastus, Commissioner of Public Works," who is probably the same man. We can see from this that the Pauline strategy for the Roman Empire as a whole was "infiltration without compromise," and not, as some would have it, "separation for the sake of perfection." This kind of thing happens naturally if we pray for, and evangelize, *everybody* (1 Tim. 2:1–2; Acts 26:29). Politics is dirty, sure enough, but so are monasteries.

For the Apostle Paul, a mystery is *not* something we do not yet know. It is something that was not widely or fully known from the creation to the resurrection of Jesus.

Some, like angels and prophets, knew it partially (1 Pet. 1:10–12), but for the most part, God kept His plans for the world hidden away in secret. How did He do this? And how is it now manifest?

When Christ rose from the dead, and His followers went out to preach that resurrection, they were not simply reporting on a remarkable fact, they were also preaching Christ as the great antitype of all the types and shadows that had come before. When Paul refers to the mysteries, he is talking in part about Adam, and David, and Sarah, and Hagar, and Abraham, and all the other types (1 Cor. 4:1; 1 Cor. 13:2; Eph. 3:9; Eph. 5:32; Col. 1:26–27).

A typological reading of the Old Testament is certainly dangerous—but it is also *absolutely necessary* to the health of gospel preaching. In order to guard ourselves against fantastical interpretations, what do we do? How do we stick close to the interpretive shore? *Christ is the shore*, and the Scriptures of the prophets are the map. If it is not aimed at the obedience of faith for all the nations, then it is an erroneous reading of the text.

Christians are to be established by the gospel, not by middle age. Christians are to feed on the preaching of Jesus Christ, Lord of Heaven and earth, and they are to glory in the sweep of God's redemptive design for the whole world.

God has established eternity in the heart of man. He has put the whole world in our heart, and He does not want us settling for petty accomplishments (Eccles. 3:11). We are certainly to glory in the mundane, knowing that nothing is really *ever* mundane. So why are so many submerged in their pettiness and blowing bubbles in it? God created you for more. Lift up your heads.

You will live forever. Shouldn't your goal be loftier than getting teenage boys to look at your body at the pool? How hard could *that* be? God intends that you be more than a curvy little dope.

Shouldn't your goal be more noble than getting the papers from this side of the desk to that side of the desk? God intended that you do more with your life than just shuffle stuff around.

Shouldn't you be less concerned about the muddy footprints your kid left on the entry mat, and more concerned about the muddy footprints you are leaving on his heart? God intended for you to be great in the law of kindness.

We are all of us small, but we were not designed to be petty.

And there is nothing better than the book of Romans to lift you up out of yourself.